For many years C. S. Lewis's dismissal of the greater part of the sixteenth century as a 'drab age' has influenced literary scholars. Andrew Hadfield offers a challenging reinterpretation, through study of the work of some of the century's most important writers, including Skelton, Bale, Sidney, Spenser, Baldwin and the Earl of Surrey. He argues that all were involved in the establishment of a vernacular literary tradition as a crucial component of English identity, yet also wished to use the category of 'literature' to create a public space for critical political debate. Conventional assumptions – that pre-modern and modern history are neatly separated by the Renaissance, and that literary history is best studied as an autonomous narrative – are called into question: this book is a study of literary texts, but also a contribution to theories and histories of politics, national identity and culture.

LITERATURE, POLITICS AND NATIONAL IDENTITY

LITERATURE, POLITICS AND NATIONAL IDENTITY

Reformation to Renaissance

ANDREW HADFIELD

University of Wales, Aberystwyth

CAMBRIDGE
UNIVERSITY PRESS

Published by the Press Syndicate of the University of Cambridge
The Pitt Building, Trumpington Street, Cambridge, CB2 1RP
40 West 20th Street, New York, NY 10011–4211, USA
10 Stamford Road, Oakleigh, Melbourne 3166, Australia

First published 1994

Printed in Great Britain at the University Press, Cambridge

A catalogue record for this book is available from the British Library

Library of Congress cataloguing in publication data

Hadfield, Andew.
Literature, politics, and national identity: Reformation to Renaissance / Andrew
Hadfield.
p. cm.
Includes bibliographical references and index.
ISBN 0 521 44207 9 (hardback)
1. English literature – Early modern, 1500–1700 – History and criticism.   2.
Politics and literature – Great Britain – History – 16th century.   3. Nationalism –
Great Britain – History – 16th century.   4. National characteristics, English, in
literature.   5. Great Britain – Politics and government – 1485–1603.   6.
Reformation – England.   7. Renaissance – England.   I. Title.
PR418.P65H33 1994
820.9′358 – dc20   93–30382   CIP

ISBN 0 521 44207 9 hardback

For Alison, Lucy, Patrick, George and Rebecca

Nationalism is a doctrine invented in Europe at the beginning of the nineteenth century.

(Elie Kedourie)

Throughout any international movement which seeks to destroy the independence of nations there must run a vein of madness.

(Rebecca West)

Nobody knows who the public is or what it wants or needs. Or whether it should be considered singular or plural. Though there are many people claiming to act on its behalf or speak in its name. And no one is quite sure what space belongs to it or to them, though that usually seems to be only what's left over when all of the other spaces have been appropriated, walled, shut, fenced, or screened off by whatever groups or individuals can enforce private claims to them.

(David Antin)[1]

Contents

List of illustrations   page xii
Preface   xiii
List of abbreviations   xvi

Introduction: the nation and public literature
in the sixteenth century   1

1   A Skelton in the closet: English literary identity
betwixt and between   23

2   John Bale and the time of the nation   51

3   Literature and history – *A Mirror for Magistrates*   81

4   Towards a national form: rhetoric and literary
theory from Wilson to Puttenham   108

5   Whose bloody country is it anyway? Sir Philip
Sidney, the nation and the public   132

6   'Who knowes not Colin Clout?' The permanent
exile of Edmund Spenser   170

Notes   202
Select bibliography   254
Index   262

Illustrations

1 Edmund Spenser, *The Shepheardes Calender*, woodcut
   accompanying 'January eclogue', in *Works* (1611).
   Reproduced by permission of the British Library. page 179
2 Edmund Spenser, *The Shepheardes Calender*, woodcut
   accompanying 'April eclogue', in *Works* (1611).
   Reproduced by permission of the British Library.   183

xii

Preface

This study has been made possible by the award of a British Academy Post-Doctoral Fellowship in the Humanities and Social Sciences held at the University of Leeds, 1989–92. The idea for the project originated whilst I was completing a PhD thesis at the University of Ulster at Coleraine on English perceptions of Ireland in the sixteenth century. I came to realise that although I felt I was asking interesting and legitimate questions regarding the relationship between politics, literature and national identity, I had not applied these thoroughly enough to an English Renaissance tradition. Like many an arrogant, putatively politically correct young Englishman, I had avoided examining a past which defined my own identity and had proceeded to scrutinise others'.[1] In effect, although my intention was to criticise and expose certain prejudices, ideologies and dogmas, I was caught up in the same process of self-inflicted blindness and repression that had afflicted many of the writers I was studying. As Bill McCormack has pointed out in his acerbic manner, many on the English left are imperialists whatever their vehement denials.[2] Clearly the research I had started to do – although I still feel it has many merits as well as shortcomings – was inadequate in itself. I completed it within the three years of my grant, but decided that it could not be shaped into a publishable form until I had followed through the project which led to this book, namely, examining the crucial link between literature and political and national identities in sixteenth-century England. In a sense, this book originated in Ireland, where English identity has always been most searchingly challenged and thrown into crisis as I can testify from experience. When revising *Language, Truth and Logic*, ten years after its original publication in 1936, A. J. Ayer remarked that being a 'young man's book', it 'had been written with more passion than most philosophers allowed themselves to show'.[3] Whilst Ayer regarded his betrayal of his feelings in a critical light, I would hope that if any reader detects any traces of 'passion' in this book, he or she will try to consider it a strength, as it is still the case that too few academic books reveal or invoke enough feeling.

A pilot article for the book, containing sections of the Introduction and chapters 2 and 3 appeared in *Leeds Studies in English* 23 (1992) and I am grateful to the editor, Dr Andrew Wawn, for permission to reproduce parts from it; another section of chapter 2 appeared in *Notes and Queries* 243 (March, 1994) and I am also grateful to the editors for permission to reproduce that. During the three and a half years it has taken to write I have incurred more debts to colleagues, friends and family than I can possibly repay. I would like to thank Kevin Taylor of Cambridge University Press for his belief in the project and help in getting it to the press. Many colleagues provided helpful comments on sections of the typescript and saved me from numerous errors; in this regard I would like to thank Michael Brennan, John Dickie, Lesley Johnson, Michael Smith, Philip Terry, Tim Woods, Blair Worden, and, especially, Paul Hammond. The encouraging but intelligently critical reports by the anonymous readers at Cambridge University Press provided further fruitful avenues of exploration. It should also be said that without the researches of scholars like David Norbrook, John King and Stephen Greenblatt, with whom I often disagree, this book would certainly have been the poorer and perhaps not even possible at all. All errors, unfortunately, are my own responsibility. Mention too should be made of David and Mary Yarnold who supplied me with many fascinating books and Ken Rowe who helped sort out some tricky problems regarding Latin and Greek translations and amazed me with his successfully dogged pursuit of one or two, unfortunately, unhelpful leads; without the last-minute help of Diane Watt and David Rabey, the typescript might well have disappeared forever. The greatest debt anyone incurs is inevitably to their families so I would like to thank my mother and father for the support they have given me over the years and to Alison, Lucy and Patrick Hadfield for going well beyond the bounds of duty in putting up with my – tortuous and sometimes tortured – intellectual and physical journeys. To them this book is affectionately dedicated.

I have followed the usual practice of leaving spelling unaltered except for modernising i/j and u/v.

Abbreviations

CL	*Comparative Literature*
DNB	*Dictionary of National Biography*
EETS	Early English Text Society
EHR	*English Historical Review*
EIC	*Essays in Criticism*
ELH	*English Literary History*
ELN	*English Language Notes*
ELR	*English Literary Renaissance*
ES	*Essays and Studies*
HJ	*Historical Journal*
HLQ	*Huntington Library Quarterly*
IHS	*Irish Historical Studies*
JEGP	*Journal of English and Germanic Philology*
JEH	*Journal of Ecclesiastical History*
JHI	*Journal of the History of Ideas*
JMRS	*Journal of the Medieval and Renaissance Society*
JRMMRS	*Journal of the Rocky Mountain Medieval and Renaissance Society*
JWCI	*Journal of the Warburg and Courtauld Institutes*
MLN	*Modern Language Notes*
MLQ	*Modern Language Quarterly*
MLR	*Modern Language Review*
N. and Q.	*Notes and Queries*
P. & P.	*Past and Present*
PMLA	*Proceedings of the Modern Language Association of America*
PQ	*Philological Quarterly*
RD	*Renaissance Drama*

xvi

RES	*Review of English Studies*
RQ	*Renaissance Quarterly*
SEL	*Studies in English Literature, 1500–1900*
S. Litt. I.	*Studies in the Literary Imagination*
SP	*Studies in Philology*
Sp. St.	*Spenser Studies*
STC	*Short Title Catalogue*
TCBS	*Transactions of the Cambridge Bibliographical Society*
Te.SLL	*Texas Studies in Language and Literature*
TP	*Textual Practice*
TRHS	*Transactions of the Royal Historical Society*
YES	*Yearbook of English Studies*

Introduction: *the nation and public literature in the sixteenth century*

The argument of this book is essentially simple, but some of the implications of its argument are not so straightforward. I want to claim that in the sixteenth century it was not obvious to many writers of 'literature' what it was they were attempting to achieve. 'Literature' was not a clear and distinctly identifiable category of writing which would be employed to deal with certain themes in a particular way. Obviously, certain modes, or types, of writing (for example, ballad, epic, romance, satire, comedy, tragedy) existed and were frequently reproduced; but it was not clear exactly how they related to each other, how they related to other forms of writing and, most importantly, what was the point of writing or reading such works.

Many writers chose to define their aims through their own particular conceptions of a public national culture for which they wrote and to which they spoke. If literature was to have a serious meaning and function, it had to be conceived of as an important constituent of a wider concern than merely fine writing. Therefore, two seemingly distinct purposes cannot easily be separated: writers had both to fashion and authorise their own utterances as literature and imagine the national community they addressed. Neither 'literature' nor 'nation' could be taken as stable entities and were always in the process of being redefined, partly as a result of their interaction and interdependence, and partly owing to other factors and relationships. Literature had to be read in relation to other kinds of discourse (some of these, of course, were also used to try to define a national identity, for example legal treatises, chronicles, maps and geographic surveys, travel writing) and the nation against both other nations and other forms of 'imagined community' (including supranational, spiritual, local or regional perceptions of identity; some of these also depending upon literary or fictional writings: see below, pp.7–8).[1]

Such a project cuts across the boundaries and assumptions of academic disciplines as they often exist within current institutions of higher education. All too often, such disciplines demand discrete, self-contained rules of engagement with evidence and specific styles of writing; in effect, part of the same problem that I have outlined above. Many historians of the concept of 'nationalism' regard the phenomenon as a modern development precipitated by the European Enlightenment. The provocative opening statement of Elie Kedourie's popular monograph, *Nationalism* (1960), 'Nationalism is a doctrine invented in Europe at the beginning of the nineteenth century', is only one instance of a common assumption.[2] It may well be possible to argue that a doctrine which can be defined as 'nationalism' post-dates the sixteenth century, but if we accept Anthony D. Smith's recent formulation, then one can clearly counter that many writers in Tudor England saw their country as a 'nation': 'A nation can...be defined as *a named human population sharing an historic territory, common myths and historical memories, a mass, public culture, a common economy and common legal rights and duties for all members*' (Smith's emphasis).[3]

Certainly, this definition would concur with the evidence to be found in the writings of such diverse writers as Sir Thomas Smith, Richard Hakluyt, Raphael Holinshed and Edward Hall, as well as the authors under consideration in this book (although their versions of the English nation would not encompass 'all' the inhabitants of England and the entire range of Smith's points would not always be fully fleshed out or properly considered; but the same could be said of many 'modern' attempts to define a nation).[4] It seems perverse that historians of nationalism have been so keen to stress only the recent history of the concept of the nation, as if the pre-history (in their terms) only led to a current state of affairs.[5] If the nation is seen as an 'imagined community' which includes some people and excludes others, then surely it must constantly be reimagined and renegotiated. The idea of a nation is predicated upon the existence of a public space – geographical and conceptual – which will always include competing voices desiring to speak for the 'nation' and fashion it according to their particular designs. Some conceptions of national identity will clearly be more successful than others and become dominant; some will disappear, as I argue in chapter 1 was the case with John Skelton's attempt to make himself the spokesman of various national communities.

Secondly, this project challenges comfortable notions of literary history which frequently assume that literature is an unchanging, ahistorical category, even when authors of such histories are obviously aware that this is not the case but have failed to pursue their own insights as rigorously as they might have done.[6] Literary history cannot be written in isolation if the writers of literature do not agree what literature is – as, I will argue, is the case with the authors considered in this volume. An attempt to write a 'pure' literary history, in the belief that a genre of writing can be isolated, will always be prone to teleological readings.[7] In this way, a traditional literary history and a history of nationalism can be seen to mirror each other in the assumption that the object of their particular studies can be isolated and separated from other phenomena.

There is another and more obvious connection between the two disciplines. If the standard error of historians of national identity is to assume that concepts can be seen to have a pre-history and a history 'proper', literary historians often seem to make the related mistake of believing that, just because certain literary styles and forms did not succeed in influencing later writers, they must have been always automatically doomed to failure; and, conversely, those which enjoyed a long history did so because they were always better adapted to survival in the hostile swamps of culture. Thus, it is often argued that the sonnet form, imported from Italy by Wyatt and Surrey in the reign of Henry VIII, led directly to the explosion of sonnets in the 1580s and 1590s.[8] This narrative ignores numerous complexities and ideologically circumscribes an intricate history of textual transmission. Italian authors like Petrarch had been adapted by Chaucer during the reign of Richard II, but the influence had not survived long after his death in 1400, ie, the sonnet form had already been adapted into English and failed to become a dominant norm before it was reintroduced in the sixteenth century. Similarly, before the publication of *Tottel's Miscellany* (1557), it had a relatively minor influence on English poetry and other verse forms (complaint, *de casibus* tragedy, Skeltonics and other related styles, rime royal and so on) played a much more dominant role in the history of an English literature. In fact, when Chaucer was re-invented as the great English poet in the Renaissance, he was usually seen as a proto-Protestant, as part of the vernacular tradition against which the courtly poets of the 1580s and 1590s were reacting in attempting to establish an English poetic style based on Italian and French models. So the forerunner of a tradition went unrecognised and actually had what he first started – the English adoption of Italian poetic forms – eventually defined against the use made of him by later writers. Such an ironic reversal illustrates the unstable nature of literary history. The willingness of literary historians to overlook this and other similar examples argues another case of a teleological narrative being applied to distinguish a pre-history from a history proper.[9] The chief desire is to create a smoothly progressive and easily manageable chronology.

More importantly still, it ignores the vast literary production of the mid-sixteenth century when very different styles of literature were sponsored at the court of Edward VI as the researches of John N. King have unearthed recently.[10] It is by no means an obvious 'fact' of literary history that such literature need only be seen in relation to the later forms which developed in the closing stages of Elizabeth's reign and can be dismissed as the 'drab' forerunner of a courtly culture which situated itself in relation to certain kinds of Henrician literature.[11] If Wyatt and Surrey seem like the harbingers of Sidney and Spenser, that is because those later authors *sometimes* read them that way. Literary history forms a discontinuous narrative even in terms of its own intra-textual process and to read it as a gradual development is absurd; who knows what might have happened had Edward VI not succumbed to consumption in 1553? It should always be remembered that some types of literature die not because they are inherently doomed, but because of the accidents and strange circumstances of a history that can never be merely 'literary'.

One might point to the perpetual suppression of a hyphen in the writing of English literary history, for, after all, to write a history of English Literature presupposes that both the nation and its literature are separate, stable entities, congruent yet unrelated bodies of empirical data which belong quite naturally together. English literary history tends far too often to concentrate upon a canon of literary texts and not upon what makes them English or why they are considered to be literary; the hyphen joining nation and literature is silently passed over so that, in an ideological manoeuvre, neither 'literariness' nor 'Englishness' are considered, only a body of works of literature. Therefore, a history of a national literature justifies itself in terms of a current imagined state of that nation, oblivious to the prospect that that state will always be open to dispute, as the acrimonious debates concerning the *national* curriculum illustrate.[12] Who, in the final analysis, speaks for the nation and decides how it has to be written?

If we examine some of the most widely read literary texts produced in the sixteenth century, it would seem that answers given to this question vary considerably. Different authors trace different genealogies, articulate various notions of literariness, adopt multifarious clusters of myths and historical memories and assume different political positions. What all the texts analysed in this book have in common is their desire to help constitute and participate within a national public sphere.

I have adopted – and adapted – this concept from Jürgen Häbermas's well-known formulation:

By the 'public sphere' we mean first of all a realm of our social life in which something approaching public opinion can be formed. Access is guaranteed to all citizens. A portion of the public sphere comes into being in every conversation in which private individuals assemble to form a public body. They then behave neither like business or professional people transacting private affairs, nor like members of a constitutional order subject to the constraints of a state bureaucracy. Citizens behave as a public body when they confer in an unrestricted fashion – that is, with the guarantee of freedom of assembly and association and the freedom to express and publish their opinions – about matters of general interest.

Häbermas alleges that such a free public space 'grew out of a specific phase of bourgeois society' and only exists in the 'modern bourgeois constitutional state', so that he too is a historian who dates modernity as a post-Enlightenment phenomenon.[13]

Häbermas has been rightly criticised for his Utopian faith in the successful operation of the public sphere in Western democracies and his apparent belief in ideologically unfettered speech acts competing to form public opinion.[14] His brief history of the development of the 'bourgeois public sphere', from the 'representative public sphere' of the high Middle Ages, which depended upon the personal power of the monarch, to the 'new sphere of "public authority"' which came into being with national and territorial states' and which consisted of private individuals who were in opposition to state structures and hierarchies, before maturing into the public sphere proper – something which 'was unique and without historical precedent' – betrays the same teleological assumptions of historians of nationalism. It might be argued, *pace* Häbermas, that the public sphere has always been an *ideal*, a hope for an unrestricted medium of debate beyond the reaches of state authority and outside the delusive confines of ideological distortion. Häbermas does not examine ancient political philosophy or any history of thought outside Europe, a strange and disturbing ethnocentrism given the grandeur of his claim that the public sphere 'was unique and without historical precedent'.[15]

Häbermas specifically contrasts the 'political public sphere' to the literary one; it should be asked why the two spheres can never overlap, especially if the place of literature within a range of discursive formations is always subject to change? To cite one example: during the Pilgrimage of Grace (1536–7), much of the propaganda produced by the rebels seeking a restoration of the traditional rights and functions of the church was in the form of ballads and poems and most produced by the Henrican authorities was in the form of proclamations and tracts.[16] However, one poem seems to have been written at the government's behest, namely Wilfrid Holme of Huntington's *The Fall and Evill Successe of Rebellion* (1536).[17] The poem is a dream vision in which the author meets the figure of Anglia who asks him to explain to her about sedition. Holme responds with a wealth of Biblical and Roman examples and a brief survey of English Medieval history, before coming to the recent 'commotion', ie, the Pilgrimage of Grace. Much of Holme's narrative is a straightforward dramatisation of Henry's response to the Pilgrims' five articles, which demanded that the Catholic Church be fully restored with its independence from the monarch left intact, unpopular laws such as the Statute of Uses be repealed, the King's Council be purged of 'villein blood' and replaced with traditional nobles, and those blamed for the Protestant onslaught (for the Pilgrims always proclaimed their loyalty to what they saw as the deluded sovereign), Cromwell and Richard Rich, be banished as heretics.[18] Henry's replies had been printed and circulated throughout the rebellious areas, Lincolnshire, Lancashire and Yorkshire, and often what Holme writes is simply a transference of these from one medium to another, so that the verses can be lined up against the original statements.[19]

But there is a point in the story where narrative strategies seem to be laid bare and illusionistic pretence turns against itself. Anglia, chiding Holme for being over-detailed in providing an exhaustive list of the principal rebels, loses her temper and demands he obey the rules of her discourse:

> Then with an ardent fury quod Anglia and frouned,
> Holme it is but *fiction* I say thou dost devise,
> Shewdest thou not me that gentlemen and men that were,
> Fled to castles & fortresses, what made them then to rise?
> (fo. 7; my emphasis)

In this poem, literary fiction and political discourse do not exist as antitheses and one does not preclude the other: rather, in this specific context, politics demands fictive treatment. Anglia is not angry because she does not believe Holme's account of events narrated in the poem, but because he has elaborated factual details at too great a length. Anglia's point is that a 'fiction', the ability to craft a narrative and tell a story, will represent her more truthfully than a chronicle of unselected information. As a reader of herself, she will understand a political situation better if it is narrated as a literary fiction rather than as a morass of confused observations. Fiction, for Anglia, is 'real' because without a conception of fiction (literature), 'facts' are meaningless, so that fictionality can be seen, paradoxically, to be both anterior and posterior to factuality. The desire of the narrator to prise the actual away from the fictional will always be frustrated.

The Fall and Evill Successe of Rebellion is a state-sponsored poem and so excludes itself from the public sphere as defined by Häbermas: 'The state and the public sphere do not overlap as one might suppose from casual language use. Rather they confront one another as opponents' (p.46). However, the crucial suggestion that literary fiction can and should be used to discuss political matters obviously opens up the possibility that literature could be used to articulate an oppositional public voice as well as a national one (something Holme achieves through his use of the prosopopoeia of Anglia). Indeed, one might suggest that many sixteenth-century writers explicitly attempted to link the 'imagined community' of the nation to a 'public sphere', in that they used their fictions to create a critical national literature.

Why, it should be asked, was this the case? I am not attempting to claim a unique status for the diverse works of Skelton, Surrey, Bale, Sidney, Spenser, the authors of the theoretical literary treatises discussed here (Wilson, Gosson and Puttenham) and the authors of *A Mirror for Magistrates*. Other sixteenth-century writers could also have been included – notably, perhaps, Wyatt, Lyly, Marlowe and Nashe.[20] I have not considered dramatic writings (excepting Gosson's tract and certain of Bale's works), partly owing to considerations of space and partly because various monographs have already started to deal with the sorts of question I have been asking.[21] I am also not attempting to assert that every sixteenth-century writer of literature has to be read in terms of their relationship to a public national culture, nor that many had not defined themselves in this way before – Chaucer, Gower, Malory and other inter- preters of Arthurian material are pertinent examples – nor that many would continue to do so after the death of Elizabeth in 1603 – Drayton, George Herbert, Ben Jonson, Milton and Dryden are only among the most obvious examples.[22] What I am suggesting is that the problem of national identity required urgent attention in the sixteenth century, principally owing to the Reformation and the consequent stress placed on the need to establish vernacular languages and cultures in each respective European country.[23] Imagined national communities had existed before the spread of Protestantism, but with the break- up of the Latinate culture of the late Middle Ages a new impetus was given to the development of national language which should become expressions of a territorial integrity. There was a greater pressure than there had been immediately before on the importance of defining identity as national and those who saw the need to write an English literature and establish this particular vernacular culture recognised that such a task involved renegotiating the relationship with the political authority under which this writing would exist.[24]

However, as the case of Skelton illustrates (chapter 1), a history of national identity – like a literary history – is dis- continuous: the Reformation served to kill off certain forms of national identity as well as to foster and proliferate new ones. It would be false to argue that the Reformation inaugurated such debates and erroneous to read Skelton's ideas solely in terms of a reaction to Protestant thought. Skelton's different visions of an English nation did not disappear because they were necessarily unfeasible, but because events which he could not have foreseen overtook him and rendered him an anachronism.

In a crucial sense, any literary discourse had an ambiguous status in the sixteenth century. On the one hand, literature affirmed a free space outside the constraints of a consciously politicised vocabulary and mode of writing; on the other, as a key component of a national culture, it played a specifically political role. An appreciation of this aporia is vital to our understanding of the relationship between the nation, literature and the public in this period. Literature could be seen as a form of ideological cement in helping to constitute the nation; but also as a public sphere in that it provided writers with a means of separating their utterances from the political constraints of state-approved discourses. It was thus a site of knowledge saturated with ideology and simultaneously a Utopian hope of a free, interactive critical space. Current arguments regarding the subversion/containment of Renaissance literary texts are all too often blind to this ambiguity and the potential for directly opposed readings of the same works which have to exist as ultimately contradictory statements. It is not always necessary – or possible – to insist on a definitely clear and distinct reading, aligning the text with one specific range of meanings.[25]

Censorship under the Tudors is a complex and thorny problem. Some scholars argue that there was a deliberate and programmatic policy, whilst others see the process as a far more random and *ad hoc* affair determined principally by luck and official sloth.[26] Whatever the truth of the matter, it is clear that literary texts often worried the authorities and the mechanisms of censorship threatened every writer who was bold, foolish or ignorant enough to challenge accepted norms. What got censored and what did not often seems surprising to a modern reader; how did the authors of the first edition of *A Mirror for Magistrates* escape when that work appears to challenge the prerogative rights of monarchs? The answer to this particular question may be that the work was not read as critical of contemporary authoritarianism but as a celebration of a British/English history, something it was to be transformed into in its later manifestations (see chapter 2). Was *The Old Arcadia* never published because of fear of censorship? There is no direct evidence for this contention, but episodes which seem to criticise the rulers of Arcadia in that text are transferred to more exotic locations in *The New Arcadia*, possibly removing a reading which both versions invite, that Arcadia can be read as Elizabethan England (see chapter 5). Why were Spenser's poems never actually censored despite the hostile attention they generated and the barely disguised attacks on the queen in the later books of *The Faerie Queene* (this should perhaps be seen in conjunction with the non-appearance of his prose tract, *A View of the Present State of Ireland*, which many assume, perhaps erroneously, to have been suppressed)?[27] Such examples might imply that just as poets and authors of literature were unsure of their position, so were the powers-that-be uncertain of their role *vis-à-vis* literary texts and unclear about how to read them. Again, one might claim that the relationship between a public sphere and the imagined community of the nation was complex and fluid.

A further problem needs to be noted: most writers considered here tend to elide the distinction between Britain and England as geographical, political and literary communities. There is an obvious nationalist motive at work here for English writers who wish to appropriate a wider heritage for their own ends, looking backwards to a dual tradition of writing. By employing both a series of national myths associated with the matter of Britain and a genealogy of English writers, sixteenth-century authors were able to assert an English hegemony within Britain, colonising the imagined space as English. One should not forget that this space also included Ireland and was thus not usually confined to mainland Britain.[28] Critical the public sphere imagined may have been, but English writers rigorously excluded other peoples and nationalities from this privileged domain, affirming it as their own and denying other forms of cultural identity the right to exist within the boundaries of the state. Such writers may not have had more than a vague conception of what audience their texts would have reached, but in constructing an implied reader they did not intend to speak to Scots, Irish or Welsh.[29] Once again, we are reminded that there is no easy separation of nation and public.[30]

I have consciously avoided certain common terms used in analysing the sixteenth century. I hope it is obvious that to have used the descriptive label 'early modern period' would have signalled the same problems of teleological reading involved in the histories of nationalism discussed above and, to a lesser extent, histories of literature. It would imply that modern men and women are of a different order from pre-modern peoples and that early modern societies had only just emerged from these dark ages. It is an arrogance of a type identical to that of many theories of 'post-modernism', which assert that the grand narratives which used to explain our lives (Marxist, feminist, psychoanalytic, scientific, Darwinian and so on) have broken down and fragmented into a multitude of local narratives so that no knowledge can ever exist without a context or without recycling previous and outmoded forms of narrative. The question is, how did we get here? To believe that the past was a series of grand narratives which have now come to an end is itself a grand narrative, blind to its own pretensions and logic.[31] In a sense such theories of post-modernism are the nemesis of comfortable assumptions of the superiority of modern society to its predecessors. It is often stated in books and articles on the development of modern historiography that truly modern methods did not occur until the scholarly revolution of the sixteenth and seventeenth centuries, ie, the early modern period. In other words the two events – the onset of modernity and the rise of 'proper' historical scholarship – occur simultaneously but are unrelated. It is argued that the works of Polydore Vergil, William Camden, Francis Bacon, Sir Robert Cotton *et al.*, inaugurated the transformation of chronicle into history proper and that similar figures in other European countries effected the same change.[32] What a post-modern analysis often does is to break down the inherent faith in the related rise of modernity and historiography, transporting the reader, in a way, back to the age of pre-history because we can no longer have the same faith in the efficacy of historical explanation, having to make do instead with 'local' narratives and chronicles.[33] The wheel has come full circle.

There are obvious problems with such stories. Both tend to take too seriously the propaganda and prejudices of writers who were keen to define themselves as distinct from those who had come before. It is a myth that in the 'Middle Ages' 'historians' wrote only chronicles and were incapable of sorting out data, were incapable of being sceptical regarding the reliability of certain source material, could not interpret the material they used in a historical manner and believed that societies had always been fundamentally the same because God had ordained

them that way.[34] Such a falsehood obviously suited sixteenth-
and seventeenth-century writers who wanted to assert their own
independence from writers of the past; what is more than a little
depressing is how keen 'early modern' historians of historiography have been to believe them.

Yet, as David Aers has often pointed out, such gullibility is
not restricted to historiographical scholarship. Many self-styled
radical critics, inspired principally by Michel Foucault's *Discipline and Punish* (1970) and his unfinished *magnum opus, The
History of Sexuality* (1970–88), have, ironically, complied with
the representations of the Middle Ages produced by the most
conservative of Medieval literary commentators. The principal
model which dominated Medieval studies from the 1950s to the
1980s was probably most influentially and forcefully pro-
pounded by D. W. Robertson in his *A Preface to Chaucer* (1963):

the medieval world was innocent of our profound concern for tension
... We project dynamic polarities on history as class struggles, balances
of power, or as conflicts between economic realities and traditional
ideals. We demand tension in art ... But the medieval world with its
quiet hierarchies knew nothing of these things.[35]

Basing a mode of historical scholarship almost exclusively on
clerical and Biblical texts represses 'the voices of dissent, the
massive and sustained struggles of tenants and labourers against
landlords and employers in late medieval England, the het-
erogeneity of experience and belief in late medieval communities, languages and rituals', as well as the economic
developments of the twelfth century when 'commodities with a
monetary value emerged as the chief force for objectifying
economic connections' (p.21).[36]

It is easy to understand why this reading of English and
European history appealed to – and still appeals to – scholars of
a conservative bias. As many 'New Historicist' and Marxist
inspired re-readings of the 'early modern period' have argued,
the same amnesia has consistently been applied to much study
of that era. One only has to think of the massive influence of T.
S. Eliot's essays on the Metaphysical poets and the Leavises'
faith in an 'organic community' as a hammer with which to

beat subsequent reading practices in an age of mass culture, or
E. M. W. Tillyard's *The Elizabethan World Picture* (1943) (still
set as background reading when I started my undergraduate
degree in English in 1981), to appreciate the influence of such
interpretations on the teaching of English literature.[37] What
particularly exasperates Aers – and myself, writing as someone
who until recently believed in the reality of the 'Renaissance'
– is that in the 1970s and 1980s 'distinctly radical critics were
propagating a version of the English Middle Ages quite
indistinguishable from that sponsored by conservatives and
grossly idealist critics' (pp.23–4).

Why has such an appalling blindness to the complexities of
'pre-modern' political, cultural and economic life prevailed for
so long, so that many iconoclastic histories of 'the subject'
argue, in all seriousness, that 'Pre-bourgeois subjection does not
properly involve subjectivity at all, but a condition of dependent
membership in which place and articulation are defined not by
an interiorized self-recognition ... but by incorporation in the
body politic which is the king's body in the social form'
(p.24)?[38] It will not have escaped the reader of this introduction
that the above statement (by Francis Barker) coincides exactly
with Häbermas's perception of the public sphere in the Middle
Ages (see above, p.6). Aers attacks his Renaissance colleagues
for their lack of curiosity and their indolence, but his fundamental diagnosis of the problem is the same as mine:

[T]hese radical critics are the victims of an institutionally trained
ignorance. Trained as literary critics they have been trained and now
work in departments which still compartmentalize our discipline,
whatever the claims to subvert received boundaries and canons: this
means that a specialist in Shakespeare and early modern English
literature simply does not read the texts of fourteenth and fifteenth
century England – the 'literary' texts, the texts around the institution
of penance and confession, the mystical texts, the political texts – let
alone study them in relation to recent social, economic and political
work being done on the period. So deeply ingrained is this compart-
mentalization that even when literary critics specializing in the early
modern period and in literary theory want to tell a story that *depends*
on claims about the period 1300–1600 they cannot erode its effects.
(p.31)

Aers's plea is principally that we suspend the master narrative
which dictates that everything interesting occurs around 1600.
Aers does not state it, but it is a premiss of his argument that
such terms as 'early modern' are ideologically motivated and
should be treated with suspicion, which is why I have avoided
using them. Defining a period as 'early modern' implies that we
are all within such a paradigm or historical epoch. Clearly it
flattens out any more diverse and discontinuous historical
narratives of time, space and place and also divides peoples into
two homogeneous categories: pre-modern and modern. More
worrying still perhaps is the ethnocentric assumption – again,
akin to Habermas's – of this belief, as it stems from an
Enlightenment faith in the progress of European civilisation, of
the growing maturity of Western society emerging from the
Dark Ages. It is hardly surprising that post-modernist theorists
of a global capitalism, which dictates the world's interests and
which cannot be escaped, have been attacked on precisely these
grounds.[39] Although, strictly speaking, such concerns are
beyond the scope of this short book, they are not irrelevant to its
argument which is intended to open up the confines of literary
study and literary history to a wider politics and a less
constricted notion of history.

Just as I have avoided the use of 'early modern', I have also
generally avoided the use of the term 'Renaissance' (except in
the book's sub-title). My reasons are fundamentally the same.
Although many scholars now recognise with Erwin Panofsky
that there was never only one real Renaissance as Burckhardt
believed, the name has remained as an institutional label within
literary studies in higher education.[40] Obviously such an
isolation of a sub-discipline encourages the same sort of
ideological confusion as 'early modern' propagates in historical
categorisation. As A. C. Spearing has pointed out, 'It was the
Renaissance that invented the Middle Ages', so that the 'post',
in the sense of what comes after, in fact comes first, as a
necessary consequence of self-definition, a process mirrored in
the need to articulate such modern critical movements as post-
structuralism and post-modernism.[41] However one attempts to
define the Renaissance – whether as 'the discovery of the world

and the discovery of man', or as 'the re-birth of learning', to name but the two most celebrated descriptions – the elastic and discontinuous nature of the phenomenon posited will defy simple synchronic classification:

There are several different Renaissances in the various cultural fields such as literature, the visual arts, architecture, philosophy and political thought, to which the term applies, and they begin at different moments, proceed at different paces, interact differently with earlier cultural traditions, and affect different parts of Europe at different times. Part of the difficulty of definition comes from the persistent and perhaps irresistible attempt to subsume these various though related phenomena under a single heading.[42]

The error of many contemporary literary scholars of the 'Renaissance' has been to take at face value the statements of self-styled Renaissance men and, particularly, their portrayal of the static Middle Ages which was a necessary correlative of their own self-fashioning.

My use of the term 'Renaissance' in the sub-title of this book is not to be regarded as an objective historical classification, but rather as an acknowledgement that the writers discussed in the last two chapters, Sir Philip Sidney and Edmund Spenser, are often represented to be the fullest expression of the English literary Renaissance, a judgement reflected in standard literary guides to the period, higher education courses and texts available from publishers. To read like this is an ideological manoeuvre which erases the complexities, ambiguities and contradictions of the role of literature in Tudor England; but to write as if it does not happen is perhaps to pretend that one has escaped the burden of a subsequent history of interpretation and hence my recognition of such reading practices in my sub-title.

The Reformation has not been invested with the same significance; it has long been recognised by historians that its progress throughout Europe was a haphazard process and there has never been the same attempt to homogenise its effects and influence.[43] Whilst many literary scholars have written about the impact of Protestant ideas upon literature – often going so far as to write highly tendentiously of Protestantism as a 'discourse' – Reformation literary texts have only ever been the preserve of a few specialists or used as 'background' information.[44] I have therefore written of my literary history as 'Reformation to Renaissance' to indicate what has been omitted in deeply ingrained assumptions and written out of other such histories.

Why has there been this convergence between a historical conception of early modernity and an assimilation of the complexities of a Tudor literary history, leading to the monolithic simplicity of the notion of the Renaissance? The straightforward answer to this question is that it is from the Tudors that our English perception of a national identity is to be dated; hence modernity, nationality and literary greatness are *made* to coincide. It is not a historical accident that Shakespeare is seen to be the greatest English author and is at the centre of current educational controversies, the Right asserting that no English schoolchild should be able to go out into the wider world without having studied at least one of his plays (strangely enough, this seems to apply to children in Northern Ireland and Wales).[45] W. B. Yeats once remarked, in a chiasmic formula redolent of many 'New Historicist' utterances, that John O'Leary had understood the intrinsic link between national identity and literature: 'He, more clearly than any one, has seen that there is no fine nationality without literature, and seen the converse also, that there is no fine literature without nationality.'[46] Quoting these words in his fascinating book, *Threshold of a Nation* (1979), Philip Edwards came to the conclusion that:

The nation does not *need* literature in the way in which ... Yeats thought it did. It uses what it wants; it needs slogans and marching-songs; it needs above all a camouflage of ideals and dreams to bewitch its followers. So it takes what it wants, corrupting the literature in the process and perhaps corrupting the writer too ... The less 'nationality' is preached, the better both theatre [and, by implication, literature in general] and nation are likely to fare [Edwards's emphasis].[47]

This idealistic statement could be accused of two related errors. Firstly, Edwards writes as if nations are objective factual entities and are not themselves written and re-written. A nation cannot write itself as Edwards's substitution of a prosopopoeia for a fictional construction suggests. Secondly, he has omitted the hyphen that exists between a nation and its literature and his attempt to dismiss nationalistic elements as propaganda, in order to assert the independence of 'true' literature from this charge, results from the false hope of being able to separate the 'imagined community' which constitutes a nation from the nation itself. It is not, *ipso facto*, absurd to state that nations can exist without literature, because of course they can – or could – but to pretend that 'proper' literature is innocent of such a reading, is to forget that nations are both imagined fictions and 'real' social forces at the same time. It is not just a collection of slogans and marching-songs which have helped to construct English national and literary identity. The conception of 'English literature' itself cannot be separated from the writing of the nation.

Many recent books, some of which have sold very well in terms of academic book sales, have reassessed the value of studying such a subject in higher education courses; notable examples being Terry Eagleton, *The Function of Criticism* (1984) and *Literary Theory* (1983), Chris Baldick, *The Social Mission of English Criticism* (1983), Brian Doyle, *English and Englishness* (1989) and Peter Widdowson, ed., *Re-Reading English* (1982).[48] Such analyses have dealt with the institutionalisation of an academic discipline, the history of its teaching and the assumptions made by those who presumed to carry out what they saw as a crucial social function. I would argue that it is just as important to analyse the complex formation of the origin of the object of analysis, ie, the attempt to establish a recognisably *English* literature and, to a large extent, that is what this book is concerned with. Whilst much 'New Historicist' research has alerted readers to the omnipresence of politics in Tudor literature, it has often been assumed that literature and politics can be separated. There has been a tendency to read politics as a sub-text of literary works, an assumption that a series of homogeneous cultural artefacts existed during that period so that the informed modern reader can identify 'structural homologies' and then produce an oppositional reading against the grain in order to recover an authentic historical meaning. This has been the case even with such stimulating works as Stephen Greenblatt's *Renaissance Self-Fashioning* (1980) and Jonathan Dollimore's *Radical Tragedy* (1984), probably the two most influential works of criticism in this area written in the last twenty years. Greenblatt frequently assumes that all literature functions to contain seemingly subversive utterances (a belief still present in his recent work), whereas Dollimore often asserts the converse case, that literature is *ipso facto* oppositional.[49] Debates carried on between 'New' Historicists and 'Cultural Materialists' in scholarly journals often do no more than reiterate these positions.[50]

My argument is that no one in the Tudor period was sure how to write such a literature or confident as to what it was supposed to do. Should authors try to produce a sophisticated literary culture to rival those of other European countries, principally France and Italy, and do so by adopting their poetic models? Or should they try to imitate a classical heritage more successfully than writers in those countries had managed? Or, could such a culture be discovered in a native vernacular? This last option has been the least explored by critics (at least until the extensive researches of John King), but to many writers outside the court or on its margins it often seemed the most attractive route, especially given the extravagant claims for the ancient purity of the English/British church made by John Bale, John Foxe and others, which were enshrined in the marginal annotations to *The Geneva Bible* (1560), the most popular Tudor translation.[51] Similarly, writers were unsure exactly what literature was supposed to do; was it a series of 'true' statements based on the Scriptures as John Bale often seems to assert (see chapter 2); a medium controlled by the demands of an absolutist state which occasionally tried to assert itself by making veiled criticisms of the monarch and his/her circle; or a forum for political discussion? How did any of these positions try to determine their 'Englishness' and that of those they addressed? Literary acts in the sixteenth century were, more often than not, political interventions and drew attention to themselves in precisely this way.

A reader will probably wonder why I chose to finish this study when I did. I should perhaps start with a disclaimer: there is no absolute, cast-iron, unchallengeable reason why I have chosen to finish with Edmund Spenser. I am suspicious of books which assert matters in such terms (as my attacks on the periodisation of literary history should indicate). As I have already stated there is no inevitability attached to my finishing point, no teleological end to a process, just as it has no clearly observable origin.[52] I am not mapping out a 'tradition' in the sense that literary historians often use this vague word (but, conversely, that does not mean that I think the authors considered existed in isolation from each other, because it seems to be the case that they did read their predecessors and did reflect upon the fact that their writings were influenced by them).[53] Spenser has been selected as a finishing point to the book for three main reasons; firstly, and most obviously, it enables me to make my conclusion coincide with the end of the Tudors for whom I have claimed such central importance in the fashioning of a distinctly 'modern' identity (it should be added that there was nothing inevitable about the end of the Tudors, but then, no one has ever claimed that there was); secondly, because Spenser's life in Ireland, as a minor public servant attempting to complete with increasing disillusionment an English national epic, serves as a telling example of the ways in which a literature which argued for its central role in public affairs came to be marginalised and reinterpreted; thirdly, because Spenser has usually been taken to be one of the most significant figures of the English Renaissance and hence has been appropriated by commentators and made to fit into conventional categories. Even John King's *Spenser and the Reformation Tradition* (1990), one of the very few books which deals with Spenser in terms of a body of native rather than of classical or European texts, reads these only as contexts and cannot see the continuity and importance of literary acts.[54] The case of Edmund Spenser's complex and contradictory literary identity is not one which solves all the problems which this book seeks to discuss, but it does serve to highlight them.

I have concentrated upon specific authors rather than

examining genres or types of discourse for similarly mixed reasons and not without a great deal of reflection. Firstly, I hope that in concentrating on authors rather than scrutinising genres and types of discourse, the false assumptions of much traditional literary history, which places authors neatly into periods, will be challenged all the more effectively by being viewed from a radically different perspective. Secondly, and more importantly, following Stephen Greenblatt, I want to look at how different writers attempted to fashion their own identities as individuals who made up a public and a nation.

Just as my choice of periodisation and classification of material is not based upon fundmental, foundationalist principles, neither is my choice of theoretical vocabulary. Like most literary critics and literary historians, I do not believe that a metahistorical, scientific discourse of inquiry can be established.[55] My concern here is to place the emphasis on the very problem of interpretation and methods of reading. Literary historians, even radical ones, often tend to posit too absolute a separation between literary texts and historical (con)texts, whilst historians are rarely concerned enough with the difficulties of close reading; hence the need to open out the field to more intertextual modes of reading history and literature.[56] This has been my aim in this book and I have employed the strategies and ideas of various literary theorists and philosophers – Derrida, Ricoeur, Bakhtin, Bhabha, Barthes, Foucault and others, as well as Häbermas – not in an attempt to be modish or eclectic, but in order to foreground the problem of interpretation in translating the foreign country of the past into a current idiom.[57] Critics who think that they are beyond the need of jargon and are free to write 'proper' English are simply in the grip of an older jargon and, consequently, older theories.[58] In attempting to explore the interrelationship between literature, the nation and the public, I cannot pretend that I do not have numerous axes to grind in choosing the subject in the first place; but then we never come to read material in a 'pure' way. In order for us to interpret anything, it must be to some extent, 'already read'.[59] But just because something has been 'already read' does not mean that it always has to be – or can be – read in the same way over and over again; or, that any text can be read in any way an individual reader wishes. We all exist within 'reading communities' which, like nations, are imagined.[60] In the final analysis both nations and literary traditions are fictions which have to be read – and re-read.

CHAPTER I

A Skelton in the closet: English literary identity betwixt and between

Stephen Jay Gould's recent book, *Wonderful Life*, which deals with the fossil record of the Burgess Shale, a small quarry high in the Canadian Rockies formed over 500 million years ago, has illustrated how the all-pervasive representation of 'the ascent of man' as 'the march of progress' – from crawling monkey to upright, relatively hairless *homo sapiens* – influenced those scientists who first attempted to reconstruct the original pre-Cambrian primal scene. Convinced by their own iconography of the increasing diversity of species, they could not countenance the possibility that a rich variety of forms of 'wonderful life' had in fact become extinct. Instead fossil remnants were made to fit 'primitive' prototypes of existing species. The most spectacular example of misreading which Gould cites is illustrated in the case of '*Anomalocaris*'. In 'the best-known reconstruction of the Burgess Shale', 'two jellyfish are shown swimming in like pineapple slices'.[1] In fact, according to the most up-to-date, less triumphalistically inspired research, the fossil represented as a jellyfish is the mouth of the large predator '*Anomalocaris*', a creature over six times the size of its nearest rival on the sea-bed.

Yet this large and sophisticated arthropod died out whilst the tiny and seemingly insignificant vertebrate '*Pikaia*' survived. And as Gould concludes, perhaps somewhat over-ornately:

Wind the tape of life back to Burgess times, and let it play again. If *Pikaia* does not survive in the replay, we are wiped out of future history … And I don't think that any handicapper, given the Burgess *evidence as known today*, would have granted very favourable odds for the persistence of *Pikaia*. The survival of *Pikaia* was a contingency of 'just history'. (pp.322–3; my emphasis)

23

The point I am making is that there is no reason why we should not apply this notion of a random history, where survival of the fittest does not mean survival of the best but merely the most suited to prevailing conditions, to literary history. Gould himself hints at this in his attempt to argue that the legacy of Darwin is an understanding that all is 'just history' dependent on contingent factors. Specifically, I want to suggest that John Skelton has been granted a role as the missing link in English poetry – to continue the evolutionary metaphor – precisely because he does not fit easily into our classifications of 'Medieval' and 'Renaissance', which are categories imposed upon the evidence. Skelton seems like an anachronism – half Medieval ape and half Renaissance man – because he tried to forge a role for himself as the poetic spokesman of a particular brand of Englishness; one which ceased to exist after the inauguration of the Reformation. With hindsight it is easy to understand why Skelton developed the strange reputation he did. But how could a contemporary observer have predicted the cataclysmic upheavals of the 1520s and 1530s?[2] How could anyone have been expected to see that the national audience which Skelton attempts to construct through his poetry would so swiftly disappear from view and very different poetic forms consumed by very different audiences come to assume a hegemonic sway in the development of English literature and public life?

In 1589 the ghost of John Skelton was summoned out of his grave to pour scorn on the defeated Spanish in the same manner that he had vented his spleen on the unfortunate poet Garnesche, Cardinal Wolsey, Lutheran heretics and, most obviously, vanquished Scots:

> O king of Spaine
> Is it not a paine
> To thy heart and braine,
> And every vaine,
> To see thy traine
> For to sustaine
> Withouten gaine

> The worldes disdaine,
> Which doth dispise
> As toies and lies,
> With shoutes and cries
> Thy enterprise.[3]

Despite the damning judgements of those like Sir George Puttenham, who dismissed Skelton as 'a sharpe Satirist, but with more rayling and Scoffery then became a Poet Lawreat',[4] or the manifest lack of enthusiasm for his verse in courtly circles,[5] there were clearly those who felt that it was worthwhile relying on the 'madbrayned knave'[6] to lead the gloating over the fate of the nation's would-be destroyers.

Skelton was indeed a much read author in the sixteenth and early seventeenth centuries, as the number of editions of his work testifies.[7] Most popular among these was his poem 'Colin Clout', a satire of the dreadful abuses which, according to the poem's eponymous narrator, plagued England during the reign of Henry VIII. Colin Clout presents himself as the homely outsider of slight poetic ability, a Juvenalian rather than a Horatian satirist, uttering the truths which cannot be told at court:

> For though my ryme be ragged,
> Tattered and jagged,
> Rudely rayne-beaten,
> Rusty and mothe-eaten,
> Yf ye take well therwith
> It hath in it some pyth.
> For as far as I can se,
> It is wronge with eche degre.
>   (lines 53–60)[8]

Greg Walker has recently argued that Skelton wrote the poem as one of a series of attempts to gain the patronage of the merchants of the city of London (see below, p.45). Towards the end of his career Skelton turned from a fundamentally aristocratic audience to speak to a bourgeois one, and it is these antagonistic class terms which partly explain his later reputation as a proto-Protestant reformer.[9] More importantly, this shift perhaps helps us understand why the anonymous author of the patriotic Armada poem in Skeltonics saw in Skelton a spokesman for a particular manifestation – one seemingly at odds with more officially sanctioned voices from the court – of the English nation.[10] Skelton and the style which bore his name had become appropriated into an oppositional, counter-culture.

Skelton had not always chosen to address such an audience, or to write in such a way. In fact, one of the few poems of his to be published in his lifetime, *The Garland of Laurel*, was not in Skeltonics but aureate diction and iambs.[11] It may also be of significance that the poem occupies pride of place in the first collected edition of Skelton's works, the *Pithy, Pleasant and Profitable Workes of Master Skelton, Poet Laureate, Now Collected and Newly Published* (1568), printed by Thomas Marsh and compiled by the antiquarian, John Stow.[12] *The Garland of Laurel*, a dream-vision,[13] is most notorious for providing readers with Skelton's curriculum vitae and re-writing the modesty topos of its Medieval models.[14] Critics disagree whether this is an arrogant 'glorification of the dreamer Skelton's career and talents' designed to justify his inclusion 'with laureate tryumphe in the Courte of Fame' (line 63); or 'one long peal of laughter at the expense of the conventions it pretends to follow ... a recognisable spoof of the modesty topos'.[15] A judgement depends on whether Skelton is to be seen as a man obsessed 'with the advancement of his own reputation', a placeman selling himself to the highest bidder; or a relatively detached imaginative writer ignoring the problems of the 'real' world in order to meditate upon the literary problems of writing and establishing a poetic voice and authority.[16]

The *Laurel*, as the recent work of F. W. Brownlow has established, was clearly revised on various occasions and was perhaps constantly re-written over a period of twenty-five to thirty years,[17] from Skelton's first period at court – when he secured the post of tutor to Prince Arthur[18] – until its publication in 1523 when the elderly cleric-poet had finally managed to win back some aristocratic patronage.[19] It was printed by Richard Facques (Fawkes) who, although he had also published Skelton's *A Ballad of the Scottish Kynge* (1513), published mainly government statutes, papal bulls and indulgences and religious works.[20] It might appear that the poem made its way into print through official court connections, drawing attention to its lofty public status.

The *Laurel* opens with the dreamer persona (Skelton) musing on the vicissitudes of fortune, before falling drunkenly asleep on the stump of a dead oak tree (itself a symbol of the poet's thoughts) in the forest of Galtres.[21] He dreams that he sees a splendidly decorated pavilion where Pallas, the goddess of wisdom, and the Queen of Fame are debating the merits of Skelton's poetic reputation. The Queen of Fame alleges that Skelton has been too lazy and needs the wisdom of Pallas to help him write: 'Skelton is wonder slake,/And, as we dare, we fynde in hym grete lake' (lines 69–70). The 'auncient poetis', in contrast 'hath bene/Them selfe to embessy with all there corage,/So that there workis myght famously be sene' (lines 65–8). Skelton, says the Queen of Fame, has not been self-promoting enough. Pallas, in contrast, is more sympathetic. She argues that if Skelton 'gloryously publisshe his matter,/ Then men wyll say how he doth but flatter' (lines 83–4); if he writes 'true and plaine,/As sometyme he must vyces remorde,/Then sum wyll say he hath but lytill brayne' (lines 85–7), or worse, he will be banished like Ovid and Juvenal; if he writes in parables 'it were harde to construe this lecture;/ ... Another manes mynde diffuse is to expounde;/Yet harde is to make but sum fawt be founde' (lines 109–12). As well as setting out the acute dangers of writing and the difficulty of interpretation (a constant theme throughout literature of the Tudor period),[22] these lines force the reader to consider the role and function of literature, its ambiguous position within the public sphere.

Similarly, they fashion Skelton's life as a public object because by this time he had already written verse which fell into all three of the categories. Both writing and writer are made to function within a public economy; one cannot naively read off an autobiography of the poet apart from the persona the poetry constructs, so that the question as to which serves as evidence for the other (poetry providing details of poet's life: poet's life explaining his poetry) becomes impossible to determine.[23] Narrated self and narrator's art exist as inseparable representations which only make sense if made legible by the audience. The message cannot function without such a mass reading and the consequent elevation of Skelton to the status of popular hero as the individual reader is forced to consider how the poet best reaches an audience.

Pallas continues the argument by alleging that many have earned favour from Fortune who have not deserved it (lines 168–210); Fame stresses that she does not wish to exclude Skelton from her chosen circle and so fall out with the goddess of wisdom, but urges that Skelton must produce 'good recorde' (line 216) to support his pretensions. Pallas agrees and the poets in the legions of honour are called by the blast of a trumpet. Phoebus comes first, lamenting Daphne's refusal of his love, but pleading that as she was transformed into a laurel tree, so should all famous poets wear the laurel as a symbol of their status and as a compensation for their malign treatment by Fortune (lines 288–322).[24] There follows a parade of poets and orators from the classical world; Quintilian, Theocritus, Cicero, Livy, Ovid, Lucian, Statius, Terence, Seneca and so on. Then comes the line of English poets, Gower, 'that first garnisshed our Englysshe rude' (line 388); Chaucer, 'that nobly enterprysed/How that our Englyshe myght fresshly be ennewed' (lines 388–9) and John Lydgate. Their tabards are covered with diamonds and rubies, 'None so ryche stones in Turkey to sell' (line 396). However, more significant is what they do not have: 'Thei wanted nothynge but the *Laurell*' (line 397; my emphasis). The three poets address Skelton: Gower tells him that he deserves his place

> In our collage above the sterry sky,
> Bycause that ye encrease and amplyfy
> The brutid Britons of Brutus Albion,
> That welny was loste when that we were gone.
> (lines 403–6)

Skelton responds with due modesty ('To yow thre this honor shalbe reserved/ ... all that I do is under refformation' (lines 409–11)), before Chaucer tells Skelton that he has supplemented ('Counterwaying your besy delygence/Or that we beganne in the supplement' (lines 414–15)) what they began and thus deserves a place in Fame's court. Skelton thanks 'noble

Chaucer, whos pullished eloquence/Oure Englysshe rude so fresshely hath set out' (lines 421-2), before Lydgate, who confesses that there is nothing left for him to say, reiterates that 'by all our holl assent', Skelton deserves to be 'Avaunced by Pallas to *laurell preferment*' (line 434; my emphasis). The poet is then conveyed into the pavilion of Pallas, ready to state his case. Skelton is indeed to supplement the work of the tradition of English poetry he has mapped out; he is both to work as an adjunct to it and to overgo it, hence his stated destiny as the first *English* laureate for the *British* people: 'predominantly, [the] concern is with England and the English tradition. The poem is infused with a sort of literary nationalism.'[25]

This passage clearly owes a great deal to Chaucer's *The House of Fame*, not least in the persona Skelton adopts, whose mock-humble refrain is 'Which glad am to please, and loth to offend' when it is clear that he is making a claim for his own importance which many would find far from innocent. In the same way the dreamer of *The House of Fame* protests his ignorance of the significance of the poem's events and his desire to shun the limelight. Emerging from the Temple of Venus, where he has read the story of Aeneas up to his settlement in Italy on the walls,[26] the dreamer asks Christ 'Fro fantome and illusion/ me save!' (lines 493-4).[27] When subsequently carried off by the garrulous eagle he speculates on his fate:

> Shal I noon other weyes dye?
> Wher Joves wol me stellyfye,
> Or what thing may this signifye?
> (lines 585-7)

Chaucer's dreamer, like Skelton's persona, is less naive than he professes to be, given that he is, ironically, being transported to the House of Fame (and, of course, writing poetry like *The House of Fame* served to make its author famous). The joke continues throughout Book 2 of the poem, which narrates the flight to the House, principally because the eagle reads the metaphor of 'stellyfye' literally and assures the dreamer that Jove 'ys not thereaboute/ ... To make of the as yet a sterre' (lines 597-9). The dreamer subsequently adopts this usage, asking innumerable, usually irritating, questions, until the eagle becomes exasperated: '"Lat be," quod he, "thy fantasye!/Wilt thou lere of sterres aught?"' (lines 901–2). The eagle promises to tell him all about the way the gods 'stellyfye' animals (line 1002), but the dreamer declines the offer, knowing enough from the books he has read.

Skelton is ostensibly a less literal and a more literary reader of the dreamer than the eagle; in the lyric 'To Maystress Jane Blenner-Haiset' which forms part of the sequence of poems to the ladies designed to win the award of the laureateship in the *Laurel*, he states that he will 'stellyfye' her (line 963) and earlier, in his translation of Poggio's Latin text of Diodorus Sicilius, *Bibliotheca Historica* (*c.* 1485), Isis had described herself as 'gloriously stellyfyed'.[28] In a sense though, the joke may be on Skelton for turning the playful irony of Chaucer's text into a solemn metaphor of immortality.[29] The point to be made is that whilst Chaucer's dream–vision portrays the dreamer playing only a detached role observing the mechanisms of Fame's strange operation, Skelton's persona is actively involved. Chaucer's dreamer wonders about being 'stellified'; Skelton's dreamer 'stellifies'. *The House of Fame* shows that the pursuit of fame is a dangerous, unstable and random game in which judgement is arbitrary.[30] Some who achieve and desire fame deserve it, whereas others either deserve it and do not get it or do not deserve it and get it. The trumpet blows willy-nilly. The *Laurel*, by way of contrast, makes the case that Skelton should join a deserving band of laureates if he can prove his worth – which, of course, he will. At the end of the poem, after Skelton has recited his poems to the ladies and listed his numerous works, the assembled laureates cry 'Triumpha, triumpha!', and trumpets and clarions sound so loud that the dreamer speculates that all will be heard in Rome. Before the Queen of Fame has shut her book of those she has favoured, 'The starry hevyn, me thought, shoke with the showte;/The grownde gronid and trembled, the noyse was so stowte' (lines 1508–9). Skelton the author has stellified himself.

Whilst it is Lydgate, a poet–propagandist for the Lancastrian dynasty, who fittingly urges that Skelton be accepted 'into the tradition of great rhetoricians and ... into the company of other writers of *public* rhetoric' (my emphasis),[31] it is clear that the *Laurel* acknowledges Chaucer as the major precursor of Skelton within an English poetic tradition, through the deliberate, creative re-writing and misreading of *The House of Fame*, paradigmatically illustrated here in the (mis)use of the word 'stellify'.[32] Harold Bloom is surely wrong to suggest that the 'anxiety of influence became central to poetic consciousness' only after the age of Shakespeare.[33] Skelton's relationship with Chaucer, his desire to 'supplement' the achievements of his master, neatly illustrates Bloom's contention that 'Poets, by the time they have grown strong, do not read the poetry of X [the precursor], for really strong poets can read *only themselves*. For them, to be judicious is to be weak, and to compare, exactly and fairly, is to be not elect' (my emphasis).[34]

Skelton, about to read himself, to push himself forward in both diachronic and synchronic terms as the pre-eminently English poet, enters the richly bejewelled Palace of Fame where poets traditionally plead for worldly glory. Poets gather there from all over Europe (Apulia to Flanders, Limerick to Portugal) (lines 492–7) and England (lines 512–13), for all sorts of motives: 'Some came to tell trueth, some came to lye,/Some came to flater, some came to spye' (lines 510–11). Superficially, the Palace of Fame resembles the 'Kafka-like' world of *The Bowge of Court*;[35] but it is only the suitors, the poetic-would-bes, who maintain a naive belief in the bounty of fortune. Skelton, in contrast, is told by Occupation, 'Famys regestary' (line 522), that the ship he has boarded is not the ship of fools[36] because she has always looked after him even when things went wrong:

> Of your acquaintaunce I was in tymes past,
> Of studious doctryne when at the part salu
> Ye fyrste aryved; whan broken was your mast
> Of wordly trust, then did I you rescu;
> Your storme dryven shyppe I repared new,
> So well entakeled, what wynde that ever blowe,
> No stormy tempeste your barge shall overthrow.
> (lines 540–6)

Unlike the other poets, Skelton is made welcome by Fame. A fleeting vision of chaos is quickly replaced by one of a providential order. Skelton's fame will spread wider than the corners of Europe whence the rest have come; from Mount Olympus to the Tower of Babel (lines 551–3). His success is pre-ordained.

Occupation then leads him to a huge field where the gates of many nations stand until they come to one with a capital 'A' which stands for 'Anglia'.[37] The lybard, heraldic symbol of England, 'As fersly frownynge as he had ben fyghtyng' (line 594), shakes a nearly incomprehensible Latin verse at the poet.[38] Skelton looks over the wall only to see a further vision of corrupt disorder in the vast crowd of people locked outside the gate marked 'Anglia'. Occupation explains that none are up to any good, but that they are a mixture of forgers, bawds, hypocrites, liars, thieves and, most significantly, in an echo of the description of the (mainly) bad motives of Skelton's rival poets a hundred lines earlier, 'medelynge spyes' (line 617) and 'Fals flaterers that fawne the' (line 619). Skelton hears gunfire and sees the locked-out and panic-stricken suitors run around frantically like the courtiers in Book 3 of *The House of Fame*, quarrelling and shouting before a mist shrouds the field in darkness, blotting out the moon.[39] When the fog clears Skelton observes a fountain 'Englistered' by the sun's beams (line 663) (a pun? 'Englis(h)tered'?) and next to it a laurel tree. In the garden which now comes into view, Jopas sings on a variety of themes.[40] Occupation asks Skelton if he is happier here and he replies that it is a paradise. As in the contrast made between the furious but pointless energy of the excluded suitors and the justly smooth progress of Skelton to the laureateship, there is a contrast made between two visions of England. The cacophony of the field of suitors has given way to the harmony of the diverse songs of Jopas which prefigure Skelton's varied lyric styles in praise of the ladies. Instead of the literally brainless sound and motion of

> With that I herd gunnis russhe out at ones,
> *Bowns, bowns, bowns!* that all they out cryde ...
> And one ther was there, I wondered of his hap,
> For a gun stone, I say, had all to-jaggid his cap.
>
> Raggid, and daggid, and cunnyngly cut;

The blaste of the brynston blew away his brayne;
Masid as a Marche hare, he ran lyke a scut.
And, sir, amonge all me thought I saw twaine,
The one was a tumblar, that afterwarde againe
Of a dysour, a devyl way, grew a jentilman,
Pers Prater, the secund, that quarillis beganne.

(lines 623–4, 628–36,)

we now have the 'natural' art of Jopas's carols:

And Iopas his instrument did avaunce,
The poemis and storis auncient inbryngis
Of Athlas astrology, and many noble thyngis,
Of wandryng of the mone, the course of the sun,
Of men and of bystis, and whereof they begone ...

                              he browght in his songe
How wrong was no ryght, and ryght was no wrong;
There was counterynge of carollis in meter and verse
So many, that long it were to reherse.

(lines 688–92, 703–6)

Numerous contrasts can be pointed out; the divisive quarrel of
Pers Prater and his opponent has given way to the harmonious
variety of the poems and stories to which all listen; the Protean
transformations of the 'tumblar'-cum-gentleman disappear and
right and wrong can be easily distinguished; opinion gives way
to true knowledge; the ragged rhythms and syntax become
smooth and regular, and so on. In the same way, if we are to
read the dream–vision allegorically, it is implied that England
will rise from the babel of voices (Occupation had said that
Skelton will become famous as far away as the Tower of Babel)
of its present poets, to a harmonious unity in diversity in
Skelton's work when he becomes *the* laureate. In case the reader
misses this possibly obscure point, Skelton interpolates a satire
against one called 'Envyous Rancour', a bad rival poet, which
he claims 'industrium postulat interpretum' (demands an
industrious interpreter) – he later complains (lines 1254–357)
that few understood his poem, *Phyllyp Sparowe*, so he was
obviously aware of the problem of overestimating his audience.[41] Like Skelton's other 'flyting' poems, 'Against Dundas',

'Against Garnesche' and 'Against Venemous Tongues', the rival is accused, among other things, of false speech: 'For when he spekyth fayrest, then thynketh he moost yll;/Full gloryously can he glose, thy minde for to fele' (lines 759–60).[42] Whilst Skelton has set himself up as the poet of national harmony and unity, 'Envyous Rancour' leads back to the dangerous divisions of the frantic suitors – and allegorically, no doubt, to the recently ended Wars of the Roses – 'by his devellysshe drift and graceless provision/ An hole realme he is able to set at devysion' (lines 757–8). Almost incidentally, Skelton has included yet another style among his panoply; the mask of satirist which was his most frequently adopted persona,[43] but which would obviously have been out of place as a lyric mode for flattering the aristocratic ladies, to whom Skelton is now led.[44] They have been weaving the garland of laurel for him, a 'goodly warke' (line 74), to reward Skelton for the 'goodly warke' of his poetry which he now recites, having first prayed to Jesus to guide his ship (again, one notes the revision of the *narrenschiff* topos). Skelton is then awarded the laurel and is brought before the other poets by Gower, Chaucer and Lydgate; Occupation produces a book of his works, names Skelton 'poete laureate/ Of Englande' (lines 1170–1), and reads out his achievements as a poet and orator. The poem ends with Skelton waking up and looking up to heaven where he sees 'Janus, with his double chere' (line 1515) making his new year's almanac. There then follows a series of envoys in both Latin and English, pointing in the direction of an international Latin culture and a native vernacular English one; a Janus-faced conclusion reflecting perhaps 'the Renaissance moment of transition to national *vernacular* standards... one crucial instance of the repeated, permanent "struggle" between two tendencies in the languages of European peoples: one a centralizing (unifying) tendency, the other a decentralizing tendency (that is, one that stratifies languages)'.[45] Skelton makes his awareness of this double vision clear: he is looking both forwards and outwards, diachronically and synchronically:

> Mens tibi sit consulta, petis? Sic consule menti;
> Emula sit Jani, retro speculetur et ante.

Skeltonis alloquitur librum suum

Ite, Britannorum lux O radiosa, Britannum
Carmina nostra pium vestrum celebrate Catullum!
Dicite, Skeltonis vester Adonis erat;
Dicite, Skeltonis vester Homerus erat.
Barbara cum Latio pariter jam currite versu.

(lines 1519–26)

Do you wish your mind to be skilful? In that case, pay attention to your mind; let it be like that of Janus which looks back and forward. Skelton speaks to his book. Go, shining light of the Britons, and celebrate, our songs, your worthy British Catullus! Say, Skelton was your Adonis; say, Skelton was your Homer. Though barbarous, you now compete in an equal race with Latin verse. (Scattergood's translation)

> For Latin warkis
> Be good for clerkis,
> Yet now and then
> Sum Latin men
> May happely loke
> Upon your boke,
> And so procede
> In you to rede,
> That so indede
> Your fame may sprede
> In length and brede.

(lines 1542–52)

The lines in Latin address an audience of English/British readers and the lines in English address an international audience who read Latin. The one claims to be able to compete on equal terms with the older language; the other humbly appeals for recognition. The paradoxical reversal of the medium of seemingly appropriate messages serves to emphasise the question of national identity which lies at the heart of the poem and which is thus what holds together the two faces of Janus.

Critics invariably have to select what they choose to read in any one poem, as Susan Schibanoff has recently pointed out with reference to analyses of Skelton's *Phyllyp Sparowe*, excluding some communities of readers by snuffing out certain modes of interpretation. But whilst it may not be anachronistic or unhistorical to claim that

a modern reader can validly interpret *Phyllyp Sparowe* as Skelton's statement that the activity of reading is a kind of rereading or rewriting, a 'personalising' or 'periodicising' of the text that may involve not-reading or even misreading or reading into... as *Phyllyp Sparowe* depicts, reading is a unique and idiosyncratic experience, as well as a highly circumstantial, contextual, and political one.[46]

The Garland of Laurel constructs a very different notion of a much less sceptical implied reader; as the last quotation from it demonstrates, such a creature belongs to a conspicuously national community. Works of literature which aspire to speak to and for this (imagined) collective identity inevitably have to project a notion of who and what the audience is and map out the boundaries between those included and excluded. Skelton is evidently making a claim, partly tongue-in-cheek no doubt,[47] to be the great English poet. Re-writing *The House of Fame* and transferring the end of Book 1 of the *Aeneid* to England requires a certain amount of panache and without self-deprecation might easily slide into self-parody;[48] but the envoys attached to the *Laurel* invite the reader to take Skelton's pretensions seriously rather than question the process of interpretation, however unstable and arbitrary we may feel it to be. Elsewhere Skelton makes the same grandiose gesture, asserting his possession of the laureateship – whatever its technical and scholastic origin[49] – to be a symbol of national greatness. Skelton claims that Calliope, the muse of epic poetry, previously summoned by Virgil to inspire his epic of *national* origins,[50] has summoned *him* to the laureateship (as the triumvirate of national poets do in the *Laurel*). In *Phyllyp Sparowe* Skelton refers to himself as 'laurigerum Britonum Skeltonida' (line 1261) – the sliding of the terms 'British' and 'English' has a long – *English* – history (see above, p.11)[51] – and, although he does not use the word here, he shows that in his verse he has 'stellified' Jane: 'Wherefore shulde I be blamed/ That I Jane have named,/And famously proclaimed?' (lines 1255-7).[52] Jane, in her wish to 'name' the dead bird in her verse, argues that although she cannot 'wryte ornately' (line 781) and imitate the classics, she can write, however unskilfully, in the English of Gower, Chaucer and Lydgate (lines 603–825). Her route to a poetic style is the same as Skelton's dreamer in the *Garland* and the literary genealogy cited substantially the same.[53] Schibanoff has argued that Jane 'personalises the liturgical text' before 'Skelton the poet rereads and rewrites Jane's text in the image of his own wishes and desires'.[54] The relationship is even closer than this judgement implies because, in poetic terms at least, Jane is the *alter ego* of Skelton and the very *imago* of his literary ambition. The female poetic voice merely ventriloquises a masculine tradition as Skelton projects his version of national literary identity through a female cipher. Skelton, like Dr Frankenstein, is imposing his power over his creation, demanding that Jane be a mirror image reflecting the creator.

Given his interest in establishing a particularly English identity and poetic tradition, it perhaps seems odd at first glance that Skelton was the sworn enemy of Protestants and humanists, those academic factions usually seen to be most keen to forge a vernacular culture and national consciousness.[55] *A Replycacion Agaynst Certayne Yong Scholars*, probably Skelton's last poem, written some time after 1527,[56] seems to have been commissioned as 'part of an officially inspired concerted attempt to destroy the heretical movement in England with the weapons of eloquence',[57] along with Thomas More's *Dialogue Concerning Heresies*.[58] Skelton's method of attacking the Lutheran scholars is to insult their learning:

> A lytell ragge of rethorike,
> A lesse lumpe of logyke,
> A pece or a patche of philosophy,
> Than forthwith by and by
> They tumble so in theology,
> Drowned in dregges of divinitie ...
> For all that they preche and teche
> Is farther than their wytte wyll reche.
> Thus by demeryttes of their abusyon,
> Finally they fall to carefull confusyon.
>
> (lines 1–6, 12–15)

Yet again, the charge Skelton makes against the 'new learning'
is that it leads to chaos and disorder through its incoherence. Its
result is babble:

> Ye are brought to 'Lo, Lo, Lo!
> Se where the heretykes go,
> Wytlesse wandring to and fro!'
> With, 'Te he, ta ha, bo ho, bo ho!'
> And suche wondringes many mo.
> Helas, ye wreches, ye may be wo!
>
> (lines 72–7)

The same insult is a constant motif in Skelton's poetry; one
thinks of 'Envyous Rancour' in the *Garland*, who can set 'An
hole reame ... at devysion'; or the heretics and schismatics in
Colin Clout who would intoxicate, contaminate, derogate and
abrogate 'The churche hygh estates' (line 708); or the
contemporary speakers of Greek who have traded-in the living
Latin culture for an incomprehensible dead language in which
they cannot even say 'How, hostler, fetche my hors a botell of
hay!' (line 147). Even more significant is the thinly disguised
portrait of Skelton's *bête-noire*, Cardinal Wolsey in *Why Come Ye
Nat to Courte?* Wolsey undermines the authority of the king (lines
437–45), the nobility (lines 622–4), the church (lines 742–9),
and his ignorance of the liberal arts (lines 513–19) means that
he too speaks gibberish: 'His Latyne tongue doth hobyll,/ He
doth but cloute and cobbill/ In Tullis faculte/Called
humanyte' (lines 526–9). Like the heretics and 'Envyous
Rancour', Wolsey precipitates national dissension, 'To cause
the commune weale/Longe to endure in heale' (lines 770–1),
bringing the 'Most royall Englyshe nacion ... almost in deso-
lation' (lines 1040–2). Whilst Skelton portrays himself as
performing the Janus-faced balancing act between international Latin and vernacular English, authorial control and
heteroglossia,[59] polyphony and monotony, his opponents and
rivals degenerate into nonsense. As he asserts in the *Laurel*, his
fame will spread as far as the Tower of Babel, presumably an
example of true speech for the barbarians.

The *Replycacion* ends with an argument for the importance of poetry within the politics of the nation. According to Skelton, his opponents believe that poetry is incapable of dealing with such lofty subjects as theology and philosophy or of renouncing heresy. Skelton refers to David, 'Poete of poetes all,/ And prophete princypall' (lines 321–2) and invokes the authority of Jerome – perhaps *the* authority for Skelton, given his allegiance to the Latin vulgate Bible and opposition to innovations like Erasmus' Greek *New Testament* (1516), satirised in *Speke Parrot* (lines 58–9)[60] – who declares David's superiority as a poet to Syminides, Pindar, Catullus and Alcaeus. Skelton's point is simply that if this is the case, then are not poets (especially 'poetes laureate' (line 358)) inspired by God and thus free to deal with subjects of national importance? Skelton uses an aureate vocabulary here, seemingly at odds with the more satirical and rude style of the main body of the poem, to argue that a mystical spirit inhabits true poets because 'of divyne myseration/God maketh his habytacion/In poetes which excelles,/And sojourns with them and dwelles' (lines 375–8). The argument is tactfully – or ironically – made. However, it is obvious that Skelton is demanding a licence for the true poet to intervene in the public sphere.

Skelton may have set himself against both Protestants and humanists; but his claims for the importance of the poet's function strongly resemble the ideas of the 'commonwealth men' and the group of Protestant intellectuals gathered around Thomas Cromwell who were to flourish in Henry VIII's court immediately after Skelton's death.[61] They also demanded that writers of literature as well as propaganda had to play a vital role in contributing to the politics of the nation or, in their terms, the health of the commonweal.[62] Skelton has too often been seen as a sort of hybrid figure, a poet on the cusp of the Renaissance, either looking forward to later developments, 'the first poet of the English Renaissance' according to Stanley Fish;[63] or backwards to Medieval times, 'the last wholly authentic utterance of the Middle Ages', according to Peter Green.[64] The alternative has been to place him within a Burgundian court culture, as Gordon Kipling has argued. Henry VII, according to Kipling, looked much more towards the Lowlands Dukes of Burgundy than he did to the Italian city states when deciding how to model the court of the Tudor dynasty. The 'Burgundian nobles taught their children that they "must become learned in order to play their part in the government of the commonwealth"',[65] just like the humanists. They also demanded translations of useful historical works, like Diodorus Sicilius' *Library of History*, which Skelton translated as a youth;[66] books of princely instruction like Skelton's *Speculum Principis*; poems commemorating the monarch like Skelton's 'A Lawde and Prayse Made for Our Sovereigne Lord the Kyng'; allegorical dream visions like the *Laurel*; comically eloquent pieces like *Speke Parrot* and *Phyllyp Sparowe*; courtly satire like the *Bowge of Court*, whose 'half-French title, immediately invites comparison with other similar *rhetoriquer* satires, such as those of Pierre Gringore, whose *Castle of Labour* was translated into English about the turn of the century'; and dramas dealing with the cardinal virtues based on a consideration of magnanimity or magnificence as the most desirable aspect of kingship (a revision of Aristotle's moral hierarchies), like Guillaume Fillastre's *La Toison d'or* (*c.* 1472) and Skelton's *Magnyfycence*.[67] Kipling claims that Skelton not only borrows the occasional line from Burgundian sources, but also that, rime royal aside, his range of verse forms, including the Skeltonic, derives principally from this literary culture.[68]

The extent of the influence of Burgundian culture on the courts of Henry VII and VIII has been questioned, as has its formative influence on Skelton.[69] Some of Kipling's arguments seem to depend less on the sort of causal priority he needs to prove, than on homologies and analogies.[70] It is by no means obvious, for example, that writing poems in praise of the monarch, translating large historical works, writing educational treatises for youthful rulers, or writing poetry in short lines (see below), necessarily proves the influence of a specific school of thought or exposure to a cultural milieu. Nevertheless, Kipling's work remains a forceful reminder that it is too simple to see a humanist Renaissance as the end of a vast continuum known rather vaguely as the Middle Ages, which brings with it new questions of national identity to inaugurate a modern world of nation states. It is undoubtedly of significance that the predominant literary figure at the English court was Bernard André, the blind poet from Toulouse, who, like Skelton, was a poet laureate and an orator.[71] André, just as Skelton had done, had received a commendatory poem from Erasmus;[72] unlike Skelton, André wrote in French and Latin rather than English and Latin. Greg Walker's contextualisation of Skelton's career takes us one step beyond Kipling's:

It must be remembered that Skelton was a native-born scholar (and a notably xenophobic one, if his later works are any indication) who was trying to establish himself in a poets' 'tribe' consisting entirely of foreign scholars, most of whom held significant papal offices and clerical appointments in this country. It would not be unreasonable to suggest that a newly arrived poet may have encountered some animosity from this 'closed shop' of continental *literati*, especially at a time when Burgundian and Italian letters were the vogue of Europe, and England was considered a cultural backwater.[73]

As we have seen, Skelton's poetic manifesto, the *Laurel*, sets him up as *the* English poet, inevitably at the expense of both his Anglophone rivals, such as Alexander Barclay – who appears to have had a running battle with Skelton[74] – and Stephen Hawes, as well as the Franco-Italian cultural hegemony which held sway at court. Skelton's frequent assertions of his English literary past (the holy trinity of Gower, Chaucer and Lydgate) and his self-fashioned role as spokesman for the Latinate heritage of the late Middle Ages – most noticeably in his defence of the traditionalist *Vulgaria* of John Stanbridge against William Lily's rival version in the 'Grammarians War', which was to earn him the scornful quip of Lily's that Skelton 'was neither learned/Nor a poet'[75] – mark him out as one who wished to be seen as the Janus-faced guardian of a specifically native, but not exclusively vernacular, culture. Or to put it another way, an English literary culture which did not demand that the English language be its single medium.

It is Skelton's pretentious assumption of this moral authority which serves to justify his intervention into public affairs and determines the roles he chooses to play, whether insulting rivals, excoriating foreigners, satirising courtly corruption or lavishing praise on the nobility and aristocratic ladies. It is this mantle, or rather laurel, of Englishness which enables Skelton to 'stellify' the ladies in the *Laurel*, vanquish Garnesche (see part v, lines 95–115), condemn the military transgressions of the Scots, and which forms the ethical backbone of the national themes of *Magnyfycence*, where the errors of the ruler allow to flourish those allegorical figures (Adversity, Courtly Abusyon) who will bring the nation to its knees.[76]

Skelton's claim that he represented the voice of English poetry partly explains the way he was appropriated by later writers and his strange and contradictory reputation in the sixteenth century. Despite his vigorous anti-Protestant polemics and the existence of two separate printed editions of the *Replycacion*, Skelton was nevertheless welcomed as a precursor by many Reformation writers and often assimilated into the tradition they mapped out (see above, p.25). John Bale, for whom true Englishness could not be separated from Protestantism,[77] whilst noting that Skelton 'was not fully in accord with Holy Scripture', argued that he 'concealed the fact deftly' (which was hardly the case!) and was to be valued as a satirist who uttered truth under the mask of laughter and 'continuously waged war on certain *babbling* friars' (my emphasis).[78] He compared Skelton to Lucian – ironically, a favourite author of both Thomas More and Erasmus.[79] Various imitations of the Skeltonics of *Colin Clout* and *Why Come Ye Nat to Courte?* were written and found their way into the Skelton canon, just as Protestant or anti-clerical works were accepted as Chaucer's, because of his popularity among Reformation Protestants.[80] The most notable entries into the Skelton apocrypha were the two satires, *The Image of Ipocrisy* and the fittingly titled, *Vox Populi, Vox Dei*.[81] Even during his lifetime Skelton attracted a series of tales which established a 'Tradition of "Merry Skelton"… a character of low comedy, ready with a jest or a witticism to confound his superiors and amuse the multitude.'[82] Such stories, the most often cited of which has Skelton brandishing his child from the pulpit in order to silence those who had impugned his manhood,[83] became incorporated with the proto-Protestant myth via the publication of a series of

'Merie Tales' depicting Skelton as a married priest continually at odds with the powers that be.[84]

Skelton's verse also influenced writers as diverse in style and purpose as Luke Shepherd and Michael Drayton;[85] but his most famous literary descendant was, of course, Edmund Spenser, who was probably introduced to Skelton's poetry by his mentor, Gabriel Harvey.[86] Spenser adopted the figure of Colin Clout as one of his personae – though the influence of Clemont Marot's pastorals must not be discounted when determining the exact nature of Spenser's antecedents.[87] Colin Clout, as in Skelton, is an outsider, but he has been translated from satire to the related genre of pastoral.[88] More to the point, Spenser, like Skelton, presumed that his poetry could speak for a nation.[89]

Skelton's poetry became absorbed into an English Protestant literary tradition. John King argues that Thomas Churchyard, a professional poet and pamphleteer whose immensely long and generally unsuccessful literary career dates from the 1540s to the early 1600s, 'sets Skelton up as a defender of native artistry against the recent fashion for Italianate poetry' in his dedication to Stow's edition of *Pithy, Pleasant and Profitable Workes* (1568):

> Peers Plowman was full plaine,
> And Chausers spreet was great;
> Earle Surrey had a goodly vayne;
> Lord Vaus the marke did beat,
> And Phaer did hit the pricke
> In thinges he did translate,
> And Edwards had a special gift;
> And divers men of late
> Hath helpt our Englishe toung,
> That first was baes and brute: –
> Ohe, shall I leave out Skeltons name,
> The blossome of the frute.
>
> (lines 82–93)[90]

For Churchyard, Skelton is the culmination of a *still developing* native English poetic tradition whose genealogy he maps out. But as King further notes, the 'nativists lost the contest' and Skelton's works went out of print after 1568 until revived, mainly for antiquarian interest, in 1736. Edward Philips, for example, writing in 1675, judges Skelton's verse to be in a 'galloping measure' and of 'a miserable loos, rambling style'. He found it 'no wonder he is so utterly forgotten at this present'.[91] King remarks, 'By the 1580s watershed, neoclassical standards of decorum had led to the denigration of Skeltonic art.'[92] Although Skelton was praised by William Webbe as 'a pleasant conceited fellowe, and of a very sharpe witte',[93] he was dismissed by George Puttenham as 'a rude, rayling rimer and all his doings ridiculous ... in *our* courtly maker we banish them utterly' (my emphasis).[94] Skelton, who railed against the usurpation of true nobility at court by the likes of the Ipswich butcher's son, Thomas Wolsey,

> How be it the primordyall
> Of his wretched originall,
> And his base progeny,
> And his gresy genealogy,
> He came of the sank royall
> That was cast out of a bochers stall!
> (*Why Come Ye Nat to Courte*, lines 489–94)

had the ignominy of his own poetry being discarded as similarly base-born. In 1622, Henry Peacham dismissed Skelton as unworthy of the title he so desperately coveted, that of poet laureate, in *The Compleat Gentleman*.[95]

Skelton's posthumous reputation is, at least, triply ironic. Absorbed into a nativist Protestant tradition, he is then dismissed as an incompetent metricist partly because of the selective reproduction of his varied poetic styles. When revived in the nineteenth century, principally after the Reverend Alexander Dyce's scholarly edition of his *Poetical Works* (1843), and made into a cult, quasi-modernist figure in the 1920s and 1930s by Robert Graves, W. H. Auden, Edmund Blunden and others, he is praised principally as an individualistic one-off whose work defies literary classification: 'Skelton is the one living poet of the fifteenth century in England. He is living *only* because he managed *without a tradition*. He is that very rare thing, an *original* artist' (my emphases).[96] Or, in C. S. Lewis's semi-accurate words, 'He has no real predecessors and no important disciples; he stands out of the streamy, historical process, an unmistakable individual, a man we have met.'[97] Contemporary scholars, as we have seen, seemingly transfixed by Huizinga's *The Waning of the Middle Ages*, feel obliged to place Skelton as either the last voice of a dying Medieval culture, or as the first voice of Renaissance humanism.[98]

Skelton's problem is that he backed the wrong historical horse. Or, to put it another way, those who write literary history have chosen to write him out. His chaotic and frequently interrupted career has been convincingly analysed by Greg Walker as a wandering journey motivated by self-interest and caught up in the politics of patronage. Walker argues that Skelton was not the important court poet depicted in his own poetry – a self-image many critics have failed to challenge, most notably in Skelton's supposed connections with the Howard family – and that it is more likely that he existed on the margins of court society.[99] Walker claims that Skelton's two major satires, *Colin Clout* and *Why Come Ye Nat to Courte?*, were written for the London commons rather than the aristocracy. According to Walker, Skelton had lost what patronage he had at court with the death of Prince Arthur in 1502, had been forced to exist as a minor cleric in the East Anglian backwater of Diss, and that ever since he had tried to regain a place at court with little success. The early 1520s saw his most sustained attempt to achieve this; when *Speke Parrot* failed to exploit the rift between Henry and Wolsey opened up by the Calais conference of 1521, Skelton turned to another audience – the London commons – changing his verse as a matter of course.[100] Skelton seemed finished, but events suddenly favoured him; the threat of the Duke of Albany's invasion, backed up by a concertedly anti-English policy and wealth of propaganda, saw Skelton back at court, possibly bought off by Wolsey or owing to his reputation as a scurrilous satirist who was known as the author of *A Ballade of the Scottyshe Kynge* and his translation of his own Latin, *Agaynst the Scottes* (1513).[101] The result was the propagandist poem, *Howe the Douty Duke of Albany* (1523). With the hope that the poem would be disseminated north of the border, Skelton could refer to himself as the 'Orator Regius', speaking on behalf of *all* the English people, for the first time in ten years.[102]

If Skelton's career does have a consistent theme, from his translation of Diodorus Sicilius 'Out of fresshe latin into owre Englysshe playne,/Recountyng commoditis of many a straunge nacyon' (the *Laurel*, lines 1498–9), to the *Replycacion*, which begins the section of the poem discussing the right of poets to deal with political matters after the model of David's *Psalms* with the heading 'The Englyshe' (lines 328–9), it must surely be his insistence on his Englishness and his ability to intervene in the 'public sphere' to speak for the English people.[103] Skelton's writings construct his audience as specifically English, whether he has been commissioned as the 'Orator Regius' he seems to have always wanted to be, or whether he has been forced to court a specific group. Hence the lonely voice of Colin Clout is directed against those who have brought the whole of civil society to its knees: for example, Colin comments that the temporal lords are unwillingly to intervene to save the abuses of the church (for example, lines 608–10). In linking these 'classes' together, *Colin Clout* could be said to belong to the tradition of Medieval estates satire, an ambitious genre which also grouped together the constituent elements of society in order to construct a national community as the object of its attack.[104] Similarly, and more specifically, *Why Come Ye Nat to Courte*?, repeatedly appeals to a nationalist consensus which the treacherous, internationalist Wolsey, who prefers his own rival power base at Hampton Court to the king's court (lines 402–10), is betraying. The anonymous narrator refers to the penchant for foreign fashions at court, remarking that '*Our* nobles' (line 922; my emphasis) have started copying the Burgundian, Spanish and Flemish styles and buying cloth from Caen at the expense of native cloth and merchants such as Thomas Smith of Lavenham lose out: 'They are happy that wynnys,/But Englande may well say/Fye on this wynnyng allway!' (lines 927–9). The move from the particular group – here the merchants angry at Wolsey's forced loans[105] – to the nation is unmistakable. The same appeal to a national identity surfaces throughout the poem, notably in the passages referring to the Scots (it again mentions the Burgundians and Spanish for good measure),[106] chastising Wolsey's diplomatic amity with the slayers of Englishmen (lines 346–76) and the lines quoted above (p.38), which accuse Wolsey of making the 'Most royall Englyssh nacion', like English clothes, go 'out of facion' (line 1040). Little needs to be said about the anti-Scots poems, which, *ipso facto*, construct a national audience of nationalist readers, although one should bear in mind Nancy Gutierrez's judgement that 'Skelton's implicit assumption in the *Ballade* [is] that his audience is a homogeneous national community which will interpret his poem not only as a diatribe against the Scots and a panegyric of the English army and king, but also as a celebration of the English people as God's chosen people.'[107]

Bernard Sharratt has pointed out that 'English', as both a language and a literature, remained 'a problematic term' at the turn of the fifteenth century.[108] William Caxton, in his preface to his translation of the *Aeneid*, praises Skelton's art as a translator and asks Skelton to oversee and correct the work: 'For hym I knowe for suffycyent to expowne and englysshe every diffyculte that is therein/ For he hath late translated the epystyls of Tulle/ and the boke of dyodorus syculus. and diverse other werkes oute of latyn in to englysshe not in rude and olde language. but in polysshed and ornate termes craftely.'[109] Skelton is credited with 1500 first usages in his translation of Diodorus (the translation of Cicero has been lost), which emphasises his role as a pioneer of an English tradition, linguistically as well as poetically. As Sharratt argues, Skelton was writing whilst 'the consolidation of "London" English as a national standard' was taking place, particularly with the crucial advent of printing.[110] 'Skelton's work comes at the very beginning of recognisably "modern" English, as it takes its place in that privileged London literary–linguistic "line" from Chaucer to Shakespeare, while at the same time it straddles and deliberately juxtaposes a variety of other classical and colloquial registers.'[111] *Pace* Roy Foster Jones's blanket generalisation that 'the age considered its own language, as well as that of an earlier age, barbarous',[112] Caxton saw in Skelton's Diodorus a 'polysshed and ornate' style and linguistic register. Skelton was viewed by at least one contemporary – as he was by Thomas Churchyard in 1568 (see above) – as a founding father of a usable and sophisticated English.

It is probable that speculations regarding the origin of the 'Skeltonic' will prove inconclusive (see above, note 68). I would argue that it is much more important to observe Skelton's innovative and varied use of poetic form, conspicuously gathered together in the *Laurel*, which employs both rime royal (the poem's major verse form), the 'Skeltonic' most famously associated with the satires, as well as the heterogeneous styles, registers and forms of the lyrics to the ladies:[113]

> The noble Pamphila, quene of the Grekis londe,
> Habilliments royall founde out industriously;
> Thamar also wrought with her goodly honde
> Many divisis passynge curyously;
> Whome ye represent and exemplify,
> Whos passynge bounte, and ryght noble astate,
> Of honour and worship it hath the formar date.
>
> ('To the ryght noble Countes of Surrey', lines 850–6)

> By saynt Mary, my Lady,
> Your mammy and your dady
> Brought forth a godely babi!
>
> My maiden Isabell,
> Reflaring rosabell,
> The flagrant camamell ...
>
> To here this nightingale,
> Amonge the brydes smale,
> Warbelynge in the vale
>
> Dug, dug,
> Jug, jug,
> Good yere and good luk,
> With chuk, chuk, chuk.
>
> ('To maystress Isabell Pennell', lines 973–8, 997–1003)

> As pacient and as styll,
> And as full of good wyll,
>
> As fayre Isaphill;
> Colyaunder,
> Swete pomaunder,
> Good Cassaunder;

Stedfast of thought
Wele made, wele wrought
('To maystress Margaret Hussey', lines 1023–30)

It was not immediately apparent to contemporaries that Skelton would later become obscure or that his poetic experiments, attempts to establish certain verse forms and what one modern critic has rather anachronistically labelled his non-standard use of English, would lead to a dead-end as far as the history of English literature or language was concerned.[114] Who, surveying the literary landscape in the 1520s or 1530s, could have predicted that the Italianate sonnets and Petrarchan translations of Wyatt and Surrey would triumph and become the dominant norm? As John King has shown, the Italophiles only finally triumphed in the 1580s, and a teleologically written English literary history, viewing history from the perspective of the winners, has been crudely selective in whom it chooses to honour. Skelton might have suggested that it is Chaucer's rather than his concept of Fame which has ruled the roost.[115] There is, of course, a lot of literary history between Wyatt and the Sidneys or Puttenham, not all of it the story of the 'Englishing of Petrarch'. Skelton's case can be read, rather interestingly, in the light of Robert Young's devastating arguments against the historicist assumptions of Western Marxism in *White Mythologies*. Young's comments on 'History' and 'histories' can be applied to the story told by modern literary history as I have described it:

What is in dispute is whether history has a meaning as 'History'. One alternative would be that history may be made up of the multiple meanings of specific, particular histories – without their necessarily being in turn part of a larger meaning of an underlying Idea or force ... why deny that history can have multiple meanings? ... We are therefore not so much talking about a single meaning as a true one versus all the others which are false ... The question about history then becomes the more interesting one of the relation between different significations, and the ways in which such differences can, or cannot, be articulated and unified under the same horizon of totalization to produce a single meaning.[116]

Skelton's version of 'Englishness' and attempt to write English literature is one amongst many: his is an English voice which defends the pre-Reformation church and state and intervenes in civil society on behalf of the 'imagined community', or implied readership, of a nebulously defined English people to preserve and adapt a continuously threatened status quo. 'History' might not have been on Skelton's side, but if makers of literary history adopted a more contingent mode of writing it should be possible to recognise his strategic importance, acknowledging that there are losers as well as winners in different games and struggles *who are not necessarily bad or wrong*. Why deny that history can have multiple meanings or be constructed into diachronic sequences which produce varied patterns? Why insist that history – including literary history – be divided rigidly into 'Medieval' and 'Renaissance', categories which seem almost deliberately designed not to deal with the likes of a Skelton, just as they tend to exclude a large part of the tradition of Protestant literature, public poetry like *A Mirror for Magistrates*, the experiments with classical metre of the Sidney circle, and the vast mass of Latin writings. Why deny that it could have taken different courses? To paraphrase Stephen Jay Gould, replay the tape of life and think of what *might have happened*.[117]

CHAPTER 2

John Bale and the time of the nation

In marked contrast to the flexible pragmatism of John Skelton's literary career, the writings of John Bale seem to be characterised by a monolithic consistency imposed upon the reader with an iron determination of will developed and hardened in youth and never altered subsequently. Bale was a vigorous – and voluminous – polemicist for a narrow range of causes: his writing is nothing if not repetitive.[1] One of his fundamental beliefs was an absolute faith in the duty of subjects to obey the monarch, who, according to Bale, could rule unhampered by any of the trappings of a moral, legal or natural code of law against which the conduct of any tyrant could be tested. This was, of course, not to argue that there were not standards of behaviour which a monarch should observe when dealing with his or her subjects; but that subjects have no rights and monarchs only duties.[2] In reaching this conclusion, Bale resembles the influential French political philosopher, Jean Bodin (1530–96), whose concept of 'natural law' was formed against the background of Huguenot dissension leading to factionalism, leading to civil war, and granted absolute – rather than autocratic – powers to the monarch.[3] Bale consistently argued that *any* resistance whatsoever to the will of the king or queen was a mortal sin against God: 'I do well remember the sayings of S. Paule, that al Princes ought to be honoured, although they be wicked and unprofitable for a common wealth, because they be placed there of God.'[4]

For Bale, to rebel against a divinely ordained monarch is to pledge allegiance to the devil. Like many Protestant writers, he reserves especial bile for the false, Catholic martyr, Thomas

Becket, who upheld the right of the church to intervene in secular matters. Becket's false 'martyrdom' is contrasted to that of the true Protestant martyrdom of Sir John Oldcastle, Lord Cobham:

Thomas Becket died upon his own seeking only, for maintaining the wanton liberties and superfluous possessions of the Romish church here within England; which are both forbidden of Christ, and also condemned by the same scriptures. 'He that forsaketh not all that he hath,' saith he, 'cannot be my disciple' (Luke xiv). And when a contention befell among the apostles for the superiority, he said also unto them: 'The kings of the world have the world's dominion with all pomp and riches belonging to the same; but you shal not so' (Luke xxiii, 1 Peter v). Sir John Oldcastle died at the importune suit of the clergy, for calling upon a christian reformation in that Romish church of theirs, and for manfully standing by the faithful testemonies of Jesu.[5]

The rhetorically pointed parallel, a favourite device of Bale's, maps out the history of true Christian consciousness versus the false worldly pomp of the Catholic church; Oldcastle tries to stop the church interfering in the affairs of state, whereas Becket tries to usurp the prerogative of worldly government and thus corrupts both church and state instead of rendering up to Caesar what is Caesar's.[6] Bale can be seen as a disciple of Martin Luther in carefully distinguishing between the two swords; one of sacred and one of secular authority:

[T]hose now called 'the religious', i.e., priests, bishops, and popes, possess no further or greater dignity than other Christians, except that their duty is to expound the word of God and administer the sacraments – that being their office. In the same way, the secular authorities 'hold the sword and the rod', their function being to punish evil-doers and protect the law-abiding.[7]

By taking such a hard and clear-cut line, Bale marked himself out as one of the first wave of Protestant thinkers. Skelton was quickly made to seem an anachronism soon after he died, but Bale was unfortunately regarded as a living fossil by many of his younger, less conservative Protestant compatriots who formed a second wave of Reformation thinkers. As W. T. Davies puts it, Bale 'was baffled by a challenge to what was the basis of his own Protestantism, a reverence for the state as represented by the temporal sovereign'.[8] The writings of Christopher Goodman, John Knox and John Ponet address a completely different set of issues from those tackled by Bale; their work formed the basis of an antagonistic political culture in its stress upon the rights and duty of citizens – not subjects – to oppose a tyrant. Whereas Bale, in common with most first-generation English Protestants, was concerned to defend the rights of monarchs against the encroachments of the papacy, Goodman, Ponet and Knox refused to equate the monarch with the national state and sought to defend the rights of citizens against the arbitrariness of the ruler's tyrannical desires.[9] The argument that no ruler was better than a tyrant and the injunction that it was the *duty* – rather than merely the right – of subjects to kill evil rulers, was anathema to the king-worshipping Bale.[10] Goodman's statement that an un-Christian ruler (ie, a Catholic one, specifically Mary) was a rebel against the laws of God, and his praise for the godly intentions of Wyatt's rebellion, was a clear attempt to invert the political concerns and language of Erastian Protestants such as Bale, most openly encountered in the official ideology of the Tudor *Books of Homilies*.[11] Furthermore, Bale did not accept John Ponet's claim that kings were answerable to the conscience of the people and that they could use the known political laws established by God to criticise their rulers.[12] For Bale, monarchs were divinely appointed.[13]

This fundamental and seemingly irreconcilable conflict, which came to a head in Frankfurt in 1554–5 when the exiled British Protestant community clashed over the relative merits of Cranmer's 1552 Prayer Book and a more Calvinist version drawn up by William Whittingham, championed by Richard Cox and John Knox respectively, can be used to illustrate Patrick Collinson's contention that there never was one elect nation of Protestants, but 'a permanently divided nation'.[14] This split can be read in many different ways: as a battle between Lutheranism and Calvinism; the result of an ossified first wave of iconoclastic fervour confronting the inevitably more radical second wave; as one of the multitude of Protestant disputes over Biblical interpretation, trying to establish the right way of reading the word of God.[15] For our purposes here,

we can foreground the obvious political division which, as many
historians have argued (albeit in rather different ways), was a
fixture of British politics until (at least) the Civil War.[16] Was the
monarch an absolute ruler as Bale and other Lutherans claimed,
who represented his or her subjects as the embodiment of
national consciousness? Or, was the monarch answerable to the
citizens who granted sovereignty in the first place, as many
English Calvinists claimed? In a sense this conflict can be read
as the battle of the king's two bodies; does the private self of the
ruler govern the entry into the public domain and leave control
resting in the personal will of the king or queen? Or does the
public body, appropriated by the people, turn back upon the
sovereign and demand that representation be more than just a
formal, empty figure? Whose property is the body of the king?[17]
Is it to be read in a metonymic relation to the political existence
of the public sphere, as Bale would have it, the private part
governing the whole; or, metaphorically, as a fictional body
politic, conceding ultimate control to those who are represented,
as the English Calvinists would have it?[18]

John Bale (1495–1563) spent his youth as a Carmelite friar
and he remained in the order, working principally as its
historian, until he became converted to the reformed faith in
1533.[19] Like Luther, Bale had decided to get married.[20] In the
1530s he was employed by Thomas Cromwell to turn out
numerous plays as part of the project to foster Reformation
propaganda through the re-writing of a morality play tradition
in addition to the Biblical translations and polemical tracts
penned by Protestant humanists like Richard Morison and
Thomas Starkey.[21] Bale's most famous play, *King John*, had
been performed at Thomas Cranmer's household at Christmas,
1538.[22] Many of Bale's other plays seem to have been designed
for performance in churches,[23] presumably as replacements for
the Corpus Christi plays (the feast was suppressed in 1548,
although the plays continued well into Elizabethan times), and
other festival performances.[24] When Cromwell was executed in
1540, Bale fled to Germany where he began to write a series of
tracts designed for domestic consumption, vilifying the latent
Catholic influence on the Henrican church and the remnants of

the monastic tradition of which he had once been a part.[25] He also wrote the widely circulated and frequently reprinted Protestant martyrologies of William Thorpe, Anne Askew and Sir John Oldcastle which were to have such a crucial influence on John Foxe's *Acts and Monuments of the Christian Church*.[26] At the same time he was busy collating the information derived from his extensive manuscript work whilst a Carmelite and, in collaboration with the antiquary John Leland, trying to recover and preserve what had been lost when the monasteries had been dissolved.[27] Bale was starting to map out a native literary tradition, the first manifestation of which was printed in Wesel in 1548, a year after his return to England on the accession of Edward VI, entitled *Illustrium Majoris Britanniae Scriptorum Summararium*. A revised, expanded edition in two volumes, *Scriptorum Illustrium Majoris Brytanniae Catalogus* (1557) appeared during his second exile and just before his return with Elizabeth's accession.[28]

Bale was appointed to various ecclesiastical livings in the south of England by Edward and in 1550 his commentary on the Book of Revelation, *The Image of Both Churches*, which he had written during his exile, was printed. The vigorous and crude typological reading of the Scriptural text divided the true Catholic church, a descendant of the apostolic designs of Christ, from the false, worldly church of Rome, and was among Bale's most popular works being frequently reprinted throughout the second half of the sixteenth century.[29] Again, its eschatological scheme was to have a profound influence on John Foxe.[30] In 1552 Bale was awarded the dubious honour of the bishopric of Ossory by Edward who came to Southampton in person to grant him the see. Bale reluctantly accepted and set off for Ireland in December (see below, p.73).

After the disastrous events of this year, Bale began his second period of exile when Mary became queen. This time he resided in Basle where he continued to produce polemical pamphlets at an impressive rate – now attacking the restoration of the hated parody of true religion, rather than its stubborn, residual survival; revised his history of British literature; and became involved in the bitter disputes among the exiled English

Protestant factions (see above, p.53). Bale was caught between two stools. On the one hand he was 'baffled by a form of Protestantism more extreme than his own and shocked by a challenge to what was the basis of his own Protestantism, a reverence for the state as represented by the temporal sovereign'.[31] On a more personal level he was perhaps shocked by John Ponet's political stance as the two had been close allies over the affair at Frankfurt and Ponet had subsequently written to Bale, suggesting that they 'blow ... boldly the trumpet of Gods trueth' together, ie, collaborate with the concerted propaganda campaign against the Marian regime.[32] Meanwhile, in England his books were banned in a royal proclamation of June 1555 prohibiting anti-papal books and on 28 March 1556, 'a man was condemned for, *inter alia*, agreeing with the *Image of Both Churches*'.[33]

Bale now began to collaborate with Foxe on the early versions of his *magnum opus*, and with Mattias Flacius Illyricus on his 'anti-papal compilations'. He published his own *Acta Romanorum Pontificum*, later translated as *The Pagent of Popes* in 1574 by John Studeley. He returned to England in 1559 as soon as possible after Elizabeth's accession, hastily dedicating the forthcoming *Catalogus* to the queen, and he took up a humble post in Canterbury. Bale hoped to recover his library which he had had to leave behind when he fled from Ireland so that he could start work on a projected history of England. But he was unable to do so (although Archbishop Parker recovered a few volumes after Bale's death)[34] and the history was to remain one of the great unwritten works of British literature, like Milton's aborted British epic planned during the 1640s, a time when the imagined community of Britain as revived by the Tudors seemed about to disintegrate.[35] Little more is known of Bale's life, although some of his works – both plays and histories – proved popular enough to merit republishing in the 1560s. He died in 1563 when 'even the mediocrities were beginning to think in an idiom quite different from Bale's'.[36]

Bale's life and literary career could be paralleled in many ways to that of Skelton: both existed on the margins of a court society; both enjoyed some initial success only to suffer long periods in the wilderness (admittedly, for different reasons and to a significantly different extent); both were notorious for the ferocity of their attacks on opponents and rivals, Bale earning the nickname of 'bilious';[37] both tried to write literature in a multitude of ways with differing functions and for different audiences; both came to seem to be hangovers from the past towards the end of their lives or very soon after their deaths. As W. T. Davies has pointed out, Barnaby Googe, a young protégé of Bale's, seems to temper his good humoured Epitaph on his mentor with 'a sort of rueful awe before this august survival from the almost incredible past' when he urges Bale to:

> Give over now
> to beat thy wearied brain
> And rest thy pen
> that long hath laboured sore.[38]

But most strikingly, one could say that it is as if Bale and Skelton face each other in the mirror of the Reformation, offering opposed and complementary images of Englishness from either side of the historical divide. Bale, no less than Skelton, sought to define a native identity throughout his long writing career.

William Haller's *Foxe's Book of Martyrs and the Elect Nation* (1963) has been widely criticised for ignoring the internationalist history that Foxe intended to write and in which his intellectual Protestant colleagues in exile firmly believed. Patrick Collinson has suggested that the book was 'all too persuasive and excessively influential' in its argument that 'Foxe was the principal architect of the conviction that the English were a people "set apart from all others".'[39] But Haller's judgement that Bale 'was ... making a start at turning national legends to the uses of propaganda in the national cause' and that

In his pages, as in those of English propagandists following him, the war between the two Churches within the Church, while still represented as filling all history, nevertheless settles down into an age-long contention of English rulers and people against the alien intruders for ever seeking to subvert the English state and corrupt the English Church by open violence or by false doctrine and evil example[40] is surely an acute one. Haller's argument depends as much on his perception of the medium as the message:

Augustine conceived the whole history of mankind as occupied with the recurring opposition of two orders within every order, two cities within every city, two churches within every Church, one ideal of grace and election, the other of nature and reprobation, one ideal and transcendent, the other material and temporal ... To express these ideas afresh for an English public in its own vernacular, and incidentally for the inspiration of John Foxe, was Bale's most important accomplishment. (p.67)

Katherine Firth is undoubtedly right to suggest that Haller was stretching a point when claiming that Foxe *intended* his martyrology to be an apocalyptic prophecy designed to persuade his fellow-countrymen that England was the elect nation chosen by Christ to be saved on the Day of Judgement and blessed with the role of serving as the haven for Biblical truth. As she points out, Foxe's Latin commentary on the Book of Revelation, the *Eicasmi*, explicitly denies that England plays this role.[41] However, she has demolished very little of importance in Haller's thesis as she effectively admits: 'That he [Foxe] did not bring with him an apocalyptic conception of England as the elect nation does not diminish the fact that he did place his nation, with other European nations, in a historical context bounded by the prophecies of the Revelation.'[42] It is clearly an irony of no small importance that Foxe's *Acts and Monuments* was originally planned as a history of radical European Protestantism in Latin; but the fact that it was eventually written in English, and deliberately advertised this as a virtue, is probably as important as what it actually said.[43] The writer who set the wheels of this great engine of national self-consciousness in motion was John Bale:

Bale's enthusiasm for the place of written history in the preservation of faith reached the heart and mind of his friend John Foxe. When Foxe undertook his great work, he answered Bale's wish that some learned Englishman should write the true history of the Church. Bale's *The Image of Bothe Churches* identified by their moral characters and actions the churches of Christ and Antichrist; Foxe undertook to write the history of both churches.[44]

One needs to add, in English.

Bale had set out to write various histories of national institutions and collect together texts to map out and thus circumscribe a national history. His scholarly enterprises prefigure not only Foxe's plea for national unity, 'because God hath so placed us Englishmen here in one commonwealth, also in one church, as in one ship together, let us not mangle or divide the ship, which, being divided perisheth';[45] but also such an enterprise as Richard Hakluyt's slightly less massive compendium, *The Principal Navigations, Voyages, Traffiques and Discoveries of the English Nation* (1589–90 and 1598–1600), which planned to rescue a forgotten history 'only of *our own nation*' (my emphasis):

Having for the benefit and honour of my country zealously bestowed so many years, so much travail and cost, to bring antiquities smothered and buried in dark silence, to light, and to preserve certain memorable exploits of late years by our English nation achieved, from the greedy and devouring jaws of oblivion: to gather likewise, and as it were to incorporate into one body the torn and scattered limbs of our ancient and late navigations by sea, our voyages by land, and traffics of merchandise by both: I do this second time (friendly reader) presume to offer unto thy view this discourse. For the bringing of which into this homely and rough-hewn shape, which here thou seest, what restless nights, what painful days, what heat, what cold I have endured ... Howbeit, the honour and benefit of this Commonweal wherein I live and breathe hath made all difficulties seem easy.[46]

Hakluyt presents himself as the loyal, suffering subject akin to the martyrs of Bale's and Foxe's histories, but rewarded by his good service to the commonwealth. The 'discourse' he seeks to establish and which he represents as emerging into the reader's field of vision in the text ('offering to thy eye'), is centred around the homogeneous empty time of the nation.[47] Such a discourse has to be written in the time of the narrative(s) collected and presented to the 'friendly reader', an inescapable paradox of a discourse of national identity.[48]

In Bale's polemical pamphlet, *An Expostulation or Complaynte Agaynste the Blasphemyes of a Franticke Papist of Hampshire* (1550), written during his period of service under the Edwardian regime and perhaps at the height of his direct, political influence, he vigorously defended the young king against his, principally Catholic, detractors, and attempted to refute the argument that a child–king was God's curse on a wicked nation by citing numerous counter-examples from the Old Testament and English history. Not every contemporary historian would have regarded Henry VI's reign as a good example to support such a case, but Bale defends him as a 'whole and parfyght kynge' like the other boy–kings Henry III and Edward IV.[49] The dedicatory epistle to the Duke of Northumberland states that 'The most Christian reformacyon of thys churche of Englande, whych is to other natyons a most wurthie spectacle' is 'very turkshely deryde & mocke[d]' by the Catholic forces of the antichrist who find it:

An intollerable griefe ... to their uncircumcysed hartes to beholde the glytterynge toyes of superstycyouse ydolatry and hipocrytycall papystrye removed from thys earthe of Englande by the kynges wurthie majestie, and hys most honourable counsell, and Gods true relygyon again restored. That oure sayde seconde & most valeaunt Josias, hath thus pourged hys Juda (hys Englande I meane) from the abhominable buggeryes and ydolatries of the great Baal Peor of Rome, earnestly sekynge for the true God of David hys forefather, to the most lyvely example of all other prynces, their ungratyouse and noughtie eyes are not a lyttle offended.[50]

Bale might not have a truly apocalyptic vision of England as an 'elect nation', but he clearly singles out his own country as a beacon of light amongst the darkness, repeating the example of God's chosen people (the Israelites) under the inspired banner of their most charismatic anointed king (comparing either Henry VIII or Edward VI to Solomon and David was a commonplace of Reformation writing).[51] The syntactic elision from the analogical 'Juda (hys Englande I meane)', which recognises the difference inherent in any comparison, to the identification of Edward and Josias implicit in 'earnestly sekynge for the true God of David hys forefather', as David becomes the common ancestor – or, rather, authentic original to be copied – reinforces this elevation of England's status. The burden of history has fallen upon the English people.

An earlier tract, *The Epistel Exhortatorye of an Inglyshe Chrystian unto his deerly beloved countrey of Inglande agaynste the pompouse popysh Bishops thereof* (1544), written as part of a series of pamphlets against the Henrican bishops he felt were destroying the newly born Reformation, again identified England as the holy land; this time, however, as a people cruelly enslaved by the tyrannical papists, who made them suffer far more than the Israelites did when enslaved by Pharaoh.[52] Bale alleged that Christian blood had been spilt through the conflicts of the various European nations because of the seditious, self-seeking and vicious attempts of papal agents to build up their own worldly power rather than save souls.[53] Priests aimed to undermine the independent sovereignty of national governments by suppressing the teaching of the gospel: 'So longe as you [ie, Catholics] shall beare rule in the parlymenthouse, the Gospell shall be kept undre, & Christ persecuted.'[54] The godly rule of the Christian monarch is contrasted to the false 'democracy' of the king's evil advisers; a common enough tactic in satire and complaint (see above p.38), but also an indication of the authoritarianism of Bale's Protestantism. The discourse of national sovereignty is centred in the power of the prince who thus becomes its vanishing point, authorising all before him, but supposedly beyond the perils of representation (here, specifically, political representation) and answerable only to the word of God. To point out his loyalty, Bale had to criticise the status quo and so risk being disloyal, a problem which dogged his political position throughout his life (see below, pp.64–5,74–5). When he accused his opponents of tyranny,[55] Bale had to except the potential for tyranny explicit in his own discourse of kingly power.[56]

Bale wrote two massive and extremely popular histories of papal abuses, *The Actes of the English Votaries* (1546) and the *Acta Romanorum Pontificum* (1558).[57] The former charts the history of monastic abuses in England and is in English; the latter, the history of the papacy and is in Latin (although it was translated into English in 1574, see above, p.56). Yet both assert that the British/English church was independent from the sway of the papal see. Bale acknowledges in the *Votaries* that the British were converted by the Roman legate, Lucius, citing Geoffrey of Monmouth, Polydore Vergil – a historian he, like most Protestants, had little time for elsewhere[58] – and Ranulph Higden as his sources.[59] But the point Bale makes is that Rome was not then attempting to hold hegemonic sway over the other Christian churches; the Pope had not yet appeared to stake his claims, the Pelagian heresy of human free will (ironically, a British invention), condemned by Jerome and Augustine, had not yet been formulated, monasticism was unknown. This was a conversion which established mutual relations between different national churches.

It also meant that Bale could condemn the subsequent expedition of Augustine, sent over by Pope Gregory, as being an attempt to bring the British church to heel and suppress the gospel. Bale transforms the famous story of Gregory seeing the fair-haired British boys in the Roman slave market and immediately deciding to bring them into the fold, into a warning against clerical celibacy, a much repeated hobby-horse.[60] Augustine is envisaged as a tyrant, raising himself above other citizens, who, nevertheless, see through his arrogant deceptions.[61] Gildas, one of Bale's favourite authors, is read as a proto-Protestant, condemning the Catholic perversions of the truth which doom the Britons in the face of the invasion of the Anglo-Saxons.[62]

In *The Pagent of Popes*, Bale again cites Geoffrey of Monmouth to show that the Britons always had the true doctrine of the primitive, apostolic church.[63] The life of Gregory the Great is more carefully fleshed out and he is seen to be one of the most significant occupants of the papal see. Although starting out as a force for good, removing graven images from churches and opposing the howling and chattering of the mass which prevented the teaching of the gospel – another of Bale's particular obsessions[64] – after his decision to make Britain subservient to Rome all his reforms were revoked and the diversity among churches he had previously encouraged was replaced by an insistence on conformity. In Bale's Apocalyptic reading of papal history, Gregory's period of office signifies a crucial development in the progress of the Antichrist; after Gregory's death, the Catholic church was afflicted with even more blindness than before, allowing human customs such as the blasphemous saying of masses for the dead to oust true doctrine. The next pope, Boniface, wanted to be head of all churches as Rome had been head of her empire; Islam began its rise to complement European developments; and in terms of Bale's classification of seven ages of the papacy, 666 years after the fall of Jerusalem the world reached the third stage of the Apocalypse.[65] A key event in Bale's eschatology – something Foxe was to modify – was the destruction of the British church by Gregory, paving the way for the invasion of the Saxons.[66] Firth is again correct to point out that the decisive break in Bale's history – and Foxe's – occurs in the year 1000 followed by the election of the arch-tyrant Hildebrand, notorious for humiliating the secular government of the emperor; but it needs to be remembered just how central the British church was to the Apocalyptic tradition of Tudor England and how much of this was derived from the work of John Bale.[67]

Bale's attempts to establish a native martyrology similarly presupposed the narration of a specifically nationalist history. In the preface to the *Chronicle of the Examination and Death of Lord Cobham* (1544), a work which was completed in exile, Bale declared that Polydore Vergil, although a man of great learning, had abused his talents and 'deformed his writings greatly, polluting our English chronicles most shamefully with his Romish lies and other Italian beggaries'. He expressed the wish that 'some learned Englishman (as there are now most excellent fresh wits) [would] set forth the English chronicles in their right shape, as certain other lands have done afore them, all affections apart'.[68] Bale was quite clearly not arguing for a privileged status for English or British identity here; rather, acknowledging the differential process of national self-definition.[69] But it is impossible, given Bale's premises, for his narrative of British subjects written in English to seem anything other than nationalistic. Cobham (Sir John Oldcastle) becomes a martyr precisely because he refuses to accept as just or godly Richard II's attempt to relinquish his authority as head of the church and submit to the papacy. Cobham is singled out by the evil and grasping clergy led by the Archbishop of Canterbury, Thomas Arnold, 'so fierce as ever was Pharaoh', because of his criticisms of the clergy. He is summoned by the king, who, under the sway of 'these blood-thirsty raveners', admonishes Cobham and tries to persuade him 'to submit himself to his mother the holy church, and as an obedient child to acknowledge himself culpable'. But 'the Christian Knight' cannot do this; he explains that he owes two types of obedience which, here, have come into conflict. On the one hand he confesses that he is willing to obey 'the christian king', 'the appointed minister of God, bearing his righteous sword, to the punishment of ill-doers, and for the safeguard of them that be virtuous'. But, on the other, he asserts that 'as touching the pope and his spirituality, truly, I owe them neither suit nor service, forsomuch as I know him by the scriptures to be the great Antichrist, the son of perdition, the open adversary of God, and the abhomination standing in the holy place'. Richard, who has in fact interceded to try to help Cobham, abandons him to the ecclesiastical powers and grants them '*full authority* to cite him, examine him, and punish him according to the devilish decrees, which they call the laws of holy church' (my emphasis).[70]

The aggressively polemical intent of the tract is evident. Richard is king and not king, because he refuses to honour the duties of his office and defend the independence of the national church. He has handed over the 'full authority' of the secular sword which should be his. Cobham can only be obedient to the public body of the king which represents the Christian nation by being disobedient to the private body. Christopher Goodman might have suggested that Richard had forfeited his rights as a holder of public office, had become a rebel against the Christian commonwealth and could thus be lawfully deposed and killed by the subjects who had to endure his diabolical tyranny.[71]

Bale carefully avoids making such a case. He seems to have been interested in a different mode of writing as it is hard not to read Cobham's life as an allegory of Bale's own circumstances:

John Bale's various activities during the years from his conversion in 1533 until the death of Cromwell in 1540 had made him a marked man. The orthodox bishops had already on two or three occasions examined him on the articles of his faith. As one who denied the real presence in the sacrament, he was not likely to receive very favourable consideration from the bishops. He was a married priest, and married priests were not in favour in orthodox circles. In addition, he was a maker of very unorthodox plays, and an actor in them. All these things explain why Bale found it expedient to shake the dust of his native land from off his feet, and seek refuge abroad.[72]

Bale was trying to make a case identical to Cobham's; he too could only show his loyalty by being disloyal and defending a position contrary to the one accepted by the king. Yet, if loyal, he dare not speak out directly against an anointed king so he reverts to a thinly disguised allegorical reading of history, a tactic used more consistently and rigorously by the authors of *A Mirror for Magistrates* (see below, chapter 3). In the preface to *The Second Examination of Anne Askew* (1547), Bale again repeats the narrative of British history which he fleshes out in greater detail elsewhere (see above, pp.61–3), dating the decline of the primitive church from the attempt of Augustine to impose the will of the Roman pontif upon it and tracing a lineage of true and false martyrs (though, here he states, perhaps with a sense of wish-fulfilment and a desire for rhetorical symmetry, that the false martyrs have all been justly put to death by the secular authorities, 'sometime for disobedience, and sometime for manifest treason', whereas the true martyrs, 'preachers of the gospel, or poor teachers hereof in corners ... were put to death by the holy spiritual fathers, bishops, priests, monks, canons, and friars, for heresy and lollardry'). Bale's stated intent is to rescue the suppressed history of the British/English church (like Skelton, Bale often seems to equate the two terms or regard them as effectively equivalent) and in doing so he is forced to foreground the national identity of his subject and, by implication, his audience: 'Now in conferring these martyrs, the old with the new, and the pope's with Christ's, I seclude first of all the British church, or *primitive church of this realm*, which never had authority of the Romish Pope' (my emphasis).[73]

The inevitability of this coincidence is as much a textual product as an authorial desire or intention. Bale's 'most influential publication', *The Image of Both Churches*, also written during this first period of exile, illustrates further the necessity that Protestantism be a national religion whatever internationalist ideology its adherents may have espoused.[74] The *Image* is a commentary on the Book of Revelation, the most frequently analysed Biblical text in Reformation Europe, and forms a crucial bridge between European and English Protestantism by 'applying to English history the twelfth-century identification of the Antichrist with the papacy made by Joachim de Fiore'.[75] Not only did Bale's millennial schema influence John Foxe and later English writers, but even after it ceased to appear the 'commentary lived on in the abridged form found in the annotations of the Geneva Bible (1560)'.[76]

I am not primarily interested here in the exact substance of Bale's interpretation of the Biblical text which has been analysed extensively elsewhere,[77] rather the grounds on which interpretation is founded. Bale establishes his subject position as a 'latter-day St. John'.[78] St John the Evangelist was exiled to the island of Patmos by the emperor 'for his preaching ... at the cruel complaints of the idolatrous priests and bishops', where the vision which is the Book of Revelation took place. Bale claims that his reading of John's book exactly figures the original, in content and in context:

Of such a nature is the message of this book with the other contents thereof, that from no place is it sent more freely, opened more clearly, nor told forth more boldly, than out of exile. And this should seem to be the cause thereof. In exile was it written ... In exile are the powers thereof most earnestly proved of them that have faith.[79]

The rhetorical parallel involves the equation of both the Biblical text with the modern interpretation of it, and the apostle with the latter-day saint; no gap is perceived to exist between text and reader.[80] Bale has placed himself as one of the elect readers of the truth of the Bible in describing his commentary as a re-enactment of the Biblical moment of revealed prophecy. Ironically, such a move depends upon a repetition, which highlights the subject's (Bale's) distance from the truth, as does the use of the rhetorical form employed to produce this reading. Concomitantly, Bale has to assert that his allegorical decoding of the Book of Revelation is beyond the wiles of rhetorical play or linguistic duplicity. It is a clear case of what Derrida calls 'the logic of the supplement', where something is presupposed and denied at the same time (here, broadly speaking, rhetoric or figurative language), a 'stitched seam', hidden yet visible, which serves to make the text function.[81]

Bale divides language into two mutually exclusive categories, figurative and plain. Whilst the papists desire to keep the true message of the Gospels 'under lock and key of unknown similitudes ... yet will it be plain enough to the faithful believers instantly calling upon him which hath the key of David to open the door of his infallible verities'.[82] Once again, the same binary opposition between 'true' and 'false' is stated as the key to Bale's reading; language can be divided as easily as martyrs, governors and the church. But whilst Bale fulminates against the use of 'figurate speech', he is seemingly blind to his own use of metaphor to establish the distinction between the literal and the figurative, ie, the key of David opening the door. Furthermore, as John King has pointed out, the very use of 'Image' in the title 'stresses the figurative nature of the Apocalypse', derived as it is from 'the Latin *imago* ("imitation, copy, likeness")'. Such a contradiction – and we remember that Bale was not averse to disguising his message when faced with a conflict of loyalties (see above, pp.64–5) – 'implicitly raises the problem of interpretation', a matter Bale was at pains to suppress in his reading of the Book of Revelation.[83] For example, XI, v, 'If any man shall hurt them (ie, God's witnesses), fire shall proceed out of their mouths and consume their enemies. And if any man will hurt them, this wise he must be killed' is interpreted as an allegory of false debate, 'the hurt' being 'subtle reasons and deceitful arguments' put forward by Medieval prelates and church fathers, eventually destroyed by 'the eternal word of the Lord that they shall declare (which is the consuming fire) [which] shall utterly destroy them'.[84] In effect such hermeneutics spirits figurative language away and the distinction between a trope and the 'truth' it signifies is rather neatly elided – does 'the Word' destroy via its own logic or 'literally' as a fire sent from God? Once God's voice has been identified, falsehood, the parodic image of 'truth', is easy to detect. The individual can be certain of God's desires through the correct reading of his word in the Bible, hence the importance of exemplary saints' lives as tales of true readers.

All signifiers lead to a stable set of already known signifieds. Revelation xvii, iv describes the whore of Babylon mounted on a scarlet beast holding a cup of gold in her hand. Bale interprets this as 'a golden cupfull of abhominations and filthiness of her execrable whoredom. This cup is the false religion that she daily ministereth.' In direct contrast, the city 'of pure gold' of xxi, xviii, is said to stand for the church of God and be without blemish.[85] 'Meaning' exists only in an oblique relation to actual words: Bale is reading Revelation in order to produce a text that, in Roland Barthes's terms, has been 'already read' because all answers are known in advance; all meaning has become confined to an allegorical code which cannot be challenged.[86] Michel Foucault's generalisation about the transformation of the Middle Ages to the Renaissance can – and should – be disputed, but his comments accurately describe what has taken place in Bale's text. Foucault states that in the Renaissance words and things became

fixed in a binary form which would render them stable; and because language, instead of existing as the material writing of things was to find its area of being restricted to the general organization of representative signs ... Things and words were to be separated from one another ... Discourse ... was no longer to be anything more than what it said.[87]

Indeed Bale provides a reading of the transformation from the Middle Ages to the Renaissance which mirrors Foucault's – albeit with an evidently different evaluation.[88] Revelation ix, i, describes a star which falls from heaven to earth when the angel blows the fifth trumpet. Bale interprets this star as the 'shining multitude of prelates, pastors and religious fathers ... fallen away from the *living word* of the lord, and from the *right conversation* of Christ' (my emphases) during the Middle Ages: 'Then was there an infinite table of sophisters and school-doctors, of reals and nominals, of sententiers and summists, of colligners and canonists, of Scotists, Thomists, Ocamists, Albertists, Baconists, Anconists'.[89] One Biblical verse justifies an almost complete summary of the English Reformation's re-writing of history (Bale also refers to the conflict of church and state, false ceremonies, murdered kings and martyrs) which emphasises further that the text has been already read. Now, in Bale's historical present, the privileged voice which can tell 'true' history because it is not subject to the constraints of history, has been restored to silence the cacophony of voices heard when the false church permitted debate, disputation, argument and dialogue.[90] Such a voice acknowledges no difference between the subject who speaks and what is said.

The *Image* posits that the 'eye of power', the transparent agent which can see all around it and escapes, via a figurative trick, beyond discourse and thus any historical constraint, belongs to the Christian saint as the spiritual representative or *imago* of God, beside the monarch as secular representative (Bale does not explore the potential conflict between these figures of authority).[91] As English is the linguistic medium for these conclusions, it is hardly surprising that anyone following Bale seriously could come to believe that 'God is English', like Bishops Aylmer and Parker.[92] After all, one of Bale's most frequent and vociferous assertions was that the word of God had to be taught in English and could never be truly told in the international medium of Latin (see below, p.73).

The confusions, tensions and evasions of Bale's dogmatic position are further highlighted in his work as a literary historian and a literary artist. Bale's massive literary history, first published in 1548 and then in a revised form in 1557 (see above, p.55), was designed to collect together all the authors of the British Isles (Bale often refers to himself as a 'compiler').[93] Bale had no native models but had to rely upon European ones such as Conrad Gesner's *Bibliotheca* (1545). Furthermore, writing the history of British or English authors – Bale is not very careful in distinguishing between the two – involved classifying texts and manuscripts written in Latin, which makes the question of a native national identity more problematic and raises the need for translation.[94] As we have seen, elsewhere in his writings Bale denies that there can be a gap or difference between the production and consumption of God's word, between the literary and the literal or between the author and the reader. Bale refuses to accept that God's word can ever be *mediated*; unlike Skelton he tries to expunge the Janus-faced legacy of his cultural heritage, something which presupposes work like his literary history.

The *Scriptorum Illustrium* is evidently not a modern literary history, like say Alistair Fowler's or George Sampson's, which perceives literature as an autonomous sphere of creative intellectual production.[95] Bale is more concerned with charting a recognisable British history of writing, a native voice, to complement the history of a distinct native church established in his other writings.[96] His catalogue of British writers covers all types of authors. They are arranged into chronological groups of one hundred (there are five of these in the *Summararium*, nine in the *Scriptorum Illustrium*), which include historians like Geoffrey of Monmouth, Gildas, Bede, John Leland; Protestant martyrs like Anne Askew (Bale's *Brief Chronicle* is based on her testimony);[97] miscellaneous ecclesiastical writers like Matthew Parker, Thomas More and John Fisher; numerous kings, as well as writers now considered literary such as the Old English poet Caedmon, Skelton, Thomas Hoccleve and Alexander Barclay. The work includes copious historical information derived from Bale's *Acta Romanorum Pontificum*, which sets each author within the enfolding apocalyptic matrix of historical development.

Bale regards apostleship as the highest form of authorship and so he claims that the apostles were the 'most important British authors ... whose true Christian authority contradicts papal claims to primacy'.[98] This evaluative classification serves two major functions: once again it elides the distinction between the literary and the literal; it also assimilates 'literature' into the nexus of the 'eye of power', denying that it can ever be other than a further manifestation of God's word and God's authority, or that it could be the site of the disturbing copia of rhetorical excess, where language no longer had to be anchored in a mimetic reality of signs, but could become figurative and, hence, duplicitous in a playful rather than a threatening way.[99]

Elsewhere, Bale argues that his own literature is 'true' and seems to make no distinction between the writing of a play and an expository tract, Scriptural commentary or polemical pamphlet. In his *An Expostulacion agaynste a papist* (1552), he vigorously defends his *Comedy of the Three Laws* (c. 1548) against the charge that it was a work of 'most perniciouse heresise' on the grounds that it declared 'how the false Antichrist of Rome with his clergye, hath bene a blemysher, darkener, confounder, and poysener, of all wholsom lawes', something 'wele knowne to al men' (certainly if they were readers of Bale's own writings).[100] Bale defends his plays in the same way that he defends his other work; that it was the true word of God.

Rather more revealing and interesting is his verse tract, *An Answere to a Papystycall Exhortacyon* (1548), written in tetrameters reminiscent of Skeltonics, which we know that Bale had read (see above, p.70). Bale begins in a style which resembles Skelton in both form and content, insulting the learning, doctrine and poetic ability of his opponents:

> Everye pylde pedlar
> Wyll be a medlar
> Though they wyttes be drowsye
> And ther lernynge lowsye
> Ther meters all mangye
> Rathe, rurall, and grangye
> Yet wyll they forwarde halte
> As menne mased in malte.
>
> These vyle cannell rakers
> Are now becumme makers
> Ther poems out they dashe
> With all ther swyber swawshe
> Ther darnell and ther chaffe
> Ther swylle and swynyshe draffe
> Soche pype soche melodye
> Soche bagge soche beggarye
> Of pylde popyshe faccyons
> They strowe exhortacions
> The people to infecte.[101]

I shall assume that the poem is by Bale; it shows a wit which is seldom in evidence elsewhere – but then, the author is consciously imitating Skelton's style. Not only does it demonstrate how easily Skelton was absorbed into a Protestant literary tradition, but also how important delineating an ancestry of Protestant literary texts involved establishing a usable form as well as content. The poem takes the form of a verbal duel between a Christian (ie, Protestant) and a papist. A few lines later, the Christian re-emphasises the connection between false language, bad poetry and false doctrine: 'Your doctrine is chaffe/ Your rhyme dyrtye draffe ... The language of lyes/ A false harlot tryes/ To seke a wycked praye.'[102] The papist, of course, is given lines which are less poetic as well as less truthful. He speaks in a lumbering pentameter which does not always scan well:

> Ther were heretykes that never wolde cease
> But from us to take unyte and peace
> So amonge us they dyd fyght.
> In ther blyndnesse to farre gone they were
> That of God they had no dought or fere.
> All to destruccion was ther delyght.[103]

Clearly the Christian has no difficulty in exposing the hypocrisy of this straw man, humiliating him in a suitable way to show that the devil does not have all the best tunes.

Needless to say, this clashes with what Bale does and writes elsewhere. The question of what would happen if the papist were to be witty and persuasive, which is implicit in the fear of figurative language central to the argument of the *Image of Both Churches*, is ignored, illustrating the pragmatic nature of Bale's inconsistent writings.

While Bale gives only the merest hint of being interested in creating a specifically Protestant poetics, he was instrumental in establishing a Protestant dramatic tradition as an employee of Thomas Cromwell (see above, p.54).[104] Bale appears to have been as prolific in his output of plays as he was in his other writings, but only five remain extant.[105]

In his lengthy self-justifying tract, *The Vocacyon of Johan Bale to the Bishopricke of Ossorie* (1553), Bale reveals, in a moment of acute personal crisis, how central his plays had become to his attempts not only to represent a public and a private self, but also to legitimise some form of agency when such constructions of self came into conflict.[106] The *Vocacyon* is related to the genre of Protestant saints' lives, using autobiographical material to transform the author into an analogous figure and make his life experience an exemplum.[107] His identification with St Paul suggests that he read his own text in the same way that he read the lives of Anne Askew and Sir John Oldcastle, as a modern 'truth' of Scriptural authority:

Saint Paul boasted much of his persecutions, and described them at large; concluding thus in the ende, 'Very gladly (saith he) will I rejoyce of my weaknesse, that the strengthe of Christe maye dwell in me. Therefore have I dilectation in infirmitees, in rebukes, in nedes, in persecution, and anguyshes, for Christe's sake'. 2. Cor. 12. If I have lykewyse felte a great manye of the same afflictions, as I have done in dede; maye not I also with him rejoyce in them? Maye I not be glad, that I am, in sorowes for the Gospell, lyke fashioned to him, and not pranked up in pompe and pleasures, lyke the wanton babes of this worlde?[108]

Having established his subject position as an authentic recorder and interpreter (see above, pp.66–8), Bale proceeds to describe his brief but eventful stay in Ireland. He recalls how Edward VI asked him to become Bishop of Ossory in August 1552, and despite grave doubts he agreed and arrived in Waterford in January 1553. He recounts his horror at the 'abhominable ydolatres maintained by the epicurish priests in the city' who were supposedly Protestant, but to Bale's eyes, still Catholic. Moving on to Dublin, he vociferously demanded the use of Edward's Second Prayer Book, arguing that '[i]f Englande and Irelande be undre one kinge, they are both bounde to the obedience of one lawe undre him'.[109] This was a significant issue in Tudor Ireland as the Second Prayer Book, unlike the first, replaced the Latin syntax of the mass with an English idiom and thus aroused particular hostility from the Irish.[110] Indeed, throughout the tract Bale fulminates against 'Latin momblings' and 'howlinge and jabberinge in a foren language' at God's service, conveniently ignoring the fact that although nominally subjects of the English king, the Irish had their own vernacular and the discarding of the Latin mass signalled a new obscurity for them rather than enlightenment from the Dark Ages. Bale's aggressive English Protestantism aroused predictable hostility in Kilkenny, especially when he tried to force the priests to take wives (p.448). When Edward died and the news of Mary's accession reached the diocese, he saw the writing on the wall and retired to his country retreat, but insisted on sending his servants out to cut hay on 8 September, Our Lady's Nativity, which was nearly fatal for him and was for the five servants. With Catholic rites firmly established in the cathedral, he decided that it was time to leave; finding no support in Dublin, he had the misfortune to be kidnapped *en route* to Scotland, having been mistaken for a rich Frenchman by a Flemish pirate. A storm drove them all to St Ives (where Bale found that Protestantism had made as little headway as in Ireland); the captain and crew threatened to leave him to face the Marian authorities in Dover, but Bale persuaded them to transport him to the continent for the sum of fifty pounds, which friends in exile paying, he made his way from Flanders to the exiled Protestant community at Wesel. In December 1553, the *Vocacyon* was published there with the provocatively satirical colophon, 'Imprinted in Rome before the Castle of S. Angell, at the signe of S. Peter.'[111]

In the *Vocacyon*, Bale has to confront the classic dilemma of sixteenth-century Protestantism; how the individual could act when the monarch was ungodly, as Bale obviously believed Mary was. His solution to the problem is illuminating. In the cathedral he preached a sermon exhorting the Irish to obey the monarch as the fundamental duty of the good citizen; in the market square, he had his plays performed:

On the xx. daye of August, was the Ladye Marye with us at Kylkennye proclaimed queene of Englande, Fraunce, and Irelande, with the greatest solempnyte, that there coulde be devysed, of processions, musters, and disguisings[112] ... I toke Christ's testament in my hande, and went to the Market Crosse; the people in great nomber followinge. There toke I the xiii. chap. of S. Paule to the Romanes, declaringe to them brevely what the authoritie was of worldly powers and magistrates, what reverence and obedience were due to the same

… The yonge men in the forenone, played a tragedye of 'God's Promyses' in the olde lawe, at the Market Crosse, with organe, plainings, and songes very aptely. In the afternone agayne they played a commedie of 'Sanct Johan Baptiste's Preachings', of Christ's baptisynge, and of his temptation in the wildernesse; to the small contentacion of the prestes and other papistes there. (p.450)

Bale, his tenure as bishop about to end, felt able to preach *and* put his art on display; a double parting gesture. Significantly, both acts point in opposite directions: his sermon demanded loyalty to the new queen, but his plays told them that her rule was godless. The trilogy referred to is completed by the comedy, *The Temptation of Our Lord*, in which the final speech of the defeated Satan Tentatour marks his self-identification with the Catholic church. Satan warns Christ of the disguises he will adopt in the future:

> Well than it helpeth not to tarry here any longar;
> Advauntage to have I se I must go farther.
> So longe as thu lyvest I am lyke to have no profyght;
> If all come to passe I maye syt as moch in your lyght.
> If ye preach Gods worde as me thynke ye do intende,
> Ere foure years be past I shall yow to your father sende.
> If Pharysees and Scrybes can do any thynge therto,
> False prestes and byshoppes with my other servauntes mo,
> Though I have hynderaunce it wyll be but for a season.
> I dought not thyne owne herafter wyll worke some treason;
> Thy vycar at Rome I thynke wyll be my frynde.
> I defye the, therfor, and take thy wordes but as wynde.
> He shall me worshypp and have the worlde to rewarde;
> That thu here forsakest he wyll most hyghlye regarde.
> Gods worde wyll he treade underneath hys fote for ever,
> And the hartes of men from the truth therof dyssever.
> Thy fayth wyll he hate and slee thy flocke in conclusyon.
> All thys wyll I worke to do the utter confusyon.[113]

Bale has made it clear that he can sanction such a performance precisely because his drama belongs to the spiritual rather than the secular or political realm; hence the seemingly contradictory emphasis of the sermon (not to mention the irony that the sermon seems to perform the political, public act and the play, paradoxically, the spiritual, private one). The autobiographical voice in the *Vocacyon* announces a double aporia, eliding both the spiritual and the political, and the literary and the literal. Bale's plays cannot avoid affirmation and refuse to tell lies because they must tell the truth or else become political and false; yet, clearly, they must also teach, if not delight, and so intervene in a public sphere. They must also, *ipso facto*, repeat or represent an original truth and exist in a metaphorical relationship to it.[114] Bale can only solve his dilemma by affirming that literature as a distinct mode of communication obeys none of the rules of other forms of discourse, but in its contrariness and ability to supplement the norm, is different, neither public nor private, but both.

A final illustration of the ways in which Bale's writings were caught between conflicting discursive fields is to be found in his important historical–morality play, *King John*. The play's complex textual history helps to make the point; *King John* exists in one manuscript transcribed soon after 22 May, 1538 and was probably written some time in the two years preceding this date and performed as part of Cromwell's attempts to promote Protestant drama 'to replace the Catholic cycles in popular esteem'.[115] The text of this version is probably a copy from a lost original and is thus named the A text. Bale then made a series of revisions to the text, probably from his first period of exile until *c.*1560, so that he worked on the text for at least a period of twenty-four years, ie, a comparable feat to Skelton's less well documented changes to *The Garland of Laurel*. These autograph revisions, the B text, leave the first part of the A text relatively little altered, apart from marginal additions and inserted sheets. But after line 1803, the A text was abandoned and a new version written (although it seems likely that Bale intended to incorporate all of the remaining A text into the new version), the play was formally divided into two acts and it seems likely that it was being prepared for publication at Wesel where his other four extant plays were published in 1547–8.[116] Most of the additions expand existing and interpolate new anti-Catholic passages, as well as developing the role of Sedition as a vice figure.[117] However, two sheets with a watermark of 1558, inserted after line 2157, add a section praising Elizabeth, and, more significantly, one attacking the

Anabaptists at Munster.[118] David Bevington has noted the irony of concluding a play primarily devoted to attacking the papacy and rescuing the reputation of a monarch whom Bale regarded as a proto-Protestant: 'The dramatic afterthought typifies the dilemma of zealous episcopal reformers like Bale or Cranmer, who never conceded and perhaps never realised that their anti-papist propaganda encouraged extremism from whatever corner it might appear.'[119] The position was a familiar one for Bale (see above, pp.52–3).

Bale's play is a concerted attempt to revive the reputation of the twelfth-century Angevin, King John, showing him to be an independent English ruler brought low by the evil conspiracies of foreign papal agents; the story is essentially the same as that of John's father, Henry II, against Thomas à Becket, except that this time the outcome for the reformed party is more tragic than comic.[120] One of Bale's lost plays was entitled, *On the Treachery of Thomas à Becket*.[121] As such, the national focus of *King John* is inescapable; in the first scene King John is approached by a suppliant widow who soon reveals herself to be England.[122] She warns King John that his clergy are to blame for the sorry state of affairs within the realm, 'mysusyng me ageynst all right and justyce'.[123] The king marvels that she has changed so much that he can no longer recognise her, his own land, which illustrates how successfully the forces of evil have disguised the real situation from the legitimate ruler John declares himself to be in his opening speech.[124] Pitted against the true speech of the female figure of England is Sedition, a false dissembling creature of the international papacy who boasts to King John that 'the Pope ableth me to subdewe bothe kyng and keyser' (line 99).[125] Stage directions indicate that the actor who played Sedition also doubled as Stephen Langton, the Archbishop of Canterbury, and later in the text they appear to merge as indistinguishable characters.[126] Sedition has exiled England's husband, 'God hym selfe' (line 109) because, according to England, 'The Popys pyggys may not abyd this word [ie, the gospel] to be hard' (line 119). God, assuming he is not dead, may not be self-evidently an Englishman, but he had taken an English wife.

Peter Womack has recently pointed out how this 'ideologically potent combination of meanings' suggests that 'the attack on the Catholic Church is being mounted in the name of the national community'. But a critical detachment is also provided for because the king is presented as '*willing* but *unable* to right her [England's] wrongs'[127] (Womack's emphasis). Bale is thus able to manipulate his representation of the historical personage to suit his propagandist Protestant aims.[128] The private historical body of the king disappears into his public one. King John rails against the 'Latyne howres, sermonyes and popetly playes/ ... tythis, ... devocyons ... offrynges,/ Mortuaryes, pardons, bequestes ... / ... halowed belles and purgatorye,/ ... relykes, confessyon and courtes of baudrye,/ Latyne mummers and sectes desseyvabyll' (lines 415–26) of the false clergy. The anachronism serves to flatten history out into the allegorical 'already read' of Bale's apocalyptic time-scale.[129] The rhetorical manoeuvre further serves as an obvious corollary to Benedict Anderson's 'homogeneous empty time' of the nation (see 'Introduction'); Bale has conflated the whole of national history into the idealised self of the monarch and the implication is that just as the devil's history can be written as a series of lives of the popes or English votaries, so can God's history be written as a series of lives of Protestant saints and good rulers.[130] The necessary form of Bale's history is inexorably metonymic and nationalistic.[131] One speculates on the never written history of England.

Ironically, given this conspicuous distortion of sources, one of Bale's strongest assertions was that the reason why King John had been given a bad name was that the true historical character of his reign had been distorted by clerical chroniclers subservient to the papacy, whose contemporary heir was Polydore Vergil.[132] Nobility makes this point during a heated exchange with Clergy:

> Yt is yowre fassyon soche kynges to dyscommend
> As yowre abuses reforme or reprehend.
> Yow pristes are the cawse that Chroncles doth defame
> So many prynces and men of notable name,
> For yow to take upon yow to wryght them evermore;

And therfor Kyng Johan ys lyke to rewe yt sore
Whan ye wryte his tyme for vexcyng of the clargy.

(lines 584–90)

The play invites the audience to read King John as an idealised Henry VIII. When Sedition is finally overthrown by Imperial Majesty he is duped by initially friendly overtures, in a manner which seems to recall the manner in which Robert Aske, the principal leader of the Pilgrimage of Grace (1536–7) was promised royal bounty and pardon before being hanged, drawn and quartered as a traitor.[133] Just as the Protestant exiles returning after the accession of Elizabeth – and this group, of course, included the elderly John Bale – were keen to manipulate the monarch by representing her as a radical Protestant and thus forcing her hand, so *King John* seems to be designed to manipulate Henry VIII.[134] At times, Bale praises (allegorically) the actions of Henry VIII (Henry's treatment of Aske); at others, he provides a model for a future perfect. Representing two figures on stage, the historical King John and the abstracted ideal of Imperial Majesty, not only solves the problem of writing a historical–morality play, but it also allows the author to exploit the hyphen connecting them and attempt to influence the future actions of the Tudor dynasty. That Bale should have had to insert a speech for Imperial Majesty in what may well have been the last performance of the play he supervised, watering down his aggressive anti-Catholic stance to turn attention to the Anabaptists, 'a secte newe rysen of late' who 'The scriptures poyseneth with their subtle allegoryes' (lines 2626–7), is a telling example of how 'Men [sic] make their own history, but not of their own free will; not under circumstances they themselves have chosen but under the given and inherited circumstances from the past with which they are confronted.'[135] Bale has to insist that his allegorical reading of history is the correct one and resolutely refuse to allow interpretative authority to spread any wider. But the revolution inaugurated by the Reformation had moved on and Bale was in no position to control the course of history. Whilst the compromise of the Elizabethan church settlement had little time for his apocalyptic readings, and the increasingly 'noble' style of writing literature favoured at court eventually shut out any attempt to forge a native style, Bale came to be most influential among those discontented with the lack of progress of Protestantism in England.[136] Bale had sought to speak for a national unity under the monarch, but his most potent influence was probably on a separatist or independent tradition which – arguably – led to the execution of the king and the disunity of civil war.[137]

CHAPTER 3

Literature and history – 'A Mirror For Magistrates'

Few texts have been relegated to the dust-heap of literary history more thoroughly than *A Mirror for Magistrates*. Although it went through numerous editions in the sixteenth and early-seventeenth centuries and was expanded by diverse hands in very different ways (see below), it is often cited as if it were no more than an extended Tudor sermon on obedience in the mode of the Elizabethan *Homilies*,[1] or as a development of the tradition of Medieval *de casibus* tragedy, named after Boccaccio's *De Casibus Illustrium Virorum*.[2] More revealingly still, the *Mirror* is frequently studied for its influence on later Renaissance literature, principally Shakespeare's histories and Elizabethan complaint, rather than as the important work it undoubtedly was. In the words of Jerry Leath Mills, 'criticism in the last forty years has been predominantly concerned with the *Mirror* as an anticipation of things much greater than itself, as a medium through which medieval concepts of history and tragedy are both perpetuated and reshaped, as a repository of potentially brilliant ideas which matured in the age of Shakespeare'.[3] The *Mirror* is the 'drab' John the Baptist unfit to kiss the 'golden' feet of those who came after it; it is the stunted boyhood of Shakespeare's histories.[4] Yet in Sidney's *An Apologie for Poetry* the *Mirror* is considered alongside *Troilus and Criseyde*, the Earl of Surrey's lyrics and *The Shepheardes Calender*, not the works of Herodotus or Xenophon, and referred to in glowing terms: 'I account the *Mirror of Magistrates* meetly furnished of beautiful parts.'[5] Clearly, for Sidney, the *Mirror* forms part of the 'golden' world of the poets rather than the 'drab' world of the histories:

where the historian in his bare *Was* [Sidney's emphasis] hath many times that which we call fortune to overrule the best wisdom. Many times he must tell events whereof he can yield no cause; or, if he do, it must be poetical.

For that a feigned example hath as much force to teach as a true example ... I conclude, therefore, that he [the poet] excelleth history, not only in furnishing the mind with knowledge, but in setting it forward to that which deserveth to be called and accounted good (*Apologie*, pp. 110 and 112)

Sidney's judgement of the relative merits of poetry and history – which might almost have been written with the *Mirror* in mind so accurately does it encapsulate the major themes of that work – should alert us to the fact that not all Tudor readers read the *Mirror* in the same way as the *Chronicles* of Fabyan and Hall from which the *Mirror* purloined most of its material (see below). Sidney refers to the tyranny of fact, the problem of fortune interfering with the didacticism literature in its broadest sense should possess, and the need for interpretation – which he equates with poetry – beyond the authority of the 'old mouse-eaten records' which can leave the historian 'better acquainted with a thousand years ago than with the present age' (*Apologie*, p. 105). The *Mirror* makes exactly the same case, distinguishing itself from history or chronicle writing:

> Unfrutfull Fabyan folowed the face
> Of time and dedes, but let the causes slip;
> Whych Hall hathe added, but with double grace,
> For feare I thinke least trouble might him trip:
> For this or that (sayeth he) he felt the whip.
> Thus story writers leave the causes out,
> Or so rehears them as they wer in dout.

> But seing causes are the chiefest thinges
> That should be noted of the story wryters,
> That men may learne what endes al causes bringes,
> They be unwurthy name of Croniclers
> That leave them cleane out of their registers,
> Or doubtfully report them: for the fruite
> Of reading stories standeth in the suite.[6]

Poetry, so it is argued, can say things which chronicles cannot, partly because it can escape the scrutiny of the censor (see below, pp. 103–7). That the *Mirror* is often regarded as historical and not literary probably says more about what the writers of an English literary history have chosen to write out of their story rather than how late sixteenth-century readers made sense of the kinds of writing available to them.

The originator of the plan for the *Mirror* was the printer, John Wayland,[7] who was keen to publish a new edition of John Lydgate's *The Fall of Princes* in 1555, described by Lily B. Campbell as a 'series of narrative tragedies in verse, tragedies in each of which the reason for the prince's fall is explained, some having fallen for disobedience to God, some for avarice, some for sloth'.[8] He approached William Baldwin, a prominent Protestant man of letters at the court of Edward VI and described by John Bale as the English Cato,[9] hoping that a continuation might be added, 'concernynge the chefe Prynces of thys Iland, penned by the best clearkes in such kind matters that be thys day lyving'.[10] Baldwin stressed the need for others to be involved and later claimed that seven worked on the original project,[11] although only the names of Baldwin and George Ferrars,[12] another well-known Edwardian Protestant, who, like Baldwin, nevertheless found a place at Mary's court, 'are identified in the 1559 text'.[13] The first edition, which used material based on the chronicles of Thomas More, Fabyan and Hall,[14] was suppressed when only partly printed with Lydgate's poem in 1555, almost certainly owing to an edict which banned seditious books, but mentioned only 'the boke commonly called Halles Chronicle'.[15] When Elizabeth came to the throne an edition was licensed through the Stationers' Register in July 1558[16] and printed in 1559, but it contained only part of the original text. A second edition appeared in 1563. Added to the text was a second part dating from the reign of Mary, which almost certainly contained tragedies from the suppressed edition. The whole was revised in 1571. A third part, containing two new tragedies, one promised since 1559, appeared in 1578, whilst the edition of 1587 added material to the first part. Meanwhile two supplementary works had appeared; one by John Higgens, entitled, *The First Part of the Mirror for Magistrates*, which made use of the matter of Britain derived from Geoffrey of Monmouth, Grafton, Stow *et al*; printed in 1574; and one in 1578 by Thomas Blenerhasset, confusingly titled *The Second Part of the Mirror for Magistrates*, containing twelve tragedies of conspicuously British/English subjects from the invasion of Caesar to the Norman Conquest. The 1587 edition included Higgens's work (but not Blenerhasset's) in an attempt to fix the canonicity of such a heterogeneous and manifestly popular text. An edition printed in 1610 put all the material together for the first time.[17]

This potted history of the text can only hint at the complexity of the *Mirror*'s history and reception.[18] The first major difficulty is placing the *Mirror* in relation to its sources; can it be read as a continuation of the *de casibus* tradition of tragedy, or does it signal a fundamental break with its generic predecessors? Lydgate's huge poem of over 36,000 lines, *The Fall of Princes*, itself a translation of Laurence de Premierfait's prose translation of Boccaccio's *De Casibus Illustrium Virorum*, mainly in rime royal,[19] was completed in the late 1430s or early 1440s at the instigation of his then patron Humphrey, Duke of Gloucester, who was an Italophile and has some claim to be the 'first humanist patron of letters in England'.[20] Indeed, *The Fall of Princes* enjoyed considerable popularity in the fifteenth and sixteenth centuries, being copied in numerous manuscripts and going into two printed editions in 1494 and 1527, both by Richard Pynson.[21] Only with the development of the plan to extend the matter of the poem to include 'Our owne countrey stories' ('Baldwin's Dedication', p.64, lines 30–1), was Lydgate's work eclipsed and neglected until reprinted in the twentieth century.[22] In other words, a self-proclaimed *nationalistic* project, of the sort Sidney encouraged in the 'Exordium' of his *Apologie* and mapped out in the 'Digression', led to the disappearance of *The Fall of Princes* as a popular literary text. It is a measure of the *Mirror*'s success that it forms a key role in Sidney's genealogy of contemporary literature, along with Gower and Chaucer, and a measure of Lydgate's own fall that he no longer rates a mention as he did when Skelton set out to trace his particular literary ancestry (see above, pp.28–31).

Lydgate's poem is by no means a straightforward translation

or adaptation of its source. In the prologue to Book 1, Lydgate
describes Laurence's purpose as desiring to teach his readers
'Fortunys variaunce,/ That othre myhte as in a merour see/ In
wordly worshepe may be no surete' (*The Fall*, 1, lines 54–6)

> And have a maner contemplacioun,
> That thynges all, wher Fortune may atteyne,
> Be transitory of condicioun;
> For she off kynde is hasti & sodeyne,
> Contrarious hir cours for to restreyne,
> Off wilfulnesse she is so variable,
> Whan men most truste, than is she most chaungable.
>
> (*The Fall*, 1, lines 106–12)

Lines such as these have led many commentators to assume that
The Fall of Princes belongs to a genre of *de casibus* tragedy which
asserts that the world is 'ruled by Fortune, the irrational spirit
of chance' so that 'there is no perceptible order of cause and
effect such as would permit an ambitious man to avoid material
misfortune by forethought, by wise judgement and action, or
even, strange to say, by the most perfect allegiance to God and
the Christian religion'. The moral of such tragedy is simple:
'Trust not at all in this world, but in the next world', which is
only 'a specially developed branch of the old argument for
Contempt of the World'.[23] In contrast to Lydgate, who portrays
'Fortune in the most orthodox tradition',[24] so this argument
generally goes, comes the *Mirror* which with its authors' greater
interest in 'establishing accurate historical accounts',[25] intro-
duces a new

conception of rational morality and of tragic justice here on earth
[which] begins to conquer Contempt of the World and brings as its
corollary a conception, not of mutable glory on earth and changeless
glory in Heaven, but of eternal glory both here and in Heaven. The
book is a 'mirror' because princes and others in authority may find in
it not so much a reflection of life's lawlessness here below, which will
repel their eyes and turn them upward, as a reflection of life's law both
here and above, which they may well take to heart.[26]

Once again, we read the same old story; the apolitical,
spiritual Middle Ages giving way to the political and human-
centred Renaissance (see 'Introduction'). There are, of course,
numerous difficulties in separating *The Fall of Princes* from the

Mirror so easily. Even if we read in generic terms of *de casibus* tragedy – a dangerous enterprise as *de casibus* definitions and classifications are modern ones[27] – it is by no means obvious that *The Fall of Princes* simply urges the reader to eschew the world. Lily Campbell has argued that in *The Fall* 'the vagaries of fortune are always directly related to the sins for which the princes fell',[28] and Derek Pearsall has pointed out that nearly all Lydgate's additions to the *de casibus* 'are in the form of moralisation', almost a quarter of Book 1, for example.[29] The following stanza, concerning the pride of princes

> God hath a thousand handis to chastise,
> A thousand dartis off punycioun,
> A thousand bowes maad in unkouth wise,
> A thousand arblastis bent in his dongoun,
> Ordeyned echon for castigacioun;
> But where he fynt meeknesse & repentaunce,
> A tour off maistresse off his ordynaunce.
>
> (*The Fall*, i, lines 1331–7)

implies that Lydgate's universe is rather more providential and comprehensible than Farnham's judgement suggests. It is also arguable that the *Mirror* consists solely of tragedies of retribution: William Peery has claimed that in the 1559 edition of the *Mirror* only two of the nineteen tragedies could be classed as tragedies of retribution *per se*, twelve demonstrating divided responsibility between the agent and the world, and five being tragedies of 'external circumstance'. Peery concludes, not unreasonably, that conceptions of fortune were a 'confused ideology' and that there were 'divergent tendencies in *De Casibus* literature from Boccaccio on'.[30]

Lydgate does set out very clearly that he believes that the world is not just an illegible text. Poets must interpret and translate it for the benefit of others less skilled in the art of reading than themselves:

> Ther cheef labour is vicis to repreve
> With a maner covert symylitude,
> And non estate with ther langage greeve
> Bi no rebukyng of termys dul and rude;
> Whatever thei write, on vertu ay conclude,

Appeire no man in no maner wise:
This th'offise of poetis that be wise.

(The Fall, III, lines 3830–6)

Lydgate's articulation of the function of poetry is not dissimilar to Sidney's. But unlike the aristocratic Sidney, Lydgate needed a patron to reward him.[31] In the world of *The Fall* poets have to rely on the other estates, hence the need not to offend them:

Lordis in erthe have domynacioun;
Men of the cherche of gold have habundaunce;
The kniht get goode thoruh his hih renoun;
Marchauntis with wynnyng have sovereyn aqueyntaunce:
But poor poetis (God sheeld hem fro myschaunce!)
May now-adaies for ther impotence,
For lakke of support go begge ther dispence.

(The Fall, III, lines 3851–7)

As Skelton did in *The Garland of Laurel,* Lydgate places himself at the head of a poetic genealogy – of an impeccably humanist cast, in contrast to that of his self-styled disciple (see chapter 1):[32] Dante, Virgil, Petrarch and Chaucer all thrived 'quieet fro, wordli mocioun' (line 3839) and 'Because thei flourede in wisdam and science,/ Support of princis fond hem ther dispense' (lines 3863–4). Poetic achievement merits mundane reward and protection from the vagaries of fortune. The poet argues a position to attain such satisfaction.[33]

There are other ways too in which *The Fall* belies any description of it as a representative example of a belief in a static, hostile universe. John Scattergood has shown that Lydgate is quite capable of altering his source to promote aggressive nationalistic sentiment.[34] Describing the capture of King John II of France at Poitiers in 1356, Boccaccio refers to the English as 'anglis, inertissimis adque pavdis et nullus valoris hominibus' ('Englishmen, the laziest, most fearful and worthless of men' (Scattergood's translation)), translated accurately by Laurence as 'des anglois, hommes faillis et vains ae de nulle valeur'. Lydgate omits these lines and instead reproves Boccaccio for his slur on English valour, suggesting that he 'Kaught a quarel in his malencolie,/ Which to his shame did aftirward rebounde' *(The Fall,* IX, lines 3171–2).

In a sense both these extracts are the logical development of the Prologue to Book 1. After describing his sources and setting out his initial aims in writing *The Fall*, Lydgate promises to deal as faithfully as he can with his authors in a 'stile nakid [...] and bare' (line 229). There is a problem, though:

> But, o allas! who shal be my muse,
> Or onto whom shal I for help calle?
> Calliope my callyng will refuse ...
>
> My maister Chaucer, with his fresh comedies,
> Is ded, allas, cheef poete of Bretyne,
> That whilom made ful pitous tragedies.
> *The Fall*, 1, lines 239–41, 246–8)

Lydgate grants fulsome praise to Chaucer for his skill in refining the English language, 'Out off our tunge tavoiden al reudnesse,/ And to refourme it with colours of suetnesse' (lines 277–8)[35] and lists his achievements – which include rendering Dante into English (line 303) – concluding, 'Sithe he off Inglissh in making was the beste' (line 356). Lydgate then turns to patrons who supported such poets: 'And these poetis I make off mencioun,/ Were bi old tyme had in gret deynte,/ With kynges, pryncis in every regioun,/ Gretli preferrid afftir ther degre' (lines 358–61). Predictably he turns to Duke Humphrey, who he claims has governed England well in Henry VI's absence,[36] maintains the church and refuses to tolerate heretics, is 'Eied as Argus with resoun and forsiht' (line 383) and, most significantly,

> In understandyng alle othir off his age,
> And hath gret joie with clerkis to commune:
> And no man is *mor expert off language*,
> Stable in study alwey he doth contune,
> Setting a-side alle chaungis of Fortune
> (*The Fall*, 1, lines 386–90; my emphasis)

Duke Humphrey is cast as the right patron, because he is powerful enough to protect the poet from fortune; because he has the ability to read what the poet will explain to him of the vicissitudes of the world; and because, so it is implied, he will, being skilled in languages, recognise another Chaucerian contribution to the establishment of a specifically English literature.

It is undoubtedly true that the *Mirror*, in concentrating on the events of recent – and controversial – history, invites readings which modify the genre from which it develops. But it is naive to imagine that it signifies a clean break with its forebears. The tradition of *de casibus* tragedy had already created a fragmented site of disharmony where mutually contradictory discourses competed for attention.

We might employ a well-known concept of Bakhtin's, the chronotope, to illuminate this generic development and follow his lead in attempting to establish a 'historical poetics'. Bakhtin notes that 'the process of assimilating real historical time and space in literature has a complicated and erratic history' and suggests that we could give 'the name *chronotope* (literally "time–space") to the intrinsic connectedness of temporal and spatial relationships that are artistically expressed in literature'. He continues: 'The chronotope in literature has an intrinsic *generic* significance. It can even be said that it is precisely the chronotope that defines generic distinctions.' The problem 'which greatly complicates the historico-literary process' is 'the simultaneous existence in literature of phenomena taken from widely separate periods of time'.[37]

Bakhtin's perceptive analysis warns us that a generic form cannot simply be read as if it existed without an external history; it is as foolish to imagine that texts can be read as if a label like epic, comedy, lyric, or in this case *de casibus* tragedy, adequately defined their existence, as it is to read them as if their form merely contained their content.[38] *The Fall* invites two incompatible types of reading, contains two very different chronotopes; a static notion of an unchanging universe which teaches mankind the same lessons regardless of historical development – a universe where the story of Oedipus or the fall of Troy can be read in the same way as that of the fate of the Knights Templar or King John of France; and an awareness of historical change which negates this certainty and is acutely conscious of a national development. In other words, an abstract didacticism versus an English nationalism. Bakhtin claims that such 'heteroglossia' only really becomes a literary norm with the development of the modern novel – Bakhtin suffers from the same myth of the static Middle Ages, dominated by an 'official' culture and ideology:

> At the time when major divisions of the poetic genres were developing under the influence of the unifying, centralizing centripetal forces of verbal-ideological life, the novel – and those artistic-prose genres that gravitate towards it – was being historically shaped by the current of decentralizing, centrifugal forces. At the time when poetry was accomplishing the task of cultural, national and political central-ization of the verbal–ideological world in higher official socio-ideological levels ... where there was to be found a lively play with the 'languages' of poets, scholars, monks, knights and others, where all 'languages' were masks and where no language could claim to be an authentic, incontestable face.[39]

Obviously Bakhtin's comments cannot be applied to *The Fall* or the *Mirror* without substantial modification. But I would suggest that in *The Fall* we can read two similar and analogous centripetal and centrifugal forces. On the one hand there is the moralistic discourse which criticises the faith of powerful men in the ways of the world; on the other, there is a celebration of a national history established through the achievements of great men. Ironically, in Bakhtin's terms both discourses could be labelled as 'official'; one echoes an age-old Christian suspicion of earthly delights,[40] the other, the need for the establishment of a national-cultural identity. In historical rather than discursive terms, we can perhaps read the conflict of church and state.[41]

Bakhtin's conflation of pre-Renaissance 'languages' under the term 'official' disguises these serious conflicts and enables him to privilege the novel and prose over poetry, as if the latter were 'by convention suspended from any mutual interaction with alien discourse, any allusion to alien discourse'. *Pace* Bakhtin, '[t]he world of poetry' is not 'always illuminated by one unitary and indisputable discourse'.[42] The public message of *de casibus* tragedy had started to pull in two directions before the *Mirror*'s complex publishing history brought the two rival discourses into the open in two distinct versions of the same work.

Lawrence Green has argued that as the *Mirror* grew and grew, the didactic function of its early editions became watered down so that the tragedies came to seem 'a celebration of admirable stances which are to be appreciated for their own sakes and not for any consequences they might have'.[43] If so, this is not in keeping with the stern moral message of the 1559 edition:

where the ambitious seeke no office, there is no doubt, offices are duly ministered: and where offices are duly ministered, it can not be chosen, but the people are good, whereof must nedes folow a good common weale. For if the officers be good, the people can not be yll. Thus the goodnes or badnes of any realme lyeth in the goodnes or badnes of the rulers. And therfore not without great cause do the holy Apostels so earnestly charge us pray for the magistrates: For in dede the welth and quiet of everye common weale, the disorder also and miseries of the same, cum specially through them. (*A Mirror for Magistrates*, p.64, lines 19–27)

Baldwin's dedication stresses that political offices are 'not gaynful spoiles for the gredy to hunt for, but payneful toyles for the heedy to be charged with' (p.63). The tragedies, nearly all addressed to Baldwin, but discussed by the group of writers in the prose links, aspire to give a genuine lesson.[44] Thus the opening tragedy represents the ghost of Robert Tresilian,[45] chief justice of England in Richard II's reign, telling the story of the growing corruption under the king and his intimate councillors. He describes how the law was used to exploit the people rather than protect them:

> So wurking lawe lyke waxe, the subjects was not sure
> Of lyfe, lande, nor goods, but at the princes wyll:
> Which caused his kingdome the shorter tyme to dure,
> For clayming power absolute both to save and spyll,
> The prince therby presumed his people for to pyll:
> And set his lustes for lawe, and will had reasons place,
> No more but hang and drawe, there was no better grace.
> (*Mirror*, p.77, lines 85–91)

The assumption of 'power absolute' by Richard is categorically condemned; the next stanza opens with the accusation that the

king was 'transcending the lymittes of *his* lawe' (p.78, line 92;
my emphasis). Eventually parliament insisted that the king's
trangressions be halted and the main offenders, Tresilian among
them, hanged. The speaker rails against the 'fyne of falsehood,
the stypende of corruption' (p.79, line 120) and urges future
councillors to tread 'the paths of equitie':

> If sum in latter dayes, had called unto mynde
> The fatall fall of us for wrestyng of the ryght,
> The statutes of this lande they should not haue defynde
> So wylfully and wyttingly agaynst the sentence quyte:
> But though they scaped paine, the falte was nothing lyght:
> Let them that cum hereafter both that and this compare,
> And wayling well the ende, they wyll I trust beware.
>   (*Mirror*, p.80, lines 141–7)

The prose link adds nothing more other than to note that the
tragedy 'semed not unfyt for the persons touched in the same'
(p.81, line 2). Two points can be made: firstly, the moral/
political focus of the work is announced and its specific target,
the would-be magistrate, unequivocally identified. Secondly, in
concentrating on material from the reign of the deposed Richard
II,[46] insisting that government makes the people what they are
and establishing a fictional universe which vindicates the rights
of subjects via their means of political representation against the
extra-legal designs of their sovereign,[47] it is easy to see why
Mary's censors might not have been acting merely out of
paranoia in refusing to license the work. It was, after all,
Shakespeare's *Richard II* that Robert Devereux, Second Earl of
Essex, had performed for him as a preface to his rebellion in
1600.[48] In the post-Reformation intensification of the debate
concerning the position of the monarch *vis-à-vis* his or her
subjects, the *Mirror* pledges an allegiance to the people which
contrasts markedly with the king-worship of John Bale (see
chapter 2), and comes perilously close to justifying the violent
overthrow of the tyrant.[49] It also unequivocally demands that
the monarch possess no representational or constitutional power
outside parliament; the position of political radicals up to the
English Civil War.[50]

Other tragedies in the 1559 edition tell related but not

identical tales. The two Roger Mortimers[51] advise magistrates not to trust in fortune because 'welth and lyfe are doubtfull to endure' (p.89, line 147); the innocent Thomas of Woodstock, Duke of Gloucester,[52] warns that fortune may seem unstable but God will strike down the unjust prince:

> For blood axeth blood as guerdon dewe,
> And vengeaunce for vengeaunce is iust rewarde,
> O ryghteous God thy iudgements are true,
> For looke what measure we other awarde,
> The same for us agayne is preparde:
> Take heed ye princes by examples past,
> Blood will haue blood, eyther fyrst or last.
>
> (*Mirror*, p.99, lines 197–203)

To read the *Mirror* in terms of an aesthetic which excludes contemporary political reference is surely to miss the point.

Eveline Feasey has suggested that the reason for the suppression of the 1554 edition centred around three tragedies, which the prose links of the first 1559 edition prepare the reader for: those of Humphrey, Duke of Gloucester, Lydgate's patron; Eleanor Cobham, his wife; and Edmund, Duke of Somerset.[53] This last was first printed in the 1563 edition, but the other two had to wait until 1578. Duke Humphrey is described as 'Protector of England, during the minoritie of his nephue kinge Henrye the sixt, (commonlye called the good Duke) by practise of enemies was brought to confusion' (p.445), presumably the original title from the suppressed edition. As Feasey notes, to describe a historical figure as the 'good duke' at this time was to allude to Edward Seymour, Duke of Somerset, and Lord Protector during the early part of the reign of his nephew, Edward VI, who was also known by the same affectionate nickname to his supporters.[54] Somerset, too, could have been said to have been 'brought to confusion' by the practice of his enemies and had been executed in 1552. It was almost certainly during the office of Somerset, a keen promoter of Protestant literature like Thomas Cromwell before him (see above, p.54), that the plan for the *Mirror* was conceived. George Ferrars, the author of this tragedy, was well known as a sympathiser of Somerset's as was William Baldwin who praised Somerset's rule in the dedication to his *A Treatise of Morall Philosophie* (1548).[55] Other more incidental details heighten the similarities; Somerset's first marriage had ended in divorce and so had Duke Humphrey's, a detail which, as Feasey notes, has no real place in the story (pp.453-4, lines 232-45);[56] both met their fates in similar ways, having been called to unexpected Council meetings of which they were suspicious:

> And though just cause I had for to suspect
> The time and place apoynted by my foes...
> Yet trust of truth with a conscience cleare
> Gave mee good heart, in that place to appeare.
> (*Mirror*, p.458, lines 393-4, 398-9)

Both were then arrested a few hours later and charged with treason (p. 458, lines 400-20).

The other two omitted tragedies encourage this historical parallel. 'Eleanor Cobham' exonerates the 'good Duke' (p.442, line 307) and the protagonist blames their fall on her ambition and necromancy.[57] The tragedy of 'Edmund, Duke of Somerset' narrates the fate of Duke Humphrey from the perspective of one of his enemies whose ghost now blames his own downfall on the part he played in framing the Lord Protector. The land described after Duke Humphrey's death strongly resembles the England under Richard II portrayed by Tresilian's ghost (see pp.91-2 above):

> Traytors dyd triumphe, true men lay in the dust,
> Reving and robbing roysted every where,
> Will stoode for skyll, and lawe obeyed lust,
> Might trode downe right, of kyng there was no feare.
> (*Mirror*, p.399, lines 260-3)

Again, any centre of legitimate authority is absent. Edmund places responsibility for the conspiracy and its disastrous effects with William de la Pole, Duke of Suffolk, who 'With glosing tongue he made us fooles to weene,/ That Humphrey dyd to Englandes crowne aspyre' (p.401, lines 293-4).[58] Humphrey is classed as one of those who have 'for their vertue been envied and murdered' ('Baldwin's Dedication', p.67, lines 72-3): 'So

long as he was Englandes dyrectour,/ Kyng Henries tytle to the
crowne was good./ This prynce as a pyller most stedfastly stood '
(p.390, lines 52–4).

It would appear that the parallels are difficult to deny and
that contemporary readers would have seen the fate of Edward
Seymour in these three tragedies.[59] Duke Humphrey stands for
the murdered 'Good Duke', the champion of the Protestants.
'Baldwin's Dedication' encourages an awareness of this chronotope in its programmatic claims:

> God can not of Justice, but plage such shameles presumption and
> hipocrisy, and that with shamefull death, diseases, or infamy. Howe he
> hath plaged evill rulers from time to time, in other nacions, you may
> see gathered in Boccas booke intituled the fall of Princes, translated
> into Englishe by Lydgate: Howe he hath delt with sum of *our
> countreymen your ancestors*, for sundrye vices *not yet left*, this booke named
> *A Mirrour for Magistrates*, can shewe. (*Mirror*, p.65, lines 49–55; my
> emphasis)

Historical information is provided in so far as it applies to the
present. The *Mirror* is designated as existing within the time-
space of the nation, pushing the critical claims of the text
beyond the general ones of *The Fall*. It is also easy to see why the
Marian authorities might take special objection to these
tragedies, even apart from the allegorical praise of a political
figure and, by implication, era so at odds with the current
regime.[60] Mary's chancellor, Stephen Gardiner, had been
imprisoned for his religious views by Seymour and 'may well
have seen in the praise of Seymour an uncomplimentary
comparison with himself'. As Feasey has observed, the unflat-
tering portrayal of Cardinal Beaufort in the tragedies of
'Humphrey' and 'Eleanor' invites a further comparison.[61]

As the narrative of the *Mirror* progresses, it keeps up its
consistent political stance. For example, the conclusion of the
tragedy of John Tiptoft, Earl of Worcester,[62] proclaims:

> Warne all men, wisely to beware,
> What offices they enterprise to beare:
> The hyest alway most maligned are,
> Of peoples grudge, and princes hate in feare.

> For princes faultes his faultors all men teare.
> Which to avoyde, let none such office take,
> Save he that can for right his prince forsake
> 　　　　　　　(*Mirror*, p.202, lines 134–40)

Such sentiments are very much in keeping with the original formulations in 'Baldwin's Dedication' in singling out a political class who must run the country. But the *Mirror*'s authors were very keen not to overstep the mark and encourage the notion that any resistance to the authorities was justified. The 1559 edition contained the tragedies of Jack Cade, the rebel who led the Kentish uprising which presented the 'Complaint of the Commons of Kent' to Henry VI in 1450; and that of Owen Glendower, who led the Welsh resistance to Henry IV until his death in 1410.[63] The former is described as one of 'fortune's whelps' (p.170, line 19) and the latter as one of 'fortune's darlings' (p.119, line 17), meaning that they trusted in fortune and were unable to read the providence of God set out in 'Baldwin's Dedication'.[64] The 1563 edition added the tragedy of 'The wilfull fall of Blacke Smyth'. All three have to admit that they are traitors.

Cade's ghost's conclusion might seem to confirm the widely held view that the *Mirror* upholds a belief in the divine right of kings. Admitting his inability to comprehend the providential plan of the universe when alive, the posthumously wise Cade speaks directly to the potentially rebellious commons:

> Full litel knowe we wretches what we do.
> Whan we presume our princes to resist.
> We war with God, against his glory to,
> That placeth in his office whom he list
> 　　　　　　　(*Mirror*, p.176, lines 148–51)

Earlier Cade had confessed that his sin was that his ambition led him beyond his estate (p.172, line 44), to pretend that he was called John Mortimer, 'Wheras in deede my fathers name was Kade/ Whose noble stocke was never wurth a sticke' (p.173, lines 52–3), and that he had thus led the valiant men of Kent to ruin with 'false perswasions' that 'they suffred to great injuryes' (p.173, lines 59–60). 'Fortunes whelp' advises that 'men folow

reason/ Subdue theyr wylles, and be not Fortunes slaves'
because 'There is no trust in rebelles, raskell knaves,/ In
Fortune lesse, whiche wurketh as the waves' (p.177, lines 162–3,
165–6). Instead they should 'flye all worldly charge' (line 168)
because

> God hath ordayned the power, all princes be
> His Lieutenants, or debities in realmes,
> Against their foes still therfore fighteth he,
> And as his enemie drives them to extremes,
> Their wise devises prove but doltish dreames.
> No subject ought for any kind of cause,
> To force the lord, but yeeld him to the lawes.
> *(Mirror*, p.176, lines 155–61)

The crucial term is 'subject'; Cade is not of the same social
significance as the magistrate. He is not permitted to enter the
public sphere and debate national policy. Rather, he is of the
order of men described by Sir Thomas Smith, as the fourth sort,
labourers, ranked below gentlemen, citizens and yeomen: 'no
account is made of them but onelie *to be ruled*, *not to rule*, and yet
they be not altogether neglected' (my emphasis).[65] The primary
duty of his estate is to obey the laws, which, according to the
Mirror, could only be established with the consent of the
political classes who assembled in parliament (see above, p.91).
Such people possess no intrinsic rights themselves; other classes
have duties towards them.

The tragedy of Glendower tells the complementary story of
the nobleman who has forfeited his political rights through
rebellion after being misled by the false predictions of prophecies.[66] Glendower is 'of a gentle blood' (p.121, line 8) and his
Welsh origin obviously links him to the Tudors and the matter
of Britain.[67] This connection is cleverly used against him to
stress his fall from grace. It is emphasised that 'neither birth nor
linage make us good' (p.121, line 10) because 'true gentry
standeth in the trade/ Of vertuous life, not in the fleshy line:/
For bloud is Brute, but Gentry is divine' (lines 26–8). The pun
on the eponymous founder of Britain is made clear thirty lines
later: 'Although he cum by due discent fro Brute,/ He is a
Chorle, ungentle, vile, and brute' (lines 55–6). Glendower's

British roots serve to emphasise his lack of inner nobility and baseness; the nobly born Glendower has made himself into a churl: 'And therfore *bent my selfe* to rob and ryve,/ And whome I could of landes and goodes depryve' (lines 62–3; my emphasis). Like Jack Cade and Thomas Smith's labourers, he has no right to represent, only to be represented.[68]

The 1559 *Mirror* text can be read as a militantly Calvinist work. Thomas Norton (1532–84) was the Elizabethan translator of Calvin's *Institution of the Christian Religion*.[69] He was yet another intellectual figure who had started off as part of Somerset's circle and in 1562 he was to collaborate with Thomas Sackville to write the influential Senecan tragedy, *Gorbaduc*, another work highly praised in Sidney's *Apologie* (pp. 133–4). Norton was thus clearly connected to the authors of the *Mirror*, both in terms of his intellectual background and through his connection with Sackville, a contributor to the 1563 edition of the *Mirror*.[70] Norton's translation of Calvin's final version of the *Institution* (1559) had appeared in 1561; but an English interest in Calvin's work had been manifest for many years. Most significantly as regards the *Mirror* Edward Seymour had been influenced by Calvin, as had William Baldwin.[71]

Calvin's contribution to intellectual life in Tudor England was not only through his particular stress on God's foreknowledge and man's predestination as is often supposed.[72] Related beliefs were commonplaces of European and English Protestant thought, held by everyone from Luther to Richard Hooker and enshrined in article seventeen of the Thirty-Nine Articles of Elizabeth (1559).[73] Calvin's doctrine of predestination is indeed complex and distinctive, but perhaps his importance lies much more in his formulation of a political public sphere or civil society.[74]

Calvin refers to the office of the magistrate in exactly the same way that Baldwin does:

[T]hough the lord testifieth that the Magistrate is a speciall great gift of his liberality for preserving of the safetie of men, and appointeth to Magistrates themselves their bounds: yet hee doth therewithall declare, that of what sort soever they be, they have not their authority but from him: that those indeed, which rule for benefit of the commonweale, are true examplars and patternes of his bountifulnesse: that they that rule unjustly and wilfully are raised up by him to punish the wickednesse of the people: that all equally have that majesty wherewith he hath furnished a lawfull power.[75]

Calvin demands that magistrates have duties as well as privileges, that they should command obedience, but also perform their roles adequately. The same argument is used in Baldwin's *A Treatise of Morall Philosophie* (1548), a work which remained popular for another century and had gone into twenty-four editions by 1651.[76]

Calvin makes a crucial distinction between the political rights and duties of private persons and those of magistrates, something we have seen is crucial to the enterprise of the *Mirror*. Referring to the question of resisting a tyrant, Calvin writes:

For though the correcting of unbridled government bee the revengement of the Lord, let us not by and by thinke that it is committed to us, to whom there is given no other commandement but to obey and suffer. I speake alway of private men. For if there bee at this time and Magistrates for the behalfe of the people... I doe not forbid them according to their office to withstand the outraging licentiousnesse of kings: that I affirme that if they winke at kings wilfully ranging over and treading downe the poore communalty, their dissembling is not without wicked breach of faith, because they decitfully betray the liberty of the people, whereof they know themselves to bee appointed protectors by the ordinance of God. (*Institution*, p.748)

It is the duty of the magistrates to oppose tyranny as the guardians of civil society and representatives of the extrapolitical masses. They must act when the populace cannot; the political message of the *Institution* is identical to that of the *Mirror*.

Such a clear focus was gradually to disappear in the subsequent editions. Sackville's much praised 'Induction', first included in the 1563 edition – which marked Baldwin's last connection with the project[77] – harks back to the less problematic versions of *de casibus* tragedy, musing on the instability of human achievement.[78] But it is really with the additions made in 1587, when tragedies written thirty years after the original plan by new authors who were of a completely different generation from the originals – Raphael Holinshed is the only one named[79] – were included, that one can chart the decline referred to by Lawrence Green (see p.91 above). For example, Thomas Churchyard's tragedy of Cardinal Wolsey opens with the lines:

> Shall I looke on, when states step on the stage,
> And play theyr parts, before the peoples face?
> Some men live now, scarce four score yeares of age,
> Who in times past, did know the Cardinalls grace.
> A gameson worlde, when Byshops run at bace,
> Yea, get a fall, in striving for the gole,
> And body loase, and hazarde seely sole.
>
> (*Mirror*, pp.495–6, lines 1–7)

Green comments: 'This tragedy is not going to be about some precept that Wolsey demonstrates. It is going to be an adventure story in an exciting world. This is already at odds with the original perspectives of the *Mirror*.'[80] And as he continues, in the second stanza the tragedy 'advertises itself as a rags-to-riches story': 'Now note my byrth, and marke how I began,/ Beholde from whence, rose all this pryde of mine,/ My father but a playne, poore honest man' (lines 15–17). The tragedy could be said to belong to a tradition of complaint – a genre which proliferated after the example of the *Mirror*[81] – rather than didactic political verse. Wolsey urges readers to copy him rather than shun his example: 'Lo what it is, to feede on daynty meate,/ And pamper up, the gorge, with suger plate:/ Nay, see how lads, in hope of higher seate/ Rise early up, and study learning late' (lines 29–32). The ghost concludes his narrative almost as if he were consciously refusing to draw a political moral from the story:

> [T]he best is wee are gone,
> And worst of all, when wee our tales haue tolde,
> Our open plagues, will warning bee to none,
> Men are by hap, and courage made so bolde:
> They thinke all is, theyr owne, they haue in holde.
> Well, let them say, and thinke what they please,
> This weltring world, both flowes and ebs like seas
>
> (*Mirror*, p.511, lines 484–90)

Wolsey, after all, was accused of high treason like Cade and Glendower, of abusing his position as a magistrate. But his fall, unlike theirs, is blamed merely upon the wiles of fortune.[82]

The change in purpose of the 1587 text of the *Mirror* is made clear in the other three tragedies added to that edition. The tragedy of Sir Nicholas Burdet, a knight slain in France in 1441, concludes:

> Let *English* Peeres abandon such contentious strife,
> It hurtes the Publique weale, decayes the state:
> It reaves the yeares too soone of longer lyfe:
> It freates the breste with ruste of baend debate:
> It gives the checke to him that gives the mate:
> Then thus I ende, that wight of all is bleste
> Which lives in love with God, his prince and country best.
> (*Mirror*, p.482, lines 595–601)[83]

The shift from a critical sense of 'public' to a nationalist one is evident: the notion of 'Publique weale' here invokes a completely different set of responses from the 'Common weale' of the magistrates.

The other two tragedies deal with the death of the Scottish king, James IV, at the battle of Flodden, a nationalist theme *par excellence* which had been the occasion of numerous poems, among them John Skelton's most xenophobic pieces (see above, pp.45–7). Both, in fact, are said to be 'pende above fifty years agone, or even shortly after the death of the sayd King' (p.488, lines 8–9), which highlights the gap between the aims and use of historical material of this edition of the *Mirror* and its earlier manifestations. In the same link between these two poems, one of the unnamed interlocutors claims that the narration of the events of the battle 'would pleasure not only such as write *our* historyes, but also encourage our Countreymen well, to the like loyall service of their Prince, and especially those who should finde therein of *their parents or auncestours* to have been praysed for valure' (lines 16–19; my emphasis). The political or didactic chronotope has given way to the nationalist one.

The additions made by Higgens and Blenerhasset (in the 1570s) are also based on a desire to re-work British and English material to form a chronological account of the nation's origins rather than to provide an advice book as such. For example, Higgens has Humber, the king of the Huns, who drowned in the river where he left his name (*Parts Added*, p.72, line 10), tell the reader:

> If thou be *forrayne* bide within thy soyle:
> That God hath giuen to thee and thine to holde,
> If thou oppression meane beware the foyle:
> Beare not thy selfe, of thee or thine to bolde:
> Or of the feates thy elders did of olde,
> For God is just, injustice will not thrive:
> He plagues the prowde, preserves the good alive
> (*Parts Added*, p.76, lines 113–19; my emphasis)

The warning is no longer addressed to would-be governors, but princes, and by implication any of their subjects. The question of conduct, how the individual governs, has been replaced by the 'imagined community' of the nation which absorbs its subjects into the metonymic figure of the sovereign who now represents (stands for) them. Humber's tale is sandwiched between the tragedy of Albanact, which tells how Brutus, his father, founded Britain as a new Troy, and his own death at the hands of the Hunnish invaders; and that of Locrinus, Brutus' eldest son, who defeated the Huns but fell for Humber's daughter, Elstride, consequently splitting his kingdom when he banished his first wife, Gwendoline, at Elstride's insistence. Albanact's tragedy warns 'worthy warriors' (p.70, line 596) that fortune is not to be trusted; Locrinus' that God will punish transgressors of the moral law. The dialogic format of the early editions and the deliberate non-identification of governors and governed which allowed critical discussion, pluralistic interpretation and the adoption of oppositional stances, has given way to an unproblematic, more crudely ideological series of narratives, ironically, just as the text becomes more cornucopian with its juxtaposition of such diverse narrative strategies.[84] The implied subject position of the reader of the *Mirror* has become as unstable as the composition of the text.

This very problem of reading and writing the text is, in fact, discussed in the tragedy of the poet Collingborne, added to the *Mirror* in the second edition of 1563 and probably a survivor of the suppressed edition.[85] This tale follows the tragedy of Henry Stafford, Duke of Buckingham,[86] approved by all the (fiction-alised) contributors, but which leads to a lively discussion. One speaker (unnamed) objects to the description of princes in hell because most would have gone to heaven and, anyway, 'it savoreth so much of Purgatory, whiche the papistes have digged thereout, that the ignorant may be deceyved' (*Mirror*, p.346, lines 6–8). Baldwin replies that what is meant is not hell, but the grave where the dead await resurrection: a usage he defends by claiming that many learned Christian writers follow such a convention. However, a third speaker argues that what is at stake is the very nature of fictional representation itself: 'Tush (quoth an other) what stand we here upon? it is a Poesie and no divinitye, and it is lawfull for poetes to fayne what they lyst, so it be appertinent to the matter: And therefore let it passe even in such sort as you have read it' (lines 14–17). Baldwin agrees, but points out that artists have not always had the freedom they should have had: '[W]here as you say a poet may faine what he list: In deede my thinke it should bee so, and ought to be well taken of the hearers: but it hath not at al times been so allowed' (lines 17–20). One notes that he neglects to include the present; a provocative question has been addressed directly to the monarch – though whether Mary or Elizabeth was the intended receiver of the message is impossible to determine.

Speaker three assents, then refers to the story of the poet, Collingborne, 'cruelly put to death for makyng of a ryme' (lines 23–4), which conveniently comes after that of Bucking-ham in the reign of Richard III. Baldwin tells his audience that they must imagine Collingborne before them, 'a mervaylous wel fauoured man' who holds in his hand, 'his own hart, newly ripped out of his brest, and smoking forth the lively spirit' (lines 24–6) beckoning to and fro to them, urging them to avoid his fate. Like Astrophel and Dante in the *Vita Nuova*, Colling-borne speaks from the heart.[87]

He tells his listeners to beware of tyrants who will act to end the ancient 'Muses freedome'. Poets can no longer be 'rough in ryme' like Juvenal, but will either be put in gaol like Jeremiah (Bale might well have appreciated this comparison and the

implied role of the poet), or made into flatterers of Caesar's
faults like Martial. Imitating a tyrant's reasoning, Collingborne
personifies them as understanding the wheel of fortune and its
danger but despising those who refuse to play their game, 'we
count him but a lowte/ That stickes to mount, and basely like
a beast/ Lyves temperately for feare of blockam feast' (p.348,
lines 27–9). Tyrants want to be seen as gods and hate those who
threaten their lofty position, ie, poets. As it seems certain that
this tragedy was written by William Baldwin, it is easy to concur
with Eveline Feasey's judgement that 'Bearing in mind what we
know of the difficulties with the licensing authorities experi-
enced by the *Mirror* writers we can only conclude that we have
an allusion to that in this poem.'[88]

Strangely enough, according to Collingborne, both poets and
tyrants agree ('We knowe our faultes as well as any other' (line
43), admits or boasts the tyrants' spokesman in Collingborne's
text); but tyrants merely want to interpret the world, poets
want to change it. However, this task is futile warns the ghost:

> Ceas therefore Baldwyn, ceas I the exhort,
> Withdrawe thy pen, for nothing shalt thou gayne
> Save hate, with loss of paper, ynke and payne...
> Thy entent I knowe is godly, playne, and good,
> To warne the wyse, to frayne the fond fro yll:
> But wycked worldelinges are so wytles wood,
> That to the wurst they all thinges construe styl
> (*Mirror*, p.349, lines 52–60)

The world is so corrupt that people will pervert the intended
message, either because they are poor readers or wilfully bad
ones. Poets' efforts are thus doomed.

Collingborne now recites the well-known lines for which he
was put to death:

> The Cat, the Rat, and Lovel the Dog,
> Do rule all England, under a Hog
> (*Mirror*, p.349, lines 69–70)

The meaning, as the author explains, was no 'dark conceit', but
'playne and true': Cat stood for Catesby, Rat for Ratcliffe, and
Lovel 'barkt and bit whom Rychard would' (hence Dog), a

word which rhymed well with Hog, signifying Richard whose symbol was a boar.[89] Unfortunately, this witty truism was not appreciated, and he was put to death with a barbarity which exceeded the usual fate of traitors (p.351, lines 106–19).[90]

The moral Collingborne draws from his bitter experience is that poets should stay aloof from politics and 'meddle not with *Magistrates* affayres,/ But praye to God to mende them if it nede' (lines 135–6; my emphasis). The message could hardly have been more carefully chosen as the opposite of the premises on which the *Mirror* was founded. A poet must be like Pegasus, flying upwards towards 'the sprynges of truth most pure'. Death has made Collingborne something of a Neoplatonist;[91] but this adoption of a mystical concept of truth is primarily because there is no suitable audience for an intersubjective, political communication to function successfully, 'For tyl affections from the fond be dryven,/ In vayne is truth tolde, or good counsayle geven' (lines 174–5). Like Raphael Hythlodaeus, he despairs of civil society, preferring to be a voice in the wilderness because no one is fit to hear his message.[92] He appeals to authorial omniscience as a principle for determining meaning, so that such confusion can be avoided: 'The authors meanyng should of ryght be heard,/ He knoweth best to what ende he endyteth:/ Wordes sometyme beare more than the hart behiteth' (lines 212–14), and further suggests that just laws should merely require a slanderer or heretic to recant what has been said. When Catesby (the Cat) objects that words are public and have a potential significance way beyond the limits of an individual's intention in uttering them ('rayling words be treason' and traitors harm the power of the prince), the poet now claims that his verse was just a 'foolyshe ryme' which meant no harm to anybody. He alleges that he stated no more than a banal series of 'true' metaphorical correspondences. It was the guiltiness of the readers who provided the treasonable interpretations and had him put to death. He concludes by exhorting Baldwin 'not to passe the bankes/ of Helicon' (lines 278–9) but to save his freedom by remaining in the streams, presumably refusing to write what might be considered 'political' by the powers that be.

This tragedy asks central and disturbing questions both about the relationship between poetry and politics and about the nature of interpretation. Collingborne's rhetorical shifts in argument, first asserting that poets should have the freedom to say what they want, then denying that his verse was political in any way but merely a statement of fact, avoids the problem of defining what poets can and cannot say. In a similar fashion he straddles the extreme possibilities of interpretation, as to whether meaning is a product of the author's intention or the reader's response[93] because although he states at one point that what he says is 'playne and true', he later alleges that he used the metaphors, 'Cat, Rat, the halfe names of the rest,/ To *hide* the sense which they so wrongly wrest' (lines 258-9; my emphasis). Who has hidden the wrongly wrested sense if not the poet? Why say metaphors hide something if, as Collingborne claims elsewhere, they do not? Is he not here appealing to a notion of allegory as unequivocal as that of John Bale, where hermeneutic unravelling depends on an agreed common-sense of correspondences (see above pp.oo–oo), judging that his interpretation of his own words is right, his executors', wrong? If so, why say 'hide' and refer to a depth below the text? Or is it that, as the authors of the *Mirror* well knew, being Protestants who had survived at Mary's court rather than gone into exile like John Bale (see above, pp.67-9),[94] that interpretation was a contentious and dangerous business?

In the colloquy, addressed 'To the Reader', that follows the tragedy, all agree on two things: firstly, that Collingborne should not have been executed, and secondly, that the ancient freedoms of poets should be restored. Indeed, yet another question is raised but not answered; whether they already have been:

Gods blessing on his heart that made thys (sayd one) specially for reviving our auncient liberties. And I pray god it may take suche place with the Magistrates, that they maye retifie our olde freedome, Amen (quod another) For that shalbe a meane bothe to staye and upholde them selves from fallyng: and also to preserve many kinde, true, zealous, and well meaning mindes from slaughter and infamie. (*Mirror*, p.359, lines 1-7)

This interchange serves to repeat the question indirectly addressed to the monarch in the prose link preceding the tragedy (see above, p.103) and places poets on the same level of political authority and with the same rights to participate in civil society, as magistrates. As discussed in these surrounding prose links, the tale of Collingborne is interpreted to demand precisely what the voice of the ghost denies; the right to political intervention. The question as to what may be considered treasonable has not been addressed (hardly surprisingly), but the message, as I interpret it, is that Collingborne *must* be wrong to try to persuade poets to avoid considerations of politics, otherwise why write the *Mirror*? The sub-text is a demand for the freedom from political control that Collingborne's ghost has condemned as naive and the implication is that if such discussions as are raised here are stamped upon by Elizabeth, as they were by Mary, then the restored Protestant dynasty may share the nemesis of Richard III whose tragedy follows Collingborne's. His fate, according to the colloquy linking the two (ie, in advance of the tale), was caused by his refusal to listen to his subjects: 'Vox populi, vox dei, in this case is not so famous a proverbe as true: The experyence of all times doth approve it' (p.359, lines 14–15). Counsel, such as that provided by the *Mirror*, is vital for good government. Poetry has to be allowed to be political if it needs to be, although what is political and what is treasonable (and who decides) is another matter. The hapless voice of Collingborne's ghost, arguing for an esoteric poetics,[95] must give way to one insisting that poetry be an interactive critical medium, free to fabricate fictions which allow for diverse – albeit limited – interpretative possibilities.[96] It is this discourse or chronotope which became mute in the later sixteenth-century editions, as the coherent didacticism of the original *Mirror* text became engulfed in the nationalist discourse of its additions and progeny.[97] And, perhaps fittingly enough – though hardly without a trace of irony – the literary history of the period, more often than not, has tended to award the laurels of victory to those who have been heard to speak like Collingborne's ghost rather than Collingborne.

CHAPTER 4

Towards a national form: rhetoric and literary theory from Wilson to Puttenham

We sware sometimes from the matter, upon just considerations, making the same to serve for our purpose, as well as if we had kept the matter still. As in making an invective against Rebelles, and largely setting out the filth of their offences, I might declare by the way of digression, what a noble countery England is, how great commodities it hath, what traffique here is used, and how much more neede other Realmes have of us, then we have neede of them.[1]

Thomas Wilson's advice to would-be orators has the appearance of a digression itself, as if in choosing an apparently random example, he were innocently illustrating a technical point. But the relationship between narration and illustration – *fabula* and *syuzhet* – can be reversed to illustrate that what seems peripheral – the example of England – is really the central concern of *The Arte of Rhetorique*.[2] In 'The Preface' Wilson tells the story of three figures, God, man and eloquence. In the beginning man was created in God's likeness, given the faculty of reason and dominion over all creatures. After the Fall, 'sinne so crept in that our knowledge was much darkened' and 'mans reason ... overwhelmed'. As a result 'all thinges waxed savage, the earth untilled, societie neglected, Gods will not knowne, man against man, one against an other, and all against order. Some lived by spoile: some like brute beastes grazed upon the ground ... none tended the education of their children: Lawes were not regarded.' In this 'brutish' state, men lived in open fields without houses, having become like the beasts they were once given to tend. To save them, God gave them the gift of eloquence and they were able to move from a state of nature to one of nurture: 'such is the power of Eloquence and reason, that

most men are forced, even to yeeld in that which most standeth
against their will'. Indeed, without the art of eloquence which
persuades men of 'that which they full oft found out by reason',
the civil society of cities would have been impossible because if
not persuaded by the art of eloquence:

Who would digge and delve from Morne till Evening? Who would
travaile and toyle with ye sweat of his browes? Yea, who would for his
Kings pleasure adventure and hassarde his life, if witte had not so won
men, that they thought nothing more needfull in this world, nor any
thing whereunto they were more bounden: then here to live in their
duetie, and to traine their whole life according to their calling.

Wilson's historical narrative is both nationalistic in the choice
of its concluding details – it finishes with an explanation as to
why citizens choose to serve their king – and in its epistemo-
logical foundations: eloquence has to be manifested in speech,
therefore it has to be in a particular language which serves to
divide that speech community from others.[3] The purpose of the
book outlined in 'The Preface' is to teach readers to use their
natural language better so that eloquent men can distance
themselves from other men in the same way that men as a
species are naturally superior to beasts: 'I thinke him most
worthie fame, and amongst all men to bee taken for halfe a GOD:
that therein doth chiefly and above all other excell men,
wherein men doe excell beastes' (Wilson's emphasis).

The Arte of Rhetorique is thus a fundamentally divided work; it
aims to foster a national greatness, teaching users of English to
develop the means by which they can acquire a sophisticated
level of eloquence whereby English can be made to rival other
more established national tongues; yet in doing so, Wilson is
forced to expose the means by which eloquent speech works and
persuade the hearer or reader to perform the task in question
– to work and die for his king and country. The reader is asked
to occupy two subject positions as addressee of the text and
belong to two separately constructed interest groups; the users
of rhetoric (the persuaders) and its consumers (the persuaded).
In eliding means and ends Wilson has set up the possibility that
the text could be read against the grain and used against itself.[4]
And it was.

The Arte of Rhetorique was first printed in 1553, the last year of Edward VI's reign. Wilson had been another intellectual promoted during the reign and his first book, *The Rule of Reason* (1551), had been dedicated to Edward. He had later moved into the orbit of the Dudley family and had dedicated *The Arte of Rhetorique* to Northumberland's eldest son, John.[5] With the fall of the Dudleys and the accession of Mary he fled to Italy rather than northern Europe where most Marian exiles went, which probably demonstrates the humanist affiliations of his Protestant beliefs and the networks of patronage within which he moved.[6] Nevertheless, in March 1557 Mary commanded that he return home and face the Privy Council and, after ignoring the letter, he was arrested and charged before the Inquisition with having written heretical works on logic and rhetoric, possibly at Mary's instigation.[7]

Wilson escaped from jail during a riot precipitated by Pope Paul IV's death in August 1559 and he returned to England in 1560. In December a second edition of *The Arte of Rhetorique* was printed, the only significant change being the addition of 'A Prologue to the Reader' which referred to the experience Wilson suffered at the hands of his hostile readers. This was placed before the preface and dedicatory poems, so that the Elizabethan reader would confront Wilson's autobiographical details before the mini-history of eloquence.[8] Wilson cites an example from Cicero's *De Oratore* in which a certain Lucius refuses to let what he has written be read by anyone, learned or ignorant, on the grounds that the former will tend to 'have a further meaning from him, then ever the authour selfe thoughte' and the latter will understand nothing, being as competent at reading as an ass playing the organ. Wilson, however, has encountered a third, more sinister, type of reader:

But I being somewhat acquainted with the world, have found out an other sort of men, whom of all others, I would bee loth should reade any of my doinges: especially such things as either touched Christ, or any good doctrine. And those are such malicious folke, that love to finde faults in other mens matters, and seven yeares together, wil keepe them in store, to the utter undoing of their Christian brother: not minding to reade for their better learning, but seeking to deprave whatsoever they finde, and watching their time, will take best advantage to undoe their neighbour.

Once again, the problem of the text's reception serves to undermine its monologic unity and didactic function; Wilson states that his book will show an orator how to teach, delight and persuade readers (p.2), but the recognition that rhetoric can be used in a variety of ways and have different effects on different addressees, forces Wilson's narratorial persona to face the dilemma that there is either no one truth, no right way of reading, or, meaning must be imposed upon a reader who may not be persuaded by the argument.[9] This split is smoothed over in the 'Prologue' via a neat rhetorical trick: Wilson describes his own delivery from the Roman jail in a language which combines a sense of divine intervention with a demagogic populism: 'In the ende by Gods grace, I was wonderfully delivered, through plain force of the Romaines (an enterprise heretofore in that sort never attempted) being then without hope of life, and much lesse of libertie.' Such a combination of causes both empowers the ordinary citizens and envisages them as empty ciphers of God's will. Wilson then proceeds to recount his feelings on his return to England: should he leave his book well alone as, after all, it started all his troubles? Will it bring harm to others who read it and act as it suggests? Eventually, he concludes that *The Arte of Rhetorique* teaches true religion and should thus be published because 'it is as great an heresie not to know God, as to erre in the knowledge of God'. Ironically enough, what he feared most in prison (fire) became his means of deliverance. The public meditation on the question of reading concludes with further thanks to the divine agency of God: 'God be praised, and thankes be given to him onely, that not onely delivered me out of the Lyons mouth, but also hath brought England my deare Countrey, out of great thraldome and forraine bondage.'

In effect, this passage is a rhetorical *tour de force* which attempts to disguise all the problems precipitated by the disjunction between writer and reader(s). A notion of truth is reintroduced, not as in 'The Preface', by asserting that there is a commonly agreed conception of truthfulness (effectively a

collapsing of any distinction between rhetorical ornamentation
and logical argument into the category of eloquence); Wilson
now accepts that only some readers will be able to interpret his
meaning correctly. The last sentence quoted makes an explicit
comparison between his delivery from jail and England's return
to a Protestant faith under Elizabeth; *The Art of Rhetorique* will
be interpreted correctly by those who understand his own
personal experience as the author.[10] This confessional link
serves to reunite the events of Wilson's life with those of the lives
of his readers; what they have in common is their shared
experience as *English* Protestants. The equation of the mir-
aculous events of an autobiography with those of a larger public
indicate that, once again, logic and rhetoric have been cemented
together, converging in the pen of an 'I' writing to signal that
the author belongs to that larger group. 'Eloquence' is proposed
as a public category in 'The Preface'; in 'The Prologue',
Wilson has transformed it into something private, a personal
possession. In the one, the writing explores the concept of a
national public; in the other, the author's own subjectivity as a
member of the nation. In each case, what is held together by an
eloquent rhetoric threatens to burst apart into the two halves of
writer and readership(s), self and public.

Throughout the main text, Wilson appeals to a general
reading community in order to validate the pedagogic intention
of the work. This is achieved in two ways. Firstly, via the use of
examples which, as often as not, illustrate an important
contemporary theme. The long discussion 'Of the figure
Amplification' provides a demonstration as to how a would-be
orator might speak about the topic, 'gentle behaviour winneth
good will, and clerely quencheth hatred'. This includes a long
series of rhetorical questions, which do not appear to follow in
an obviously logical sequence, as in the following transposition:

If God warneth us to love one an other, and learne of him to bee
gentle, because he was gentle and humble in heart: How cruell are
they that dare withstand his Commaundement? If the Subject rebell
against his King, wee crye with one voyce, hang him, hang him, and
shall we not think him worthie the vilest of death of all, that being a
creature, contemneth his Creatour, being a mortall man, neglecteth

his heavenly maker, beeing a vilde moulde of Clay, setteth light by so mightie a GOD, and ever living King? (p.116)

The homologous relationship between man and God/man and king does not present any problem and is obviously far from unusual.[11] But each question is elaborated to make a substantially different point: the first emphasises the enormity of the transgression of those who fail to honour their duties, whereas the second moves from the vertical link of the necessity of obedience to superior powers to a horizontal one in urging citizens to join with the orator in condemning the crime. *Vox populi, vox Dei*. Who is speaking to whom here? Who are 'wee'? It would seem that the example serves a dual function within the economy of the text: it works both to instruct the interested scholar (a formal level) and also to draw him or her into an imagined national community who unite to condemn the rebel (a level of rhetorical persuasion). What appears to be marginal to the handbook of rhetoric – an illustration – is actually central to its discourse, exhorting its readers to improve their technical ability to manipulate their natural language to weld together an eloquent society and expel what threatens its rigidly hierarchical power structure.[12] Wilson is acutely conscious of social and national status. He draws up lists and genealogies of relative merit: as he puts it, 'The Realme declares the nature of the people. So that some Countrey bringeth more honour with it, then an other doth' (p.12). It is better to be a noble Frenchman than an Irishman, to be English than Scottish, to be born in Paris rather than Picardy, or London rather than Lincoln (where Wilson was born). The third paragraph of *The Arte of Rhetorique* impresses upon the would-be orator the importance of asking questions: here, in asking how an audience would deal with rebellion, Wilson speaks free indirect discourse, eliding his role as instructor of rhetorical arts and as rhetorician.[13]

The second way that Wilson draws his audience into his discursive world is in his advocation of a plain English free of 'ynkhorne terms'. His position in the long debate about English diction as a 'moderate purist' – someone who was suspicious of loan words but not in favour of removing them altogether – is well established.[14] Again, Wilson employs the first person plural to convey his message:

> Among all other lessons this should first be learned, that wee never affect any straunge ynkehorne termes, but to speake as is commonly received: neither seeking to be over fine, nor yet living over-carelesse using our speeche as most men doe, and ordering our wittes as the fewest have done. Some seeke so far for outlandish English, that they forget altogether their mothers language. (p.162)

The terms used in this passage carefully divide English into two mutually hostile forms: against a language composed of '*straunge* ynkhorne termes', an '*outlandish* English', is placed an instruction to 'speake as is *commonly* received', to use '*our* speech as most men doe'. One type of speech is clearly marked as artificially acquired by perverse effort, spoken by those who 'forget ... their *mothers language*', the other as a natural possession. Wilson is quite explicit in refusing to reject the purist's position of not accepting any loan words:

> Now whereas wordes be received, aswell Greeke as Latine, to set forth our meaning in the English tongue, either for lacke of store, or els because we would enrich the language: it is well doen to use them, and no man therein can be charged for any affectation, when all other are agreed to followe the same waie. (p.165)

He appeals to a commonly accepted speech employed by a public made up of both the writer and his readers. That community can then decide what is a correct usage and what is alien and foreign; or, rather, the passages imply, they instinctively recognise already and are thus in a position to judge between a natural English and an artificial imported foreign word or phrase.

Richard Foster Jones has pointed to this lacuna in Wilson's analysis: '[He] recognises the necessity of neologisms, and he sanctions those which have been received into the language and appear familiar and natural. He does not, however, reveal how a new term can become familiar without passing through a period of strangeness.'[15] Such a comment is to miss the essential point: Wilson appeals to what readers already know in order to make use of this gap. A detailed analysis of English diction would draw out the vast differences in dialect and sociolect, but the appeal to a common knowledge – or, a common sense – specifically enables the author to disguise an actual knowledge.[16] The implication is that at the end of the book the reader will have joined this exclusive yet common club of those who employ 'the best kind of speech' made up of 'such words as are commonly received, and such as properly may expresse in plaine manner, the whole conceipt of their minde' (p.165). Words should describe things and correspond exactly with the objects they name: Wilson's notion of mimesis is used to suggest that in speaking properly and correctly 'the whole conceit of... minde' enters the public domain.[17] *The Arte of Rhetorique* seeks to control a language which could be appropriated by transgressive individual users to subvert the stable and rigidly hierarchical society the book proffers: private speech acts cannot be admitted.[18] The vanishing point of Wilson's discourse is the assumption of a national readership, a factor which may have contributed to its popularity as much as its obvious virtue as a handbook of rhetoric.[19]

It might be objected that *The Arte of Rhetorique* is not a specifically literary work, which was the reason the editor of the most comprehensive collection of sixteenth-century critical essays excluded it and all other pre-Elizabethan treatises from his edition.[20] However, it becomes clear that Wilson's use of the concept of mimesis in his theory of ideal language forces him to shift his attention towards a consideration of literariness as his central focus.[21] It must be emphasised that this shift is fundamentally a logical progression of argument not an arbitrary or empirically motivated switch on Wilson's part. In 'The Third Book, Of apt chusing and framing of words and sentences together, called Elocution', tropes and figures are considered. As is usual in sixteenth-century manuals of rhetoric, metaphor is considered first as the master-trope being defined as 'an alteration of a worde, from the *proper* and *naturall* meaning, to that which is not proper, and yet agreeth thereunto by some likenesse' (p.172; my emphasis).[22] Wilson comments that an oration is not merely 'wonderfully enriched' when apt metaphors are used, but, in fact, will not function unless they are:

'Neither can any one perswade effectuously, and winne men by weight of his Oration, without the helpe of wordes altered and translated' (pp.172–3).

This statement obviously contradicts and undermines Wilson's comments on the proper form of English as a truthful, mimetic language: to write persuasively one has to abandon what is proper, ie, a proper oration involves the use of transformed, improper language, a speech act the form of which may threaten the very stability its content supposedly supports. Wilson's discussion, unsurprisingly, leads him to a consideration of literature as a copy or similitude. Poetry, according to Wilson, enables orators ('we') to 'talke at large, and win men by perswasion' because such 'tales were not fained without cause':

> For undoubtedly there is no one tale among all the Poetes, but under the same is comprehended some thing that partaineth, either to the amendment of maners, to the knowledge of the trueth, to the setting forth of Natures work, or els the understanding of some notable thing done. (p.195)

Poetry, in other words, has to be read allegorically, signifying something which it is not. Two points can be made regarding allegory: firstly, as Wilson defines it, 'An Allegorie is none other thing, but a Metaphore, used throughout a whole sentence, or Oration' (p.176), so that literature and oratory are ultimately fused in their reliance upon the resemblance of metaphoricity. Secondly, for allegory to work in the manner in which Wilson describes, as a didactic method, there has to be a tacit understanding between author and reader, so that signifier and secondary signified coincide.[23] Wilson's list of examples – Jupiter, Hercules, Tantalus – illustrates his desire to control his readership and appeal to a common stock of readings by pre-empting divergent, improper interpretations. Once again, the strategy employed is to argue a space for the text's discourse through the very act of creating an audience; but, again, the fear that this audience may subvert and fragment what is ideally unified, returns. Wilson likens the labours of Hercules, which deliver the message that 'reason should withstand affection, and the spirit for ever should fight against the flesh', to early

Christian saints' lives: 'Wee Christians had like Fables here-tofore of joyly felowes, the Images whereof were set up (in Gods name) even in our Churches. But is any man so madde to think that ever there was such a one as Saint Christopher was painted unto us? Mary God forbid' (p.196). Of course, people had been 'so madde' and Wilson has to acknowledge that God's commands had to be carried out by his spiritual police on earth: 'But who gave our Cleargie any such authoritie that those Monsters should be in Churches, as lay mens bookes? God forbad by expresse worde, to make any graven image, and shall wee bee so bold to breake Gods will for a good intent, and call these Idolles laie mens bookes?' (p.197). At what point can the authority to permit copying and imitation be fixed? When does an image teach and when does it subvert true doctrine? Wilson appeals to the common experience of his readers to decide matters: the problem is that the history of their experiences continually threatens to divide his ideal speech community into a multiplicity of different groups.

Wilson's difficulties with literature's status within a national culture were reproduced in virtually every sixteenth-century treatise on rhetoric and poetry in English. Wilson's contemporary, Richard Sherry, stated that no learned nation existed without schemes and figures, defined these as devices which made language new or strange, yet insisted that orators spoke plainly not 'darkeley'.[24] The 'foremost English critic' who opposed contemporary literature because of its duplicitous nature was Stephen Gosson, a humanist intellectual who turned the tenets of the 'new learning' against itself to make his case.[25] Gosson's argument, based on many sources but primarily Plato and Tertullian, is that English literature has become idolatrous, the signifier of the allegorical vehicle has served to delight the senses of the reader or playgoer so that the allegorical signified does not register in the mind:

I cannot but commend his wisdome, which in banqueting feedes most upon that, that doth nourish best; so must I disprayse his methode in writing, which following the course of amarous Poets, dwelleth longest in those pointes, that profite least; and like a wanton whelpe, leaveth the game, to runne riot. (p.76)[26]

An excess of uncontrollable response threatens to overwhelm and drown the desired stability of meaning. Poets are like cooks: 'the pleasures of the one winnes the body from labour, & conquereth the sense; the allurement of the other drawes the mind from vertue, and confoundeth wit' (p.79).[27] If used correctly each nourishes the mind by keeping the demands of the body at bay, if not, the desires of the body prevent the mind from functioning.

Gosson makes quite clear that he is not against literature or drama *per se* (although he was to adopt this position in his later writings after having complained that he had been caricatured as a hostile critic): he boasts that he was himself a skilled poet in his youth ('I have bene matriculated my selfe in the schoole' (p.81)) and argues, in traditional humanist fashion, that the form and content of good literature should provide counsel and instruction:

The right use of auncient Poetrie was too have the notable exploytes of woorthy Captaines, the holesome councels of good fathers, and vertuous lives of predecessors set downe in numbers, and song to the Instrument at solemne feastes, that the sound of the one might draw the hearers from kissing the cupp too often; the sense of the other put them in minde of things past, and chaulk out the way to do the like. (p.82)[28]

Gosson emphasises that although the foppishness and blatant sensuality of most theatre has to be condemned, some drama is good if it teaches a useful lesson. Like Wilson and the authors of the *Mirror*, he is particularly keen that the malign effects of rebellion be impressed upon his readers. He speaks highly of a 'lively play' which describes, 'howe seditious estates, with their own devises, false friendes, with their owne swoordes, & rebellious commons in their owne snares are overthrowne' (p.97).

The Schoole of Abuse is a treatise designed to separate desirable and undesirable literature: good literature is masculine and martial, encouraging its listeners to be the same, bad literature is feminine and wanton, teaching its listeners to be ill-disciplined and subversive. The poetry of the military societies of Sparta and Scythia is praised as 'without vice' (p.79) and contrasted in the next paragraph to the protean writings of Sempronia who 'coulde frame her selfe to all companies ... [and] versifie, sing, and daunce, better than became an honest woman' and Sappho who 'was skillfull in Poetrie and sung wel, but she was whorish' (pp.79–80).[29] Bad literature is that which does not instruct the reader; it is noticeable that Gosson praises the abilities of both female poets whilst condemning the content and implications of their talents.[30] Just as Sappho is said to challenge any fixed notion of fidelity in marriage being described as 'whorish', Sempronia undermines a fixed conception of truth, through refusing to possess a stable self which corresponds to a real subjectivity and consequently adopting the personality of her audience. She talks 'discretely with wyse men, and vaynely with wantons, taking a quip ere it came too grounde, and returning it back without a faulte' (p.79). In contemporary England those without land or 'good occupation to get their breade, desirous to strowt it with the beste, yet disdayning too live by the sweate of their browes' (p.93) become vagabonds, wandering musicians and players who choose to avoid any stable possession of their own self or property in their constant shifting from place to place and identity to identity.[31] In effect, they have emasculated themselves and become wanton.[32]

Set in contrast to such feminised men is the figure of the ancient British queen, Bunduica (Boudicca), who has adopted specifically masculine values. In an oration to the invading Roman troops of Nero she states that she 'accounted them unwoorthy the name of men, or title of Souldiers, because they were smoothly appareled, soft lodged, daintely feasted, bathed in warme waters, rubbed with sweet oyntments, strewd with fine poulders, wine swillers, singers, Dauncers, and Players' (p.95). Gosson has linked together a series of descriptions which depict both courtiers and players who are therefore targeted as those who have brought about the present lamentable state of England. His accusation is that both the military might and the literature of the country have simultaneously declined. England in 'olde time' consisted of:

men in valure not yeelding to Scythia, the women in courage passing the Amazons. The exercise of both was shootyng and darting, running

& wrestling, and trying suche maisteries, as eyther consisted in swiftnesse of feete, agilitie of body, strength of arms, or Martiall discipline. But the exercise that is nowe among us, is banqueting, playing, pipyng, and dauncing, and all suche delightes, as may win us to pleasur, or rocke us a sleepe. (p.91)

England used to be as hard and well-defined as Scythia but now it has become as soft, luxurious and effeminate as Greece in its worst days of decay.[33] Although there is now a queen on the throne, Elizabeth, who is a second Boudicca, her subjects are not worthy of her rule and abuse her government (pp.95–6).

The story that *The Schoole of Abuse* tells could be read as one which is the complementary opposite to that narrated in the preface to *The Arte of Rhetorique*. For Wilson, the dawn of eloquence led to the establishment of civil and civilised society; for Gosson, the separation of poetry and the arts of rhetoric from a military machine lead to degeneration and the overthrow of truth as a use value. Gosson regards the discipline of Sparta and Scythia more than the culture of Greece and Rome; the primitive England of Boudicca is to be preferred to its current decadence.

The Schoole of Abuse is a witty, provocative text, rigorously using the methods of humanist study in order to reverse the usual conclusions of humanists. Gosson makes the case that the oldest source is the best because it is the most authentic and so sweeps aside what humanists valued, the contemporary revival of a classical culture.[34] Nevertheless, it is difficult to read the text as a sophisticated joke for initiates in the light of his own later writings on the theatre, the responses of Gosson's contemporaries and his own stated desire to promote the Church of England as a bellicose ideological state apparatus in *The Trumpet of Warre* (1598).[35] *The Schoole of Abuse* demands that if literature is to exist at all it must exist for the good of the nation. But, whose nation? Wilson's notion of the public sphere varied from a seemingly indiscriminate populism to a rigid elitism; however, such a statement risks turning the question on its head because *The Arte of Rhetorique* appeals to the common knowledge or sense of its readers to form the national community the text requires. Gosson's project is different in that its aim is to persuade readers that one manifestation of the nation was superior to another. England had been a man but had become a woman, its subjects – who are identified with the land – are bad sons to their queen, 'unnatural children of so good a mother' (p.96).[36] The well-worn metaphor of the commonwealth as a body politic is used to attack what Gosson saw as the break-up of a unified and disciplined public. This has come about through the segregation of men into distinct classes: 'the whole body of the common wealth [should] consist of fellow laborers, all generally serving one head, & particularly following their trade, without re-pining. From the head to the foote, from the top to the toe, there should nothing be vaine, no body idle' (p.107). Two marginal notes read 'labourers' and 'Loyterers'; only the former unite as subjects to 'sweat in obedience to their Prince' (p.108).

The attack is principally aimed at courtiers who do no proper work: the achievements of virtuous nations – Spartans, Scythians, Persians, Thracians, Cathaginians – are contrasted to the conspicuous consumption and lack of visible endeavour performed by this parasitic class:

If our Gallants of Englande might carry no more linkes in their Chaynes nor ringes on their fingers, then they have fought feeldes, their necks should not bee very often wreathed in Golde, not their handes embrodered with pretious stones. If none but they might be suffered to drinke out of plate, that have in skirmish slain one of her majesties enemyes, many thousands shoulde bring earthen pots to the table. (p.105)

Like Wilson, Gosson is perturbed by the possibility of excess or superfluity. Whilst courtiers surround themselves with self-referential signs, ie, false trappings which serve only to signify their supposed superiority, soldiers are singled out for special praise as the 'Images of GOD' (a phrase repeated twice in the same paragraph) (p.104). Soldiers are emblems of truth who allow the economy of the sign to function: 'they are the Welsprings of Justice which giveth to every man his owne'. The existence of courtiers results in – and from – a disfunction in the symbolic economy; the signifier no longer corresponds to a stable and 'real' signified. Proper value is obscured by a series of false values, so that gold and jewellery – which actually hinder work – come to be regarded more highly than the humble but clearly more useful plate and earthen pots. The art of the courtier is the art of idolatry.

The preferred model for a state is a watchful military machine, a system of government which abolishes class distinctions, social mobility and other forms of differentiation (the assumption that all citizens are male enables sexual difference to be used as a means of condemning societies which tolerate or encourage social mobility and difference). The ideal England depicted in *The Schoole of Abuse* resembles nothing more than the austere directions for the establishment of colonies in Ireland and the Americas.[37] Gosson's statement that there is 'more perill ... in civil discord, than forraine warres' (p.94) is a neat illustration of the value system operating throughout *The Schoole of Abuse*: concord at home so that aggression can be directed abroad. The aim is that 'the word and the sword be knit together' in the martial metaphors of the poets who will spur the nation on to military glory. Poets are told to:

Play the good captaines, exhort your souldiers with your tonges to fight, & bring the first ladder to the wall your selves. Sound like bells, and shine like Lanternes; Thunder in words, and glister in works; so shall you please God, profite your country, honor your prince, discharge your duetie, give up a good account of your stewardship, and leave no sinne untouched, no abuse unrebuked, no fault unpunished. (p.109)[38]

In marked contrast to the austere militarism of Gosson's nationalism is that of George Puttenham's *The Arte of English Poesie* (1589).[39] *The Schoole of Abuse* argues that just as the false kinds of poetry and drama have misled worthy men to vice, so have the wrong people become successful in reaching the apex of a warped society, ie, the court. Such a problem does not shadow Puttenham's frequent historical summaries; his narrative is implicitly progressive.[40] The sketch of English poetry provided in the last chapter of Book 1 (No. 31) makes the claim that English poetry is now as good as French and Italian, but has only matured in recent times. Puttenham explains that he:

will not reach above the time of king Edward the third and Richard the second for any that wrote in English meeter, because before their times, by reason of the late Normaine conquest, which had brought into this Realme much alteration both of our language and lawes, and there withall a certain *martiall barbarousness*, whereby the study of all good learning was so much decayd as long time after no man or very few entended to write in any laudable science: so as beyond that time there is litle or nothing worth commendation to be founde written in this arte. (My emphasis)[41]

This refuses to countenance precisely what Gosson held most dear, a Spartan, military style of poetry (although the same crudely dialectical relationship between society and literature is repeated).[42] Instead, Puttenham values what literary historians have valued ever since, poetry written after 1580 which has come to represent the English Renaissance.[43] There may be problems with Puttenham's logic but it has held a hegemonic sway ever since. In *The Arte of English Poesie* the triumvirate of Chaucer, Gower and Lydgate are still honoured (as is 'that nameless' who wrote *Piers Plowman*), but Skelton is dismissed and the teleological development of an Italianate English poetic form is assumed. With hindsight, the experimental work of Wyatt and Surrey is seen to presage the triumph of the 1580s:

In the latter end of the same kings raigne [Henry VIII] sprong up a new company of courtly makers, of whom Sir Thomas Wyat th'elder & Henry Earl of Surrey were the two chieftanes, who having travailed into Italie, and there tasted the sweete and stately measures and stile of the Italian Poesie, as novices newly crept out of the schooles of Dante, Arioste, and Petrarch, they greatly polished our rude & homely maner of vulgar Poesie from that it had bene before, and for that cause may justly be sayd the first reformers of our English meetre and stile. (pp.62–3)

This praise is repeated towards the end of the chapter, merging the poets as 'the two chief lanternes of light to all others that have since employed their pennes upon English Poesie', owing to their conceits, style, correct use of terms and accurate metres, 'all imitating very naturally and studiously their Maister Francis Petrarcha' (p.76).

The contrast to the thought of Gosson is again marked: Puttenham carelessly (or cunningly?) slides between praising Wyatt and Surrey for their elite skill as 'courtly makers' and their success in reforming 'our English meetre and stile'. Does the 'we' addressed here have access to this verse in the same way that they formed the public who possessed 'our language and lawes' in the previous quotation? If not, as is likely, then Puttenham is clearly not distinguishing between two distinct communities both of which are claimed as representative of the nation: subjects who obey laws and speak English, and the court.

These aesthetic judgements are evidently not made in isolation but are part of a complex system of literary and socio-political-historical reasoning. It is important to note that Puttenham's views were by no means the only ones available to readers in the 1580s. A treatise which superficially resembles *The Arte of English Poesie* in its arguments is William Webbe's *A Discourse of English Poesie* (1586). Like Puttenham and Wilson, Webbe claimed that the invention of poetry led mankind from barbarousness to civilisation; that poetry should teach what is virtuous; that rules for English poetry were badly needed; that English poetry could be as good as that of any other nation; and that the only poetry which met this standard had been written in the last few years (in Webbe's case, twenty).[44] But, unlike Puttenham, Webbe was not as keen to dismiss certain genres (satire, eclogues); was prepared to accept varieties of English in poetry more readily (and for both of these reasons did not dislike Skelton so much); and was not so strongly in favour of rhymed verse as the natural English form.[45] Webbe and Puttenham both agreed that the first forms of poetry rhymed, but they draw radically different conclusions from this observation. Webbe distinguished between a received definition of rhyme, 'The falling out of verses together in one like sounde is commonly called, in English, Rhyme ... which surely in my judgement is verye abusivelye applyed to such a sence', and a 'proper' one, 'the just proportion of a clause or sentence, whether it be in prose or meeter, aptly comprised together' (p.267). According to Webbe, although the first definition of rhyme is more ancient it has never led to the writing of poetry of significant merit. The earliest recorded example, 'a foolish attempt', to write about Jupiter and Leda with every verse ending in the same rhyme, 'was so contemed and dyspysed that the people would neither admitte the Author nor Booke any place in memory of learning'. The Greeks went on to write 'proper' rhyme, so that rhymed verse is more accurately associated with the Goths and Huns. Rhyme works as well in English as in any other language, but 'our speeche be capable of a farre more learned manner of versifying' (pp.267–8).

Puttenham, also loath to be exclusive, clearly signals his preference for rhymed verse which he terms 'natural' or 'vulgar': 'The naturall Poesie therefore, being aided and amended by Art, and not utterly altered or obscured, but some signe left of it (as the Greekes and Latines have left none), is no lesse to be allowed and commended than theirs.' His argument is that because rhymed verse pre-dates Greek and Latin 'verse numerous and metrical' it is therefore more authentic (natural). The logic becomes circular and folds over itself:

So as it [rhymed poetry] was notwithstanding the first and most ancient Poesie, and the most universall, which two points do otherwise give to all humane inventions and affaires no small credit. This is proved by certificate of marchants & travellers, who by late navigations have surveyed the whole world, and discovered large countries and strange peoples wild and savage, affirming that the American, the Peruvian & the very Canniball, do sing and also say, their highest and holiest matters in certaine riming versicles and not in prose, which proves also that our manner of vulgar Poesie is more ancient then the artificial of the Greeks and Latines, ours comming by instinct of nature ... and used with the savage and the uncivill. (p.7)

The time-scale referred to here is contradictory. It is claimed that rhymed poetry is superior because it is both the oldest and the most modern form; the most primitive peoples write it as do the most civilised, so its adoption signifies a universal human nature, 'comming by instinct'. Puttenham's teleological model also conflates time and space into the static progression of known historicity; contemporary primitive peoples observed by travellers (Americans, Peruvians and cannibals) are equated with ancient pre-civilisations ('the Hebrues & Chaldees who were more ancient than the Greeks, did not only use a metricall Poesie, but also with the same a manner of rime') in contrast to 'our maner of vulgar Poesie', ie, 'us' moderns.[46] Just as John Bale (and other Protestant theologians) regarded the Reformation as a return to the principles of the true Catholic church, so does Puttenham regard the re-adoption of rhyming poetry.[47]

As Lawrence Manley has observed, Puttenham, like many other literary theorists in the Renaissance, employs the concept of 'convention' in order to mediate between a 'natural' and an 'artificial' art.[48] His theory of a suitable national form of literature corresponds to a received idea of historical and social hierarchy, inevitable trends which must be recognised and cannot be resisted. *The Arte of English Poesie* takes as its starting point the existing status quo; unlike *The Arte of Rhetorique*, it does not argue for its own significance in trying to create its own audience and unlike *The Schoole of Abuse* it does not launch an attack on what is conventional to articulate an oppositional discourse. In the opening chapter to his work, Puttenham equates poetry with the power structure within the nation by referring to Elizabeth as 'the most excellent Poet':

Forsooth by your Princely purse favours and countenance, making in maner what ye list, the poore man rich, the lewd well learned, the coward couragious, and vile both noble and valient. Then for imitation no lesse, your person as a most cunning counterfaitor lively representing Venus in countenance, in life Diana, Pallas for government, and Juno in all honour and regall magnificence. (p.2)

Elizabeth is both the rightly appointed apex of society and a 'counterfeitor', possessing an authority which is simultaneously natural and artificial but nonetheless legitimate because it is conventional. The queen is an artist and a work of art writ large. Puttenham's description of the ruling monarch serves to empower her (in the former role), but also emphasise the limits of her power. Like Wilson's description of right reading, these lines leave room for a politics of resistance; the need for the queen to be represented enables writers to manipulate even the most formal instance of encomium and turn images of praise against themselves, a possibility exploited by John Foxe and Puttenham's contemporary, Edmund Spenser.[49] But in *The Arte of English Poesie*, the correct (conventional) relationship between poet and prince is seemingly less problematic:

Princes may give a good Poet such convenient countenance and also benefite as are due to an excellent artificer, though they neither kisse nor cokes them, and the discret Poet lookes for no such extraordinarie favours, and aswell doth he honour by his pen the just, liberall, or magnanimous Prince, as the valient, aimiable or bewtifull though they be every one of them the good giftes of God. (pp. 15–16)

The poet and the prince complement each other in a mutually dependent relationship; but, Puttenham suggests, 'in this iron and malitious age of ours', princes have had to be more interested in the arts of war, 'being over earnestly bent and affected to the affaires of Empirs & ambition'. Consequently they have not been able to pay attention to 'any other civill or delectable Art of naturall or morall doctrine' (p. 16).

The Arte of English Poesie can be read as a massive position paper promoting the author and advancing his claim for preferment.[50] It also represents the transformation of a potentially critical literary medium and poetics into the art of a 'cunning princepleaser'.[51] Puttenham's major criticism of princes is that they neglect to listen to the arts of poetry, but he recommends that poets only tell the prince what exists by dint of agreed convention.

Although Puttenham's implied readers are constructed more homogeneously than Gosson's or Wilson's, the text can be read as fundamentally split in function(s). On the one hand it can be read as a masque, positioning the monarch as the best reader (as in the prefatory comments cited above); on the other, as a manual advising aspiring courtiers how to write poetry.[52] The first position counsels the stasis of order, the latter encourages the mobility of the social climber (one of whom is almost certainly the author).[53]

The homology between the poet and the courtier points to a further ambiguity: is the primary purpose of the text to instruct poets or courtiers? The two roles are elided throughout the work. Just as Wilson was forced to concede that his definition of the function of rhetoric necessarily made literature (poetry) the most highly charged form of persuasion because it is the most imitative, so Puttenham has to concede that his definition of art cannot distinguish between the actions of courtier and poet. In the last chapter he discusses how the good poet ought to 'dissemble his art' and negotiate between the artificial and the natural. The dichotomy, nature/culture, and the homology, poet/courtier, are both united through the 'figure allegoria' which has already been defined in an earlier chapter:

the Courtly figure Allegoria, which is when we speake one thing and thinke another, and that our wordes and our meanings meete not. The use of this figure is so large, and his vertue of so great efficacie as it is supposed no man can pleasantly utter and perswade without it, but in effect is sure never or very seldome to thrive and prosper in the world, that cannot skilfully put in use, in somuch as not onely every common Courtier, but also the gravest Counsellour, yea and most noble and wisest Prince of them all are many times enforced to use it. (p.155)

Like Wilson, Puttenham regards this cultural form of deception as an inevitable consequence of civilisation and civilised behaviour and for both writers the fundamental trope is metaphor: 'such inversion of sense in one single worde is by the figure Metaphore, of whom we spake before, and this manner of inversion extending to whole and large speaches, it maketh the figure allegorie to be called a long and perpetuall Metaphore' (p.156). At such points *The Arte of English Poesie* explains that nothing can ever be what it seems and abandons any formal quest for truth. A duplicitous epistemology necessitates the fashioning of a life of deception and both concerns are united in the form of the courtier–poet. Puttenham asks – clearly manipulating the imagined reader into assenting as the question comes last in a list – if it is not better that 'our courtly Poet do dissemble not onely his countenances & conceits, but also all his ordinary actions of behaviour, or the most part of them, whereby the better to winne his purposes & good advantages[?]' (p.251).

This concluding section can be read as a recommendation that the complete text be read as an exercise in the semiotics of duplicity.[54] Is the work to be read as an elaborate hoax which deconstructs the certain and stable hierarchies it sets up or is it blind to the 'mobile flaw' in its argument? Should we read it as an allegory of Puttenham's own life and his supposed desire to elevate himself to a higher status? At what point can the reader know how to decipher such a radically indeterminate text?[55]

The answer is that *The Arte of English Poesie* is split between scepticism and certainty, an infinitely cynical doubt and a naive faith in a definite order. In the same Book, Puttenham deals with the figure of 'Amphibologia or the Ambiguous' which he condemns as 'vicious speech' principally used by 'false Prophets'. In the discussion of false prophecy, which serves by way of illustration, Puttenham concludes with a rare example from recent political history. He claims that 'blind prophecies' have led to 'many insurrections and rebellions ... in this Realme', namely those of 'Jacke Strawe, & Jacke Cade in Richard the seconds time' and, in 'our time', Kett's rebellion in Norfolk.[56] As a result 'our maker shall therefore avoyde all such ambiguous speaches unlesse it be when he doth it for the nonce and for some purpose' (p.218).

The Arte of English Poesie is a multivalent and contradictory text, but the discourses it employs all centre around the figure of the 'courtly maker' whose own purposes transcend and suspend the usual rules of writing and behaviour. He is able to mediate between the series of oppositions crucial to the functioning of the narrative: art and nature, deceit and truth, stasis and change. His private desires serve to make up the public sphere. In Book I Puttenham provides a brief history of poetic genres which he relates directly to a social history.[57] The first type to emerge was satire, used as 'bitter invective against vice and vicious men';[58] however, the limitation of having only one speaker led to the development of comedy which gradually became less aggressive and personal and 'more civil and pleasant a great deal and not touching any man by name' so that 'old' and 'new' comedy may be distinguished. When comedies were written there were no kings or emperors, 'al men being yet for the most part rude, & in a manner popularly egall', but with the emergence of such rulers the new genre of tragedy developed to accommodate the lives of great men, principally those who had become tyrants, had fallen from power and thus 'might worke a secret reprehension to others' (p.28). Later came the pastoral or

eclogue which was 'not of purpose to counterfeit or represent
the rusticall manner of loves and communication : but under the
vaile of homely persons, and in rude speeches to insinuate and
glaunce at greater matters, and such as perchance had not bene
safe to have bene disclosed in any other sort' (pp.30–1). Finally
historical poetry evolved which, in contrast to pastoral, represented a reality that did not require decoding :

Now because the actions of meane & base personages, tend in very few
cases to any great good example: for who passeth to follow the steps,
and manner of life of a crafts man, shepheard or sailer, though he were
his father or dearest frend?... Therefore was nothing committed to
historie, but matters of great and excellent persons & things that the
same by irritation of good courages (such as emulation causeth) might
worke more effectually, which occasioned the story writer to chuse an
higher stile fit for his subject. (p.33)

Puttenham's narrative tells the story of an increasingly
complex and stratified society which requires an ever greater
range and sophistication of poetic genres to represent it. In the
earliest societies equality led to crude satire and comedy:
classlessness and democratic political participation produced
bad art. Tragedy resulted from the onset of tyranny. But, for
Puttenham, the most interesting developments – socially and
aesthetically – occur later as 'society' advances to resemble that
of the Elizabethans. The characterisation of these last two forms
could be read as a diptych to parallel the divided role of the
queen as both poet and muse, representer and represented. On
the one hand there are the eclogues where 'greater matters' are
insinuated 'under the vaile of homely persons'. These demand
to be read as allegory. On the other, there is historical poetry
which is not disguised but a truthful mimesis, describing
'matters of great and excellent persons & things'. Only a society
which has developed and recognised the value of a coterie of
great men could produce these types of poetry; both forms as
defined by Puttenham presuppose distinctions between the
homely and the great, and the writer and the centres of power.
In doing so they herald the arrival of the figure of the
courtier–poet, a man able to dissemble and tell the truth, whose
role fuses literature and politics. In a sense one of the poetic

functions of courtiers is to tell the story of their own class and serve as apologists for their existence; the perpetual fear of needing to disguise what they really mean illustrates that, like the queen, they cannot fully authorise their own narrative.

The Arte of English Poesie in all its tangled, varied and contradictory strategies of argument centres around the Janus-faced figure of the courtier–poet and is a vindication of this class who by rights claim the English public sphere, as well as its more obvious functions as a position paper and an instruction manual. Modern commentators have generally been complicit with Puttenham's text, even when dismissing it.[59] As a result – although the achievement cannot be credited to Puttenham alone – the voice of the courtier–poet has become hegemonic and, just as experiments with accentual metre in English are generally assumed to be faulty because they did not become a dominant norm, other voices and traditions have been silenced.[60] It might be argued that Gosson, in opposing what he saw as a courtly literature and dismissing it as effeminate, was playing King Canute; but Wilson's vociferously Protestant poetics and very different conception of the relationship between court and public might well have been of greater interest to contemporary scholars had Edward VI survived beyond 1553.[61] Taking the Renaissance at face value is a dangerous and widespread habit.[62]

CHAPTER 5

Whose bloody country is it anyway? Sir Philip Sidney, the nation and the public

It has become something of a commonplace of recent critical writing on Sidney that *An Apologie for Poetry* speaks with two voices.[1] Having summarised the argument of his carefully crafted oration and concluded that poetry is an art of 'true doctrine' and not lies, worthy of praise not censure, Sidney launches into a digression on the poetry of his native land.[2] O. B. Hardison Jr has argued that not only does the *Apologie* appear to be finished before the digression starts, but that there is no precedent for such a departure in the classical models Sidney has carefully followed in the text and the 'passage clearly does not contribute to the defense of poetry...if anything, it undermines the defense by suggesting that English poets are guilty of many – if not most – of the charges that the enemies of poetry have levelled against it'.[3]

Why does this passage exist? Hardison has suggested that Sidney changed his mind about poetic theory: the major part of the *Apologie* conforms to a traditionally humanist approach, a standard mixture of Plato, Aristotle and Horace; the digression turns from this 'to the critical and rationalistic poetic of neoclassicism that was gaining favour in Italy and France between 1560 and 1580' (p.94). According to Hardison, the two sections cannot be reconciled: at some point in the 1580s Sidney revised his theoretical approach whilst he was revising the *Arcadia*, but '[b]efore a thorough revision was possible Sidney died, and when the *Apologie* was printed the newer material remained incompletely harmonized with the old' (p.98).

Hardison's speculations are in many ways convincing; but they are a salutary reminder that once again we are dealing with a work with a complex textual history – like *The Garland of Laurel* and *A Mirror for Magistrates* – and that interpretations often depend upon attempts to establish the intentions of dead poets, a task fraught with both historical and methodological pitfalls. Some critics suggest that Sidney was revising both the *Apologie* and the *Arcadia* for publication;[4] yet Sidney pours sarcastic scorn upon the decayed state of current national poetry where poets 'are almost as good in reputation as the mountebanks at Venice'. He marks a pointed contrast between the 'bastard poets', 'base men with servile wits ... who think it enough if they can be rewarded of the *printer*' and true poets, presumably those mistakenly believed to be mountebanks, who 'are less grateful to idle England, which can now scarce endure the pain of a *pen*' (pp.131–2; my emphasis). The opposition pen/printer in such an ornately rhetorical work, is surely not accidental and suggests that Sidney's constructed reader is someone with access to manuscript rather than print, ie, a courtier.[5] It also highlights how little is still known about Tudor reading practices and that overtly Ramist readings of Sidney which presume his close relation to print may need to be qualified given Ramism's dependence on print culture.[6]

It is possible that the digression on the need for a revitalised national poetry is perhaps less at odds with the main body of the *Apologie* than Hardison claims. It may well signal a departure from more familiar forms of the classical oration; but it is not as if Sidney was unwilling to experiment elsewhere in his writings (see below, pp.148, 154). Throughout the *Apologie* Sidney makes comments which seem to be preparing the reader for the concluding digression. Early in the tract he makes grand claims for the role of poetry in the history of nations, showing how it precedes all other learning:

And first, truly, to all them that, professing learning, inveigh against poetry may justly be objected that they go very near to ungratefulness, to seek to deface that which, in the noblest nations and languages that are known, hath been the first nurse whose milk by little and little enabled them to feed afterwards of tougher knowledges. (p.96)

Critics have frequently commented upon Sidney's use of the Latin term '*vates*', or the Greek 'ποιεῖν', translated as 'maker', definitions (etymologies) which lead on to the well-known grand claims for the efficacy of poetry as a 'feigning' which delivers a golden world beyond the brazen one of nature and leads men to virtue.[7] Less recognised is the syntactic and logical connection drawn up between knowledge, national identity and poetry. Poetry stands as the originating foundation of *Ur*-knowledge in the particular community of the nation: logically, it must also be the first form of knowledge of that nation so that 'tougher knowledges' are *ipso facto* offshoots of this literary nationalism. In a way, Sidney has thought through the problem that confronted John Bale in his desire for a universal language of truth, which, nevertheless, could never escape the inevitability of culturally specific articulation.[8] However, this can only be at the cost of a recognition that there can be no universal discourse of truth. There can, of course, be translation and the negotiation between languages and national forms – Sidney equates languages and nations in the sentence quoted above. Much of the *Apologie* is a translation and adaptation of classical and contemporary continental critical theory – Plutarch, Minturno and Zuccaro, as well as Aristotle and Plato[9] – to a specifically English context; but, I would argue, Sidney's famous dismissal of history and philosophy may well stem from their dependence on a 'regime of truth' which falsely claims to go beyond the national.[10]

One other word from this sentence deserves attention, 'noblest'. For Sidney, not all nations are equal; they do not have an equivalent access to knowledge and truth. In the same paragraph Sidney starts to draw up a genealogy of these 'noblest nations'. He starts with Greece and pays homage to Orpheus, Linus and some others (not named) who were 'the first of that country that made pens deliverers of their *knowledge* to their posterity' (my emphasis) and so 'may justly challenge to be called their fathers in learning'.[11] Again, the syntax invites the reader to make the connection between nation and knowledge, as does the second half of this sentence which states that they caused 'to draw with their charming sweetness the wild untamed wits to an admiration of knowledge' (p.96). The Orphic myth of cultural transformation, a ubiquitous motif in sixteenth- and seventeenth-century literature, is used to narrate the story of the birth of a nation and its knowledge.[12] In a series of rhetorically paralleled sentences, the development of Greek self-consciousness is shown to have served as the model for events in Rome, Italy and England:

So, as Amphion was said to move stones with his poetry to build Thebes, and Orpheus to be listened to by beasts – indeed stony and beastly people – so among the Romans were Livius Andronicus, and Ennius. So in the Italian language the first that made it aspire to be a treasure-house of science were the poets Dante, Boccaccio, and Petrarch. So in our English were Gower and Chaucer, after whom, encouraged and delighted with their excellent fore-going, others have followed, to beautify our mother tongue, as well in the same kind as in other arts. (p.96)

Such patterning serves to flatten out a history; England has its equivalents not only of Orpheus and Amphion, but also of the first Roman poets and Dante *et al*. English poetry as established by Chaucer and Gower can look back to a classical heritage and simultaneously across to the foremost poets of contemporary Europe. Sidney seems to be consciously picking up the line of poetry established by the Earl of Surrey, the contemporary of Skelton and Wyatt, whose experiments in his sonnets and translation of the *Aeneid*, sought to establish a courtly, aristocratic literary voice based specifically on the deployment of an Italianate and Roman style. In mapping out his genealogy of English poetry in the 'Digression', which obviously complements the genealogy of the poetry of noble nations in the 'Narration', Sidney does not mention Wyatt or Skelton, though the former was as well represented in *Tottel's Miscellany* (1557) as Surrey, and editions of the latter's verse were freely available and must have been known to Sidney.[13] He does, however, refer to the Earl of Surrey's lyrics after Chaucer's *Troilus and Criseyde* and the *Mirror for Magistrates* and before the *Shepheardes Calender*, stating that they are 'many things tasting of a noble birth, and worthy of a noble mind' (p.133). If England is worthy to exist within the line of noble nations, it is clearly partly due to the literary efforts of the Earl of Surrey in refining and polishing a style Sidney was to adopt when performing his own poetic experiments in writing the first English sonnet sequence, *Astrophil and Stella*.[14]

The ostensible purpose of the *Apologie* is not to praise but to revitalise English poetry 'which from the highest estimation of learning is fallen to be the laughing stock of children' (p.96). A conspicuous sign of this national shame and ignorant expunging of the origins of knowledge is the fact that poets are honoured highly even in the most barbarous of countries. Having completed the contracted survey of noble nations and given a brief rehearsal of the arguments he will later bring to bear against philosophers and historians, Sidney balances his praise of the highest with a counter-genealogy of the barbarian to emphasise the extent of England's current shame and, presumably, to spur his audience to action, to move the reader to supplement gnosis with praxis, and thus illustrate his central concern that poetic feigning is the highest form of knowledge whatever the form of the writing.[15] Sidney alleges that in Turkey the only writers they have are 'law-giving divines' and poets; in Ireland, 'where truly learning goeth very bare, yet are their poets held in a devout reverence'; that 'Even the most barbarous and simple Indians where no writing is ... have their poets'; in Wales, 'the true remnant of the ancient Britons', 'good authorities' show that 'they had poets, which they called bards' who have survived the attempts by the Romans, Saxons, Danes and Normans to suppress them so that they survive 'even to day last' (pp.97–8).

This cluster of nationalities forms a complex sign of barbarousness to serve as the antithesis of the sign of nobility – or civility – connoted by the signifiers, 'Greece', 'Rome', 'Italy'. The comparison between the Irish and the native Americans of the New World was a common one, as was the belief that both these forms of 'savage' could be equated with the ancient Britons, illustrating that civilised nations had once had a common past with primitive peoples, but that now they had progressed beyond this early stage and left their origins behind. The Turks were demonised as the irreligious infidels who threatened Christianity; the Irish were Catholic as well as savage; the suggestion that the marginalised peoples of the

Celtic fringe (Welsh, Irish) cared more about poetry than their English metropolitan counterparts was a further insult.[16] If even these lowliest of peoples valued poetry, Sidney is saying, why does not England? How can ignoramuses like Stephen Gossen not only be allowed to write against poetry unchallenged, but also be foolish enough to dedicate their work to a literary man like Sidney in the mistaken belief that a serious Protestant faith went hand in hand with an iconoclasm and a mistrust of the 'speaking pictures' of poetry?[17]

I have commented at length on the first few pages of the *Apologie* in order to demonstrate how it announces itself as a treatise bound up with the question of nationality from the very start, something which seems to have escaped the attention of virtually every commentator.[18] When Sidney, in the most often-quoted pages of the book – the end of the 'Narration' and the beginning of the 'Divisions' – refers to the poet exploring 'the zodiac of his own wit' in order to bring forth a 'golden world' which outdoes the brazen one of factual reality, a process which bridges the gap in the life of fallen man in elevating the reader's 'infected will' to match 'our erected wit', we are confronted with a specific knowledge which belongs to the history of the nation, past, present and future. Sidney defines the poet as a 'maker', an English word which 'whether by luck or wisdom' parallels the term used by the originators of Western knowledge, the Greeks.[19] The 'truth' derives from etymology, a form of knowledge which can accommodate fortuitous accidents, as the indifference to an explicitly causal relationship implies: luck and wisdom (often a synonym for 'knowledge') are both offered as explanations for the coincidence of names.[20] No way of distinguishing between them is suggested, in itself a mark of randomness, so that Jonathan Culler's comments on the relationship between etymologies and puns is challenged by the *Apologie*:

Etymologies – whether sanctioned or unsanctioned by current philology – are valued for the punlike quality, as they forge unexpected connections, whose suggestiveness shimmers on the borders of concepts, threatening to transform them: *christian* and *cretin* are the same word … Etymologies, we might say, give us respectable puns, endowing pun-like effects with the authority of science and even of truth.[21]

Sidney is making the claims Culler outlines; but what needs to be emphasised is that he is using the pun/etymology in contradistinction to the scientific authorities of history and philosophy in order to establish poetry as a conscious discourse of knowledge.[22]

Sidney confesses that few will swallow his bold claims and will require further, more traditional proof:

> Now let us go to a more *ordinary* opening of him [ie, the definition of poetry], that the truth may be more palpable: and so I hope, though we get not so unmatched a praise as the etymology of his names will grant, yet his very description, which no man will deny, shall not justly be barred from a principal commendation. (p.101; my emphasis)[23]

Paradoxically, Sidney is again using the *Apology* as a poetic text, an example of what it discusses; in elaborating on 'the truth' to make it more palpable, he is teaching and delighting the reader as a 'right popular philosopher', preparing 'food for the tenderest stomachs' (p.109), those unable to read the truth of philosophy.[24] He is also demonstrating that the 'truth' of poetry's foundational role can be found in the past, related in the present via the recovery of an authentic etymology and looks forward to the future in being defined as the representation of images, 'counterfeiting, or figuring forth' which leads men to virtue: 'to move men to take that goodness in hand' (p.103). Poetry, the most skilful use of language, is the site of national knowledge, remembering the most ancient truth, making it visible and therefore knowable, before urging that it be projected into the future by the reader who is 'made' or fashioned in the process.[25] In the *Apology*, 'English poetry' contains an unseen but nevertheless permanent hyphen; literariness cannot be separated from Englishness because the history of one presupposes the other, something which, according to Sidney, contemporary England has foolishly forgotten. To be cut off from the origins of knowledge is to risk knowing nothing, being without history, philosophy and a national identity. For Sidney, as much as for Samuel Beckett or any theorist of postmodernism, in the beginning was the pun.[26]

It has to be asked, does Sidney recognise this form of knowledge he has defined? How much does he know about it? In his discussion of the merits of poetry versus those of history, Sidney seems to read poetry in a radically different light from that outlined above. Whilst paraphrasing what Aristotle has to say about poetry in his *Poetics*, Sidney notes with approval that the Greek philosopher values poetry more than history 'because poesy dealeth with *Katholou, that is to say, with the universal consideration*' (my emphasis), whereas history only deals with the particular: 'Thus far Aristotle: which reason of his (as all his) is most full reason' (p.109).[27] Sidney, following Aristotle, claims that poetry teaches us what we know before we read, that it functions in the same way as Bale's allegorical decoding of scripture, as the 'already read' (see above, p.68):

If the poet do his part aright, he will show you in Tantalus, Atreus, and such like, nothing that is not to be shunned; in Cyrus, Aeneas, Ulysses, each thing to be followed; where the historian, bound to tell you as things were, cannot be liberal (without he will poetical) of a perfect pattern, but, as in Alexander or Scipio himself, show doings, some to be liked, some to be misliked. (p.110)

History, with its ability to impart messages which are not decided in advance, might appear to be the more liberal art in being more particular. What Sidney claims here quite manifestly contradicts his opening remarks on the value of poetry. The *Apologie* indeed speaks with a forked tongue, announces an aporia as many critics have maintained, one not solved by the attempt to unite the old Medieval division of life into active and contemplative parallel to the desire to drive a wedge between history and philosophy:

Where the philosophers, as they scorn to delight, so must they be content little to move – saving wrangling whether *virtus* be the chief or only good, whether the contemplative or the active life do excell – which Plato and Boethius well knew, and therefore made mistress Philosophy very often borrow the masking raiment of poesy. (p.114)[28]

What philosophers merely talk about, poets actually do. As with history, philosophy is only good philosophy when it is really poetry, the most eminent form of knowledge.

Sidney's concern with national identity is never forgotten even if it is largely absent from the substance of the analysis in the main body of the text. In the discussion dealing with 'the parts of poetry' ('Examination 2'), Sidney praises the lyric, and confesses to a certain 'barbarousness' in enjoying the old songs of Percy and Douglas which move his heart 'more than with a trumpet'. Immediately following this autobiographical detail is the sentence: 'In Hungary I have seen it the manner at all feasts, and other such meetings, to have songs of their ancestors' valour, which that right soldierlike nation think one of the chiefest kindlers of brave courage' (p. 118). The lyric is being cast as a specifically national form; the juxtaposition of its effect on the noble Philip Sidney with its use by the Hungarians, invites the reader to equate the two experiences – a comparison further encouraged by the subsequent comments on the Lacedemonians and the Greeks, who had the supreme lyricist, Pindar, to praise their martial exploits.[29] The lyric is shown to form a link with the past and move the hearer to virtue; Sidney, affected by a poetic form from his nation's own past is thus able to empathise with the experience of the Greeks and Hungarians, though clearly he cannot translate any more closely than this because the knowledge each nation possesses is local and specific.[30]

The comments on heroic poetry concentrate mainly on the example of the *Aeneid*, which Sidney argues should be 'worn in the tablet of [the reader's] memory', primarily because it shows how Aeneas, among other things, 'governeth himself in the ruin of his *country*' (my emphasis) and 'how in his inward self, and how in his outward government ... he will be found in excellency fruitful' (pp. 119–20).[31] As Sidney would have been aware, Aeneas' epic journey led to the foundation of Rome – and from his progeny, Britain – so that from the ruin of one country came the line of civilisation which followed on from the achievements of the Greeks.[32] The explicit link between the personal and public behaviour ('inward self ... outward government') of Aeneas illustrates how the fate of nations can depend upon the character of one heroic man; Sidney cites the case of Aeneas as a 'speaking picture' which tells a story of national and civilised self-discovery to spur others on to virtue. The implication is that this epic (heroic) narrative must teach as well as delight because the same may be true of future events, ie, the fate of nations could depend on the acts of significant individuals.[33] Lyric and epic could thus be seen to complement each other in function: lyric works sentimentally to evoke a mood of national fervour; epic tells of the fate of nations from which the reader learns both a general lesson and the specific knowledge of how Western civilisation came to be.

Edward Berry has pointed out how much of Sidney's argument in the *Apologie* depends upon the use of martial metaphors. Berry suggests that this is due to a necessary displacement of values in Sidney: unable to pursue the public, military career he had always desired because of his tactlessness and the opposition of the queen, Sidney put all his energies into writing poetry and in doing so he 'tends to identify the poet with the heroes he celebrates and to combine images of seduction and aggression ... The poet, no longer enticer, becomes the epic hero, defending his prince and country'.[34] One need not accept all of Berry's psychologistic speculation to accept that Sidney elevates the role of the poet to that of national hero. Sidney's argument may be as much supplement as displacement in recognising that drawing up the boundaries and representing the form of the nation was a task every bit as necessary as performing more obvious heroics for its honour, a notion which underpins the rationale of Fulke Greville's *Life of Sidney*.[35]

Berry makes the important point that Sidney conceives the nation in explicitly gendered terms, reversing the claims of those who allege that poetry is an art of 'effeminateness' and arguing that martial and literary vigour go hand in hand like Venus and Mars. Poetry 'is not the cause of effeminacy, but its potential cure' and should thus inspire national renewal: 'For heretofore poets have in England also flourished, and, which is to be noted, even in those times when the trumpet of Mars did sound loudest' (p.131).[36]

Literature as a national form is indisputably masculine; it is also aristocratic, or, as Sidney puts it, 'noble'. Hardison is correct to note that Sidney is almost exclusively derogatory in his comments on previous English literature: 'the tone becomes negative, even garrulous'.[37] Chaucer – again cast in the role of founding father – is regarded as an anachronism for writing *Troilus and Criseyde* so well, 'yet he had great wants, fit to be forgiven in so reverent an antiquity'; *The Shepheardes Calender* is damned with faint praise, judged to be 'worth the reading' but of 'an old rustic language' which cannot be permitted; *Gorboduc* stands out amongst English comedy and tragedy which observe 'rules neither of honest civility nor skilful poetry', but despite being 'full of notable morality, which it doth most delightfully teach... in truth it is very defectious in the circumstances' (pp. 133–4). Sidney cannot even bear to name any more poetry, claiming that 'Other sort of poetry almost have we none, but that lyrical kind of songs and sonnets' (p. 137) and he continues to attack the native tradition's diction and prosody, ending the *Apologie* with the reminder that poets were the 'first bringers-in of civility' but 'the cause why it [poetry] is not esteemed in England is the fault of poet-apes, not poets' (p. 141).[38] Hardison neglects to mention that the *Apologie* concludes in the form of a manual for writing English poetry and that the only poet Sidney really praises from the previous generation of poets is Surrey, precisely for his nobility, a word he significantly uses twice.[39] The argument is perhaps less a case of Neo-Classical tenets sitting uneasily with unoriginal humanist ones than the *Apologie* having an absent centre which then reappears at the end as a digression, but which has always been present signalled by small hints, odd phrases and statements leading the reader on towards it. Sidney is copying a standard form of the Oration and Hardison seems to be wrong to claim that he has adapted it in an unusual manner: concluding with a digression which actually relates to the central purpose of the treatise was a usual practice.[40]

More to the point is the disjunction between a treatise discussing the function of rhetoric – or, at least, certain branches of it – and one which aims to provide a blueprint for those who wish to write the nation: the dangerous and suppressed hyphen between English and literature.[41] Sidney's complex and contradictory account of imitation – what many critics regard as

an attempt to unite Aristotelian and Platonic theories of art[42] –
is ultimately resolved by the claim that the purpose of poetry is
to 'move men to take goodness in hand', to re-fashion the
national culture, go out and write as well as perform acts of
heroism. Hence, the digression on English poetry is actually the
most useful part, but depends upon the reader being persuaded
by the philosophical core. A similar dilemma haunts Fulke
Greville's biographical experiment and his attempt to use
Sidney's life for a similar purpose of inspiring active heroism in
the name of England. This text, I would argue, ends up caught
between four competing figures: Sidney, Elizabeth, Essex and
Greville's own fictionalised self, continually asking who represents national identity most truthfully, can it ever be fixed, or
does it have to be constantly re-written and re-performed?[43] In
both cases it is impossible for the controlling narrative voice not
to split and announce an aporia and the only resolution of the
problem is via an appeal to imitative action of the narrative on
the part of the reader.[44]

What Sidney is doing in the *Apologie*, I would suggest, is
trying to establish literature as a series of national forms, which
are both masculine and noble, with the goal of providing models
for other writers to copy, notably himself. In neglecting to
mention poets he must have read – Wyatt, Lodge, Gascoigne,
Googe, Churchyard, Rich, Heywood, Harington and all those
collected in the highly influential *Tottel's Miscellany* (1557) –
Sidney is automatically relegating them to the status of
'poet–apes'. But why single out Surrey?

In many ways Surrey was the obvious choice for Sidney to use
as a model for the lyric; *Tottel's Miscellany* was properly entitled,
*Songes and Sonettes, written by the ryght honorable Lorde Henry Howard
late Earle of Surrey, and other*, showing that Surrey was generally
accounted the most influential poet in the development of
English verse. The brief introduction, 'The Printer to the
Reader', made it clear that the collection was just as concerned
with the establishment of an English literary culture as the
Apologie:

That to have wel written in verse, yea & in small parcelles, deserveth
great praise, the workes of divers Latines, Italians, and other, doe

prove sufficiently. That our tong is able in that kynde to do as praiseworthely as ye rest, the honourable stile of the noble earle of Surrey, and the weightinesse of the depe witted sir Thomas Wyat the elders verse, with severall graces in sondry good Englishe writers, doe show abundantly. It resteth nowe (gentle reder) that thou thinke it not evill doon, to publish, to the honor of the Englishe tong, and for profit of the stacions of Englishe eloquence, those workes which the ungentle holders up, of such treasures have heretofore envied thee.

Richard Tottel's manifesto makes the familiar comparison between a native English tradition, classical Latin and contemporary Italian; the description of Surrey as 'honourable' and 'noble' relates closely to Sidney's estimation of his precursor.

Comparisons do not stop here. Surrey, like Sidney, was also keen to experiment with numerous forms of versification, notably the heroic quatrain in his elegy on Wyatt, blank verse in his translation of the *Aeneid* and invention of the sonnet form in English; he spent his career oscillating between a military career and a literary one; like Wyatt and Petrarch, he was closely associated with the Protestant cause, paraphrasing sections of the Bible which appealed specifically to reformers – Ecclesiastes and the Psalms – which were read by no less a Protestant icon than the martyr Anne Askew (see above, p.70).[45] Surrey was also executed, as was Wyatt's son; but whilst the latter died in a rebellion specifically for the Protestant cause, it is hard to regard Surrey's death as a religious martyrdom.[46] Nevertheless, Surrey had 'become representative of the age' for a later sixteenth-century audience; just as Sidney was to be for a nostalgic Jacobean one, harking back to the glorious days of Elizabeth.[47]

Bill Sessions has attempted to characterise how Surrey appeared to the generation of the 1580s rather than the 1550s. According to Sessions, the 'really revolutionary dimension' of the importation of the sonnet as articulated in statements like Tottel's (cited above), was its 'economy' of concentrated poetic form because writers and readers were well aware that Petrarch had been used by Chaucer – most notably translated in crucial sections of *Troilus and Criseyde* – a tradition revised by Surrey.

However, by 1589 'what had been viewed as technical originality was characterized by Puttenham as a virtual revolution'.[48] Surrey's 'inventions for his courtly audience, in one sense self-aggrandizement – like his portraits – came to be read as the way to write a noble, courtly English poetry', one which deliberately set itself against other verse forms and constructions of literary identity, eg, Skelton's, the varied voices of the *Mirror* and the rest of the Reformation tradition mapped out so carefully by John King. Sidney may well have been a Protestant, as was Surrey, but the *Apologie*'s argument for a 'noble' poetic voice based on the poetry of Surrey was designed to kill off a vernacular Protestant literary tradition and replace it with a consciously aristocratic one.[49] To this end, Sidney was instrumental in telescoping, restricting and making more class-bound a varied vernacular poetic tradition and attempting to use the legacy of Surrey to establish a dominant form of national literature.

Sessions's comments on one of Surrey's most well-known lyrics, 'When raging love with extreme payne', printed on folio six of *Tottel's Miscellany*, illustrate why Sidney probably chose to adopt Surrey's sonnet form and construction of the lyric 'I' in writing *Astrophil and Stella*, probably written alongside the *Apologie* and the *Old Arcadia* (early 1580s):

The love poem combines the motifs of Petrarch with the motifs of the Trojan war to produce an original text ... structuring a Petrarchan subject within a network of allusions, almost all of them Vergilian rather than Ovidian, is a technique that had seldom appeared before, certainly not so positively in English or Continental love poetry. In 'When ragyng love', the ancient myth of Troy – itself translated for Surrey through Homer, Vergil, and Chaucer – is made contemporary because its universal themes are related to the immediate voice of the male persona.[50]

In Petrarchan translations before Surrey – as, for example, in Troilus' celebrations of his love with Criseyde – the Ovidian lyric mode had been dominant.[51] In linking Petrarch with Virgil and specifically the fall of Troy, Surrey was producing his own version of a subject and a form which looked across to contemporary Europe and simultaneously back to an English/

British tradition and a classical past. The fall of Troy led not only to the *Aeneid*, but the foundation of Britain, so that it forms the mediation point between an epic of British national origins and the classical world, a relationship of which Sidney was also clearly aware (see above, p.140). Surrey's lyric 'I' is thus fashioned as inherently national:

> When ragyng love with extreme payne
> Most cruelly distrains my hart;
> When that my teares, as floudes of rayne,
> Beare witnes of my wofull smart:
> When sighes have wasted so my breath
> That I lye at the poynte of death:
> I cal to minde the navye greate
>
> That the Grekes brought to Troye towne:
> And how the boystrous windes did beate
> Their shyps, and rente their sayles adowne,
> Till Agamemnons daughters bloode
> Appeasde the goddes that them withstode.[52]

As Sessions notes, it is the male voice the poet assumes which forges the link between Troy and the contemporary English court. Stanza 1 refuses to announce any link with a particular past or personal history, appealing to the reader to recognise the lyric form.[53] What holds the series of phrases and images together – 'ragyng love', 'extreme payne', distrained heart, 'teares...floudes of rayne', 'wofull smart', sighs wasting breath, 'poynte of death' – are five personal pronouns (only the first line lacks one). The poem announces its own voice; it speaks as an apostrophe, a disembodied lyric 'I' fashioning itself in English.[54] The persona of the (male) poet speaks in 'homogeneous empty time', a time without origins, which is the desired time of the nation.

Stanza 2 preserves this uncertainty and lack of historical fixity. Although we learn that the poet remembers the Trojan war ('I cal to minde'), we do not discover whether he is speaking as a former participant close to the events or the reader of a book; all we know is that his poem comes after the war because he translates it into his own experience, but what that

experience is, beyond his construction as a lyric 'I', is impossible
to determine. The Trojan War could be said to exist as an
origin; however, the true origin of the poem is the consciousness
of the poet who remembers it, so the argument becomes circular
and we are back to the problem of identifying the poet who does
no more than announce his existence as an English speaker
living after the Trojan War, a period of time which includes the
complete history of Britain, the British and the English.[55]

The poetic voice Surrey establishes in this lyric is probably
the most self-consciously nationalistic in all his short verse, but
it does not stand alone and serves to emphasise how Surrey has
combined and negotiated various possibilities to produce a
noble, national style. In his translation of Petrarch's *Canzioniere*
140 (*Tottel*, p.6), Surrey highlights the first person pronoun
which is significantly less prominent in the Italian:

> Love, that liveth, and reigneth in *my* thought,
> That built his seat within *my* captive breast,
> Clad in the armes, wherin with *me* he fought,
> Oft in *my* face he doth his banner rest.   4
> She, that *me* taught to love, and suffer payne,
> *My* doubtfull hope, and eke *my* hote desire
> With shamefast cloke to shadowe, and refraine,
> Her smilyng grace converteth straight to yre.   8
> And cowarde Love then to the hart apace
> Taketh his flight, whereas he lurkes, and plaines
> His purpose lost, and dare not shewe his face.
> For my lordes gilt thus faultless byde I paynes,   12
> Yet from my lorde shall not my foote remove.
> Swete is his death, that takes his end by love.

> Amor, che nel penser *mio* vive e regna
> e 'l suo seggio maggior nel *mio* cor tene,
> talor armato ne la fronte vene;
> ivi si loca et ivi pon sua insegna.   4
> Quella ch'amare e sofferir ne 'nsegna,
> e vol che 'l gran desio, l'accesa spene,
> ragion, vergogna e reverenza affrene,
> di nostra ardir fra se stessa si sdegna.   8
> Onde Amor paventoso fugge al core,
> lasciando ogni sua impressa, e piange e trema;
> ivi s'asconde e non appar piu fore.

Che poss'io far, temendo il mio signore,   12
se non star seco infin a l'ora estrma?
che bel fin fa chi ben amando more.[56]

The Italian contains only two first person pronouns in the first
six lines, whereas Surrey's translation has at least one in each
line; Petrarch speaks of love coming armed to his forehead ('la
fronte'), Surrey elaborates and stresses the active collaboration
of the speaker in the battle with the lady ('with me he fought');
the second quatrain of Surrey's sonnet also transforms a first
person plural pronoun ('ne') and neutral construction ('l
gran desio, l'accesa spene') to the first person singular ('She,
that me taught to love/... my hote desire'); in Petrarch's sonnet
love is a prosopopoeia alongside the poet, in Surrey's, love starts
as a similar separate figure but soon becomes a homunculus
absorbed within the lyric 'I'; there is no equivalent in Petrarch
of Surrey's 'For my lordes gilt thus faultless byde I paynes' and
as Emrys Jones has pointed out, in changing the concluding
couplet and including the word 'foote', Surrey may well be
recalling Aeneas' attempt to rescue the reluctant Priam in Book
2 of the *Aeneid* which he translated as '"Father, thoughtest thow
that I may ones remove",/ Quod I, "a foote, and leave thee
here behinde"' (lines 864–5).[57] Such an allusion further
illustrates that Surrey is writing verse which speaks with a noble
'I' for the nation. Constructing this voice in a love lyric invites
the reader to assume that the putative nation addressed was a
woman.

In writing a sonnet sequence and thus making a whole out of
what had been isolated fragments, Sidney would seem to have
been trying to elevate the Italianate sonnet form imported by
Surrey back to the sophisticated and interlaced whole of the
Canzioniere as well as 'proving, in his native country, Du Bellay's
claim that the sonnet sequence could be an effective means of
demonstrating the artful versatility of the vernacular'.[58] Nevertheless, the opening sonnet of *Astrophil and Stella* forces the reader
to confront the question of the speaker's constructed identity, in
itself a recollection of the concerns of the originator of the form
in English. The first lines emphasise that the identity of the
subject will be written in the poems and will engage the energies

of the reader more than the ostensible object of that subject's desire:

> Loving in truth, and faine in verse *my* love to show,
> That she (deare she) might take some pleasure of *my* paine;
> Pleasure might cause her reade, reading might make her know,
> Knowledge might pitie winne, and pitie grace obtaine,
> *I* sought fit words to paint the blackest face of woe,
> Studying inentions fine her wits to entertaine.[59]

The problem for Astrophil (and Sidney) is that the 'truth' he wishes to tell cannot exist outside 'inventions', 'fit words' or wit. In telling of his passion not only does he have to rely on existing conventions and thus run the risk of insincere untruth, but he also has to invent a self to tell it, a point brought out forcefully in the paradox of the concluding couplet, itself a literary cliché: 'Biting *my* trewand pen, beating *my* selfe for spite,/ "Foole", said *my* Muse to *me*, "looke in thy heart and write."'[60] The production of Stella in the sequence depends upon the prior articulation of the male voice.[61]

Maurice Evans has argued that this opening sonnet is deliberately and perversely unusual in its argument: 'It is interesting – and a point which an educated reader of Sidney's time would easily recognize – that Astrophil approaches his composition in entirely the wrong order: he seeks fit words before he has chosen his basic materials or considered their presentation; he jumps straight to Elocution, leaving out Invention and Disposition, and this is why he finds it so hard to write.'[62] The unusual nature of the sonnet is further highlighted in the fact that it is the first in alexandrines in English and its reversal of rhetorical norms contrasts to the careful form of the *Apologie*.[63] Evans's observation illustrates how the sonnet is deliberately written to force the reader to become aware of the writer writing, searching through the forms of invention and hypothesising how they might be used before coming to the cliché of introspection, something which has, ironically, been put on display. Astrophil's tortured and confused search is the very opposite of Barthes's '*écriture blanc*' into which the author disappears.[64] *Astrophil and Stella* advertises itself as a quest for the lyric 'I'.[65]

Much recent critical writing has emphasised that the sonnet sequence is not simply the narration of the unrequited love of a frustrated aristocratic suitor for an unobtainable would-be mistress. Furthermore, Sidney draws attention to the impossibility of distinguishing between the 'private' and the 'public' at a court where the Petrarchan language of love was used to address the queen in the hope of political advancement and the gaining of favour. As Arthur Marotti has pointed out, when Sidney wrote *Astrophil and Stella* he was known as a 'politically, economically and socially disappointed young man'; the small 'coterie audience' who would have seen the manuscripts of the sequence would have been able 'to appreciate a subtly ironic interplay of text and context'.[66] Marotti's reading is a salutary reminder that one cannot hope to isolate a public world from a private one; but he is too keen to set up a simple opposition between the language of love and the language of ambition. Such a dichotomy ignores the possibility that the language of love might not be *standing for* a political reality; it could also be the means of an attempt to articulate a political language itself, ie, *Astrophil and Stella* can be read as a fictional reality rather than an elaborate disguise or a displaced set of motives.

In the octave of sonnet 3, Astrophil provides a series of examples of the models 'daintie wits' have used to describe their 'fancies'. Many show themselves to be no more than '*Pindare's* Apes', flaunting their wit in phrases fine, 'new found Tropes', 'Or with strange similes enrich each line,/ Of herbes or beastes, which *Inde* or *Afrike* hold'. The sestet, by way of contrast, asserts that he knows only one muse: 'in *Stella*'s face I reed/ What love and Beutie be; then all my deed/ But Copying is what in her Nature writes'. This concluding triplet places the 'I' of the poet in direct contact with the object of his affection; the octave has dismissed all foreign or exotic poetry ('Inde or Afrike') and affected style. The implication is that in describing Stella's face he can fashion his own poetic self and speak with his natural, native voice. Such a poem is not necessarily *about* frustrated ambition diverted into poetry – though, of course, it could be – but it quite clearly announces a desire to speak in an authentic English literary style, articulating something which can only be stated in the form of a fiction, a 'nature' which can only ever exist as a copy.

Such a reading, although on one level logical and formal, would be strengthened if it could be demonstrated that Stella was read by contemporaries as Elizabeth or a female representation of the nation to complement the male poetic voice.[67] Unfortunately there is no direct evidence of this having been the case; nevertheless throughout the sequence the reader is encouraged to make this connection. Sonnet 8 describes how love has fled from Greece, 'his native place', after the aggressive Turks have invaded, and come to England 'pleasd with our soft peace'. Unused to the cold of the North, he has 'perch'd himself in *Stella*'s joyfull face'; unfortunately she is also too cold and he flies to Astrophil's heart for sanctuary. This might seem to be easy to decode in terms of the oppositions interpreted by Marotti. However, sonnet 9 describes her face as 'Queene *Vertue*'s court', a metaphor which is by no means a straightforward compliment to Elizabeth from an aspiring courtier; instead, it envisages Stella as the physical form of the court and thus, by implication, the courtiers rather than the queen. The sonnet is perhaps more obviously read as an address to the would-be readership of the poem – the courtiers – who make up the substance of what Stella forms as an empty abstract symbol, the nation.

In sonnet 30 Astrophil addresses Stella directly for the first time and simultaneously confesses that the 'star-gazer' is really Sidney himself: 'How *Ulster* likes of that same golden bit,/ Wherewith my father once made it halfe tame.'[68] The sonnet takes the form of one sentence divided up into units of relative clauses which each occupy one couplet. The finite verb ('answer do') does not appear until the concluding couplet, as does the subject ('I'); as in Surrey's sonnets, the rearrangement of syntax serves to force the reader's attention towards the speaker and his identity and away from the addressee. The sonnet lists a series of questions which Astrophil/Sidney answers but without understanding how he can do so: whether the Turks will attack Christendom, how the Polish invasion of Russia is succeeding, whether religious factions in France are in agreement yet, what has been decided by the Germans at the diet of Augsburg, how William of Orange's leadership of the Dutch revolt against the Spanish is progressing, what the situation is in Ulster since his father left and which faction has the upper hand at the Scottish court. The conclusion, 'These questions busie wits to me do frame;/ I, cumbered with good manners, answer do,/ But know not how, for still I thinke of you' has usually been read as an acknowledgement that the love-sick poet cannot concentrate on the affairs of state which used to be his province (or as a reminder that Sidney is still interested in what he affects to be rejecting).[69] But the sonnet may be more witty, more polysemous and more radical still; its grammatical form forces the reader to consider both the subject of the utterance, the first which is addressed neither directly nor indirectly to this imagined reader, and the knowledge which he knows. By dismissing the political affairs of Europe as matters which he can speak about but does not *know*, he implies that what he does know is constructed in the fiction of the linguistic form of the sonnet and it is of the same order. He may not know the addressee who does not appear, but he does come to know himself through writing it and thinking of Stella. She becomes the vanishing point of a discourse of a national identity which is never explicitly stated but depends upon the identity of the poet speaking; she authorises his 'I' and enables him to fabricate his 'real' fiction. On one level, literature is fashioned into a special knowledge of national identity in this sonnet, something practised by Surrey in his verse and a claim made by Sidney in the *Apologie*.

The small group of sonnets, 68–72, is often seen as the turning point of the sequence.[70] Astrophil, resigned to copying Stella's virtue, believes that she has consented to be his lover, only to realise that he has misinterpreted and his hopes of uniting physical desire with spiritual advancement are an illusion: 'As fast thy Vertue bends that love to good:/ "But ah," Desire still cries, "give me some food"' (sonnet 71). Sonnet 69 is the centre of this group, being the poem where Astrophil believes that Stella has said yes. The terms in which his supposed triumph is described link it to the themes outlined above. Before we know what has happened, Astrophil speaks of his joy being too high for his 'low stile' to convey and his bliss being 'fit for a nobler state than me', so that the descriptive terms employed are metaphorically concerned with class, birth and poetry ('low stile'). As Paul Ricoeur has argued, what distinguishes metaphor from simile is that its terms are semantically reversible; Sidney is referring to the success of his poetry and his courtly career in this imagined triumph: 'Come, come, and let *me* powre *my* selfe on thee;/ Gone is the winter of *my* miserie' (my emphasis).[71] Although the reader can easily guess what the cause of his joy is, the fact that it is left unstated emphasises Ricoeur's point.

The sestet reinforces this inherent ambiguity (or reversibility); whilst it is made clear that Stella's consent is the cause of Astrophil's joy, the metaphorical enactment of this state continues in political language, once again, focusing upon the subjectivity of the speaker rather than his objective knowledge of the addressee:

> For *Stella* hath with words where faith doth shine,
> Of her high heart giv'n me the monarchie:
> I, I, O, I may say that she is mine.
> And though she give but thus conditionally
> This realme of blisse, while vertuous course I take,
> No kings be crown'd, but they some covenants make.

Astrophil thinks he has become king, the ruler of Stella's heart. If this were the case (which it is not), he would not only have solved the problem of equating the pull of desire and the quest for virtue, but also answered the question of who can speak for the nation; the poets like Sidney who attempt to write a national literature, the courtiers who surround the monarch (in sonnet 9 they metonymically occupy Stella's face), or the ruling monarch herself? In sonnet 69, Astrophil/Sidney finds a way of combining all three roles, a union borne out by the exclamation in line 11, which is the only place in the sequence where the first personal pronoun is repeated ('I, I, O, I'). Were Astrophil's fantasy a reality, the gap demanded by the representation of power would automatically close; Astrophil and Stella would be as closely united as Donne's lovers in 'The Sunne Rising': 'She is all states, and all princes, I,/ Nothing else is./ Princes do but play us.'[72] Astrophil is 'playing' the king, whilst Stella – in some ways a representation of Elizabeth – stands for the nation (state).

This sonnet seems almost studied in its ambiguity; should it be read as a desirable fantasy, a political criticism of Elizabethan despotism, or as an absurd chimera which serves to undercut Astrophil and demand that he be perceived ironically? Is his identification with the monarch a veiled demand for the political representation of an elite class of courtiers, or a dismissal of such ambitions? If, as I would argue, it is impossible to determine which of these readings is the most plausible, then the possibility of political criticism is at least entertained.[73]

Obviously such comments on *Astrophil and Stella* neither exhaust possible readings of the sequence nor invalidate much previous criticism. What is important to note is that ignoring the nationalistic and political aspects of certain poems, attempting to isolate 'literary' and aesthetic questions as if they were automatically separate from other discourses, is to blind criticism to both formal, logical and intertextual relations, as well as intentional ones. In both senses – and it is usually impossible to separate them – Stella, rather than being the national form itself, is cast as the addressee of the national voice, the listener who makes its articulation possible.

Such ideas are explored more thoroughly in the *Arcadia*, Sidney's most ambitious literary experiment. As has frequently been observed, the work does not fit into any recognised generic category; *The Old Arcadia* owes much to the five-act structure of Terentian comedy, but the unfinished revisions which form *The New Arcadia* would seem to undermine the homologous pattern; the pastoral setting demonstrates the influence of Heliodorus, Montemayor and, most importantly, Sannazarius' *Arcadia*, though Sidney rejects any simple notion of pastoral retirement and forces the reader to rethink carefully the relationship between action, contemplation and literary symbolism.[74] The *Arcadia* advertises the fact that it is a literary experiment in more than a formal sense. Specifically, the reader is encouraged to think of the relationship between Arcadia and contemporary England, just as the reader of the *Mirror for Magistrates* is invited to regard England's present in terms of its past. *The Old Arcadia* opens with a description of the country:

Arcadia among all provinces of Greece was ever had in singular reputation, partly for the sweetness of the air and other natural benefits, but principally for the moderate and well tempered minds of the people ... were the only people which, as by their justice and providence gave neither cause nor hope to their neighbours to annoy them, so were they not stirred with false praise to trouble others' quiet ... Even the muses seemes to approve their good determination by choosing that country as their chiefest repairing place, and by bestowing their perfections so largely there that the very shepherds themselves had their fancies opened to so high conceits as the most learned of other nations have been long time since content both to borrow their names and imitate their cunning.[75]

The peacefulness of Arcadia corresponds to 'our soft peace' of *Astrophil and Stella*, sonnet 8; the flourishing of poetry contrasts to England's neglect of literature described in the *Apologie*. The fiction of Arcadia describes both an ideal and a real England, demanding that the reader make the effort to distinguish between the two types of representation; *The Old Arcadia* is a Utopian work.[76]

By way of contrast, *The New Arcadia* begins *in medias res* with a scene in which the two virtuous shepherds, Claius and Strephon, discuss their mutual separation from their love object, Urania, and their native land, Arcadia.[77] Their talk is interrupted by the need to rescue the shipwrecked Musidorus and they all set off to find his cousin, Pyrochles. The revised text immediately foregrounds the love plot of the two disguised nobles; the original began with the decision of Basilius, Arcadia's ruler, to consult the oracle at Delphos in order to learn what the future held in store for his two daughters, and, having done so, retiring to a retreat 'to prevent all these inconveniences of the loss of his crown and children' (p.6). The narrator emphasises the folly of Basilius' actions: he is described as 'a prince of sufficient skill to govern so quiet a country where the good minds of the former princes had set down good laws';

in other words, Basilius is a competent ruler when he is following precedent, but probably lacks 'sufficient skill' (p.4) to govern if he asserts his independence or Arcadia, for whatever reason, should become unruly. Basilius' desire to consult the oracle is described as being for base motives, 'not so much stirred with the care for his country and children as with the vanity [of those who] ... are desirous to know the certainty of things to come' (p.5), which implies that the very reason for his retreating into the country may well threaten what the action was designed to prevent. Although he places his trust wisely in Philanax, 'a friend not only in affection but judgement, and no less of the duke than the dukedom – a rare temper, whilst most men either servilely yield to all appetites, or with an obstinate austerity, looking to that they fancy good, wholly neglect the prince's person' (pp.5–6), to act as regent in his absence, he makes the horrendous error of assigning his elder daughter Pamela to the illiterate shepherd, Dametas, 'thinking it a contrary salve against the destiny threatening her mishap by a prince to place her with a shepherd' (p.6). The latter judgement implies a deal of whimsy on Basilius' part and provides the humorous plot in which Pamela is easily lured away from Dametas with an absurd bribe in Act 3. Dametas is exactly the sort of subject who, yielding to his appetites, neglects the prince's person in the hope of personal gain.[78]

The more serious problem, both for Basilius in the fictional world of the *Arcadia* and for the reader comparing the politicised pastoral to the conditions of sixteenth-century England, comes towards the end of Act 4, the darkest phase of the narrative. After the supposed death of Basilius, Philanax, suspecting a plot, imprisons the queen, Pamela and Philoclea. The result is confusion, but the narrator exonerates Philanax:

[A]lready was all the whole multitude fallen into confused and dangerous divisions. There was a notable example how great dissipations monarchical governments are subject unto; for now that the prince and guide had left them, they had not experience to rule, and had not whom to obey. Public matters had ever been privately governed, so that they had no lively taste what was good for themselves, but everything was either vehemently desirable or extremely terrible. Neighbours' invasions, civil dissension, cruelty of the coming prince, and whatsoever in common sense carries a dreadful show, was all in men's heads, but in few how to prevent them'. (p.277) If a ruler neglects to politically educate his – or her – citizens and relies on personal government, then a malign act of fortune will result in chaos. Basilius' trust in oracles is the logical corollary of his benign despotism, signalled at the start of the *Old Arcadia*, and demonstrates his desire to control what his conspicuously irrational form of government cannot bargain for. The sentence which provides the reader with the character of Philanax distinguishes first carefully between duke and dukedom, but then elides the separation between the king's two bodies, stating that Philanax will not 'neglect the prince's person'. Does this mean the prince as an individual or the prince as head of state? From the start of the book, the reader is forced to ask two related questions: firstly, how drastically have the actions of Basilius in seeking to protect his own dynastic succession affected the ordinary life of the country he rules? Has he placed his own personal fortune as ruler ahead of that of the office he occupies? In other words, is he guilty of confusing the relationship of the king's two bodies? Secondly, what is the connection between the fictional world of the *Arcadia* and the reality of Elizabethan England? Has Elizabeth adequately educated her citizens and does she allow them to participate in the nation's political life as fully as they should? If the answer to this is 'No' then what should be done?

There has been much excellent critical analysis of Sidney's politics in the *Arcadia* which has served readers well.[79] In general, two episodes have been singled out for special attention; the rebellion of the commons in Book 2 and the beast fable told by Philisides (like Astrophil an obvious fictionalisation of Sidney himself) in the Fourth Eclogues.[80] What these two incidents reveal is that Sidney was opposed to both tyranny and the possibility of rule by the commons in formulating how a national public sphere of political participation should be established.[81]

The first episode describes the aftermath of a celebration of the duke's birthday which gets seriously out of hand when the commoners have too much to drink and start to accuse the foreign princess, the Amazon Cleophila (Pyrochles disguised), of attempting to seize 'their prince and government' (p.112) after the temporary abdication of Basilius. They attack the court party and force them to retreat into the palace, but Cleophila delivers a clever speech which disperses the rebels.

Most analyses of this incident have concentrated on Sidney's scorn for 'the many-headed multitude' (p.115), their inability to sustain serious political discussion, 'At length the prince's person fell to be their table-talk; and to speak licentiously of that was a tickling point of courage to them' (p.111) (the confusion of the person of the ruler and his office is, not surprisingly, repeated) and the heady progress of their passage from politics to full-blooded rebellion:

But as mischief is of such nature that it cannot stand but with strengthening one evil by another, and so multiply in itself till it come to the highest, and then fall with his own weight, so to their minds once past the bounds of obedience more and more wickedness opened itself, and they which sought to succour him, then to reform him, now thought no safety to themselves without killing him. (pp.112–13)

The commons cannot engage in the reasonable criticism of political discourse; for them, all questioning leads *inevitably* to mindless violence. Cleophila/Pyrocles' speech emphasises their neglect of 'due points of subjection' (p.114).

The speech itself is shrouded in irony: Cleophila/Pyrocles announces that for her to speak at all is an aberration:

'An unused thing it is, and I think not heretofore seen, O Arcadians, that a woman should give public counsel to men; a stranger to the country people; and that lastly in such a presence a private person, as I am, should possess the regal throne. But the strangeness of your action makes that used for virtue which your violent necessity imposeth. For certainly a woman may well speak to such men who have forgotten all manly government'. (pp.113–14)

The joke is not only that Pyrocles is a man, but also that he is a very public one, who will inherit the kingdom of Thrace in due course (p.361). The equation of women with the feminine

private and men with the masculine public ('manly government') is ironic in a referential rather than a narrative context
because England was ruled by a woman, something Sidney and
his audience were hardly likely to forget and which made
possible the sophisticated figurative language of *Astrophil and
Stella*. Elizabeth herself referred to this gender-based exclusion
when she claimed that beneath her feminine guise she had the
heart of a man.[82] Pyrocles can be seen as a transposed,
transvestite Elizabeth, similarly a man disguised as a woman.[83]

Is Sidney tacitly agreeing with John Knox's famous judgement – actually written against Mary, but published on the
accession of Elizabeth – that women should be excluded from
public politics?[84] Does the speech serve to criticise political life
during her reign, with its attendant disguises, role-playing and
elaborate compliments; or is it to be read as a sympathetic
comment on the problems political women have to confront and
the games they have to play?[85] Once again, interpretation can
be seen to depend upon the stance of the reader, what he or she
has 'already read'; but the very ambiguity opens up the
possibility of a critical position.

The potential disjunction between gender and political
representation is reproduced in a related tension between
national and political identity, an issue which is often attributed
to the composition of the *Old Arcadia* after Sidney's withdrawal
from court and retirement to Penshurst resulting from his active
opposition to the projected Alençon marriage.[86] One of the fears
of the commons is that their country will be taken over by
foreigners through the wiles of Cleophila/Pyrocles:

[I]t were tedious to write their far-fetched constructions ... Who will
call him duke if he had not a people? When certain of them of
wretched estates (and worse minds), whose fortunes change could not
impair, began to say a strange woman had now possessed their prince
and government; Arcadians were too plain-headed to give their
prince counsel. What need from henceforward to fear foreign enemies,
since they were conquered without stroke striking, their secrets
opened, their treasures abused, themselves triumphed over, and never
overthrown? ... *Since the country was theirs* and that the government was
an adherent to the country, why should they that needed not be
partakers with the cause of the danger? (pp. 111–12; my emphasis)

The commons reason that only direct action can serve their cause as events have gone too far for persuasion or political discussion.

The crucial phrase is 'Since the country was theirs', which implies a straightforward contract theory of sovereignty, the government being simply 'an adherent to the country', ie, metonymically, the people who occupy the land.[87] As usual, the reader has to ask whether this is being advocated by Sidney, or whether it is undercut by a number of ironies. It is no good appealing to Sidney's intellectual milieu for an answer because he could have acquired conflicting notions from a variety of sources: Machiavelli, the radical Protestantism of Christopher Goodman, Jean Bodin.[88] Commenting on the effect of Cleophila/Pyrocles' appearance on the crowd, the narrator appears to condemn them: 'the goodness of her shape, with that quiet magnanimity represented in her face in this uttermost peril, did even fix the eyes of the *barbarous* people with admiration for her' (p.113; my emphasis). By referring to the people as 'barbarous', Sidney's narrator employs a discourse of civilised/savage, one which distinguishes between those inside the boundaries of the state, acceptable, cultured natives and those outside who threaten to break down these barriers and so bring about chaos, whether they be exotic Indians, Irish, or, as in this case, the lower classes: 'one man's tinker is another man's Indian'.[89] Arcadia is part of Greece, but a knowledge of the Greek etymology of 'barbarian' ('foreigner') is not necessary to appreciate that the narrator is answering the question of the Arcadian commons by effectively excluding them from the public life of the nation, denying that they have a right to be *zoon politikon*.[90]

But this by no means exhausts the problems of contextualisation: just because the commons are excluded does not mean that they are always wrong or their ideas never to be taken into account (Sir Thomas Smith's distinction, see above, p.97). Cleophila/Pyrocles assures the crowd that 'In this harmless lodge there are harboured no Trojans, your ancient enemies; nor Persians, whom you have in present fear' (p.114). Katherine Duncan-Jones notes that this is 'not a well-developed theme', but the point is perhaps more of a topical than a narrative nature.[91] The commons have no reason to know that they are not being betrayed, especially given the fact that, unknown to them, they are being addressed by a foreign prince in drag. Does s/he have any more right to their country than they do? Does Queen Elizabeth have the right to give over the fate of the nation she rules to a French prince in the teeth of popular opposition?[92]

The episode ends harmlessly enough with the rebels dispersing having been persuaded by Cleophila/Pyrocles' speech that they have really been displaying excess affection for the duke and that he will thus choose to pardon them. It is quite likely that the incident is intended to amuse its aristocratic audience, demonstrating the absurd fickleness of the multitude even when they are potentially dangerous and have a serious point to make (when government is based solely on the private matters of its rulers, hidden from the public and so beyond their knowledge and control, how can ordinary citizens feel at ease and trust that future events will be planned in their interest?). As the crowd drift away some still feel disgruntled and their looks of disappointment and dismay demonstrate that for them the outcome is 'but a sheeps draught' (p.115), ie, a bitter medicine. A few dozen others wait even after the duke has issued a general pardon, 'where they kept themselves to see how the pardon should be observed; where feeding wildly upon grass and such other food, drinking only water, they were well disciplined from their drunken riot' (p.116). Mesmerised by authority, these members of the 'many-headed multitude' have ceased to be rebels and have become sheep.[93]

In the *New Arcadia* the episode has been altered quite dramatically. No explanation is offered for the sudden attack of the mob:

Yet before they could win the lodge by twenty paces, they were overtaken by the unruly sort of clowns and other rebels which, like a violent flood, were carried they themselves knew not whither. But as soon as they came within perfect discerning these ladies, like enraged beasts, without respect of their estates or pity of their sex, they began to run against them, as right villains thinking ability to do hurt to be a great advancement; yet so many as they were, so many almost were their minds, all knit together in madness. (p.280)[94]

The description and imagery serve to demonise the crowd: they are 'enraged beasts' out of control in their collective madness unable to influence the course of events they have set in motion because they have no idea what they are doing. This provides a neat link with the irresponsible behaviour of Basilius in consulting the oracle and so creating the problems which the narrative of the *Arcadia* has to resolve; but it also serves to empty the episode of its political content.[95] They are unable to distinguish between rank or sex – something which would severely hamper any aspiring Elizabethan courtier – and are similarly indistinguishable as individuals, quite unlike the crowd in the *Old Arcadia*.

Violence is legion in the revised version, and the humour is viciously spiteful in a manner alien to the joke about the sheep in the original.[96] Whilst that could be read as ambiguous in its effect, criticising commoners for being sheep and nobles for making them, and thus implying that change might be possible and desirable, the wit of the *New Arcadia* is designed to dehumanise and maim:

'Oh,' said a miller that was half drunk, 'see the luck of a good fellow,' and with that word ran with a pitchfork at Dorus; but the nimbleness of the wine carried his head so fast that it made it over-run his feet, so that he fell withal just between the legs of Dorus, who, setting his foot on his neck (though he offered two milch kine and four fat hogs for his life) thrust his sword quite through from one ear to the other; which took it very unkindly, to feel such news before they heard of them, instead of hearing, to be put to such feeling. But Dorus, leaving the miller to vomit his soul out in wine and blood, with his two-handed sword strake off another quite by the waist who the night before had dreamed he was grown a couple, and, interpreting it that he should be married, had bragged of his dream that morning among his neighbours. (pp.281–2)

Such 'cruel laughter' serves to dismiss out of hand the peasant revolt and the entire episode has seemingly been re-written in order to efface the original ambiguity and political edge.[97] Sidney's wit is designed to exclude non-noble readers rather

than include them as the *Old Arcadia* did. The rebels no longer
have a cause and the comments about 'the weak-headed trust of
the many-headed multitude' are now spoken by Clinias, a
cowardly and corrupt servant of Basilius' sister-in-law, Cecropia, working as an *agent provocateur*, rather than the narrator.
What in the *Old Arcadia* possibly implied that the rebels should
have stuck to their guns in the *New Arcadia* serves merely to
reveal the base motives of the speaker.

Whilst this crucial incident has been severely bowdlerised in
its expansions, the addition of other incidents which move the
narrative sideways rather than forwards suggests that Sidney's
revisions might have been prompted by more than simply
formal or aesthetic judgements.[98] The *New Arcadia* opens with
Musidorus shipwrecked in Laconia and being led to Arcadia by
the two shepherds, Strephon and Claius; as in the *Old Arcadia*,
the reader is invited to compare Arcadia to Elizabeth's England,
but the opening words of the original are now spoken by the
gentleman, Kalander. Two consecutive paragraphs contrast
Arcadia and Laconia: whilst Arcadia can boast happy shepherds, suffers no distinction between city and country and is
'thus decked with peace (and the child of peace) good
husbandry', Laconia is barren, not through a natural deficiency
but because of 'a civil war, which being these two years within
the bowels of that estate between the gentlemen and the
peasants (by them named Helots) hath in this sort as it were
disfigured the face of nature' (p.11). Jon Lawry's comment that
Laconia, as the enemy of Arcadia, signifies 'the condition to
which Arcadia may slide if she indulges in her own rebellious
passions' is surely apt, given the rhetorical paralleling of the two
descriptions.[99] Emphasis falls on the class basis of the civil war
which corrupts the natural fertility of the land; although the
capture of Cliophon and Argalus by the Helots is the event
which leads to a struggle between the Arcadians and the Helots,
the solution to the conflict secured by Pyrocles, disguised as
Diaphantus, is wholly in favour of the oppressed Helots who are
to be made free men, 'and so capable both to give and receive
voice in the election of magistrates', all children are to be
brought up under the same Spartan system of education, and

the distinction between the aristocracy (Lacedemons) and the peasants (Helots) is to be abolished. The Helots are told to forget the past 'since the cause of war is finished', love the Lacedemons like brothers whom they previously hated as oppressors and, most significantly, 'to take care of their estate *because it is yours*' (p.41; my emphasis). The sentiment of the last phrase echoes that of the rebel Arcadians who assert that the country is theirs.

Irving Ribner's suggestion that the war represents 'not a rebellion against tyranny within a state, but rather the struggle of a conquered people who had formerly been free to overthrow its conquerors and regain its lost liberty' and that the war in Sparta refers to 'the struggle of the Netherlands against Spain' is, in many ways, an attractive and persuasive one. However, it is a reading which relies on the *Arcadia* being an inflexible allegory and it is impossible to fit the fictional events to the course of the war (who would Cliophon and Argalus, Arcadians fighting for the Lacedemons stand for?).[100] More seriously, such a reading ignores the deliberate merging of estates and the forgetting of a history which includes the very names which distinguish national/political/social identities. The reading of the episode against the domestic rebellion in the *New Arcadia* and the overtly political description of that event in the *Old Arcadia* perhaps leads to the conclusion that the exploratory Utopian fiction contained in the original has been transferred from a domestic setting to an international one. The Helots are integrated into the public sphere of the new imagined community of the nation because the country is theirs as well now. Pyrocles/Zelmane informs the rebellious Arcadians that if their fellow subjects are allowed to displace the present royal dynasty the result will be tyranny because 'the innate meanness will bring forth ravenous covetousness and the newness of his estate, suspectful cruelty'. He also argues that 'there could be no government without a magistrate, and no magistrate without obedience, and no obedience where everyone upon his own private passion may interpret the doings of rulers' (p.286). Such a comment resembles the arguments and style of such works as *The Homily Against Disobedience and Wilful Rebellion* (1571) or

John Cheke's *The Hurt of Sedition* (1549), but that does not mean that Pyrocles/Zelmane/Cleophila is right and Pyrocles/Diaphantus wrong.[101] The latter emphasises the need for estates to merge and the general responsibility for the appointment of magistrates; the former emphasises the inevitable hierarchy of class society. In the *New Arcadia* an episode of ambiguous, possibly subversive, political significance is replaced by a series of related and verbally connected episodes. Ironically, Sparta, which virtually disappears from the narrative after Book 1, chapter 7, is arguably a potentially more stable political entity than Arcadia, which places the flattering comparison between Arcadia and Elizabethan England in a harsher light.[102]

Both versions demonstrate an extreme anxiety regarding the form of public/national political participation and representation which is never clearly resolved and which prevents the *Arcadia* from taking the strong didactic stance of the *Mirror*. The aristocratic rebellion led by Amphialus in Book 3 is roundly condemned, but it does not raise the constitutional issues that the commons' revolt or the Spartan War does because the motives of Amphialus are no more praiseworthy than those of the *agent provocateur*, Cecropia (indeed, they are part of the same plot).[103] More prominent as obvious political comments are the struggles Musidorus and Pyrocles have with foreign tyrants: Plexitus, Tiridates and the king of Phrygia.[104] These additions also seem to be designed to deflect serious political discussion from the domestic arena but make it available for the alert reader who can then perceive the disguised connection. To take but one obvious example: the description of the sycophantic courtiers who attend the king of Phrygia could well have come from the pen of an Elizabethan satirist:

[A]ccursed sycophants, of all men, did best sort to his [the king's] nature; but therefore not seeming sycophants, because of no evil they said, they could bring any new or doubtful thing unto him but such as already he had been apt to determine, so as they came but as proofs of his wisdom: fearful, and never secure, while the fear he had figured in his mind had any possibility of event: a toad-like retiredness and closeness of mind, nature teaching the odiousness of poison and the danger of odiousness. (pp.169–70)[105]

Such a court causes extreme anxiety in its courtiers (it may apply to Sidney's own perilous position, or that of his family); it suppresses all political discussion and so leaves the subject, whether aristocratic or common, with the stark choice of obedience or rebellion.[106] The king, suitably enough, comes to a sticky end.[107]

As Annabel Patterson has argued, '[t]hat actual censorship was on Sidney's mind as the *Old Arcadia* took shape seems indisputable'. At the heart of the work he placed a beast-fable loosely based on the Aesopian tale of *The Frogs Desiring a King*, which serves as a 'metafable', suggesting that 'the theory of monarchy's acceptance is dependent on two conflicting premises, divine origin and that particular version of contract theory that supposes a people, initially capable of self-government, consenting to transfer the common sovereignty to a single figure'.[108] The fable tells how the animals, despite the harmony of their lives in ancient times, desire to be ruled by a king. They petition Jove, who agrees, but warns them that 'Rulers will think all things made them to please,/ And soon forget the swink due to their hire', and after a parade of each creature's talents, man is chosen. Initially he includes every creature in his decisions, 'Not in his sayings saying "I" but "we";/ As if he meant his lordship common be'; eventually, however, man rules by dividing up his subjects into competing factions so that a hierarchy is established, excluding the majority of creatures from the decisions of government.[109] The warning of the last stanza is directly aimed at the abuse of power and suppression of debate:

> But yet, O man, rage not beyond thy need;
> Deeme it no gloire to swell in tyranny.
> Thou art of blood; joy not to make things bleed.
> Thou fearest death; think they are loath to die.
> A plaint of guiltless hurt doth pierce the sky.
> And you, poor beasts, in patience bide your hell,
> Or know your strengths, and then you shall do well.

The contradictory nature of the problem has resulted in a tyrannous authority which pays as little respect to freedom of speech as the court of the king of Phrygia. The sharing of political responsibility, reminiscent of the hopes for the post-civil war Spartan state, has given way to its antithesis. Once again, the stark choice for citizens is between quietism and the possibility of direct action. Such direct criticism of censorship and suppression gives way to the 'arcane representation' of the *New Arcadia*, a far harder text for the reader to decode.[110]

One of the rebels mutilated during the ferocious onslaught of Pyrocles/Zelmane and Musidorus/Dorus, is 'a poor painter', standing by and holding a pike:

This painter was to counterfeit the skirmish between the Centaurs and Lapithes, and had been very desirous to see some notable wounds, to be able the more lively to express them; and this morning, being carried by the stream of this company, the foolish fellow was even delighted to see the effect of blows. But this last, happening near him, so amazed him that he stood stock still, while Dorus, with a turn of his sword, strake off both his hands. And so the painter returned well skilled in wounds, but with never a hand to perform his skill. (p.282)

Both Edward Berry and Stephen Greenblatt have provided illuminating readings of this incident, noting the painter's vocational affiliation with Sidney as an artist. Both have also stated that Sidney affirms a crucial distance between himself and the painter: for Berry, the painter is too inept aesthetically, socially (he is poor) and politically (he holds a pike and thus supports the rebellion) to 'awaken the nation' and so stands in the way of good art which will perform this function; for Greenblatt, Sidney 'attacks the professional as opposed to the amateur', mutilating the artist by cutting off his hands in symbolic punishment.[111] Both assume that the painter is a bad comic artist, principally because his desire to see a reality ('some notable wounds') before he 'counterfeits' the Ovidian story of the battle between the Centaurs and Lapithes goes against Sidney's statement concerning the zodiac of poets' wits (see above, p.137).[112] The problem with such interpretations is that we do not know what the painter had intended to paint before he lost the means of representation; observing an extra-fictional world does not mean that the artist has to be bound by these observations when representing a fictional one. If we conjecture that in revising the *Arcadia* Sidney felt obliged – or was forced – to transfer some of his political statements and explorations, then it may be that the painter without hands resembles a gagged Sidney whose aesthetic work has been mutilated.

That the *Arcadia* became 'a site of class conflict during the Civil War' is hardly surprising; Sidney's sense of a nation and a public in this and other works is elastic and by no means consistent, varying between an inclusive and an exclusive notion of political representation.[113] Greville's famous statement that

in all these creatures of his making, his intent, and scope was, to turn the barren philosophy into pregnant images of life; and in them, first on the Monarch's part, lively to represent the growth, state, and declination of Princes, change of Government, and lawes: vicissitudes of sedition, faction, succession, confederacies, plantations, with all other errors, or alterations in publique affaires. Then again in the subjects case; the state of favor, disfavor, prosperitie, adversity, emulation, quarrell, undertaking, retiring, hospitality, travail, and all other modes of private fortunes, or misfortunes.[114]

acknowledges that Sidney was concerned with both governors and governed and the problematic relationship between them in the *Arcadia*, implying that the 'pregnant images of life' are as much about political as aesthetic representation. The statement also confirms that to look for one coherent strand of political thinking in Sidney's writings is to ignore the experimental and exploratory nature of the criticism and fiction. Sidney seems to be arguing that literature must possess a certain autonomy if it is to serve as the form of national self-definition and not fall prey to the flattering nonsense of poet-apes rather than the truth of poets. Poets cannot be treated as the 'poor painter' was if this is to happen.[115]

Sidney's work can be seen to follow on from the concerns of the *Mirror*, but whilst that text was always intended for publication, his writings were only printed after his death and circulated in manuscript to a limited, familiar audience. The reasons for this are not clear and may have had as much to do with the fear of censorship as the traditional assumption that Sidney thought publication beneath a gentleman.[116] We still know very little about the relationship between manuscript and print culture in the late sixteenth century; but certainly by the late seventeenth century an elaborate cat and mouse game between censors and writers of fiction in manuscript had developed and it is by no means unlikely that Sidney either operated within a similar mode of literary production or calculated that he could speak more truthfully if he avoided print.[117] Nevertheless, the effect was that unlike the *Mirror* and Spenser's writings, Sidney's work addressed a tiny public sphere until his death helped to create a legend and his writings went into print to eclipse his unsuccessful career as a would-be statesman.[118] At last, Sidney became the national figure he had always wanted to be.

CHAPTER 6

'*Who knowes not Colin Clout?*' *The permanent exile of Edmund Spenser*

If Sidney's perception of the importance of his own literary output and the status of his self-appointed role as a poet of national significance are patently ambiguous and difficult to determine, the same cannot be said for his exact contemporary, Edmund Spenser. Richard Helgerson has argued that Spenser was the only one of his generation of poets who had the talent and ambition to claim to be a national laureate and that in his representation of himself as the shepherd, Colin Clout, he illustrated that he had no sense of abandoning an alternative career in order to become a poet.[1] According to Helgerson, different rules applied to the aristocratic Sidney who demonstrated rather more amateurish attitudes towards his poetry, delighting in its pleasurable rhetoric rather than its persuasive truth. It was Spenser's approach to his work which was to prevail in the forthcoming years as society ceased to be dominated by those possessing hereditary wealth and consequently a new literary ethos developed.

Helgerson's analysis merits serious consideration but is questionable in terms of its teleological and over-schematic distinctions. It is by no means clear that the writers of the *Mirror* did not regard themselves as professional writers and abjure the rhetorical *an sich* Helgerson locates in the works of courtly authors; John Bale certainly took his role as national literary historian seriously and tried to expunge rhetorical copia from his own literary works – whether he put the two tasks together is debatable. It might seem that Helgerson is yet another critic guilty of a blindness to the complexities of literary history in reading back the situation of writers in the 1570s and 1580s into the first seventy years of the century. He cites Spenser's oft-quoted line, 'who knowes not Colin Clout?' (*Faerie Queene*, VI, X, 16) as evidence that Spenser knew he had made himself famous in this literary guise. But Spenser's adoption of Skelton's most celebrated mask is both fraught with ironies and could in fact be used to undermine Helgerson's argument that the rise of the professional poet took place between 1570 and 1590. Firstly, Skelton, as I have argued in chapter 1, crowned himself as the English laureate seemingly determined to displace and assimilate all previous poetic models in English. Spenser, who was unlikely not to have had an opportunity to familiarise himself with Skelton's ambition, variety of styles and self-appointed national status given the publication of the *Pithy, Pleasant and Profitable Workes of Master Skelton, Poet Laureate* (1568), is apparently acknowledging a precursor. Secondly, Helgerson's attempt to read the question as self-evidently rhetorical is not secure. In the 'Mutabilitie Cantos' Jove and the goddess Mutability agree to be judged by Nature in a debate on Arlo Hill. The narrator asks exactly the same question, 'Who knows not Arlo Hill?' (VII, VI, 36). It seems unlikely that anyone outside Spenser's immediate neighbours on the Munster Plantation where he made his home in the late 1580s would have recognised the poet's mythological sobriquet for Galtymore, a small peak in the Galty mountains, visible from Spenser's house at Kilcolman castle.[2] This would suggest that the question could have been read as ironic in intent, isolating a small group of addressees with local knowledge, ie, English settlers on the Munster Plantation, who could answer in the affirmative, unlike a courtly audience back in London.[3] The use of the negative form of the interrogative places the emphasis on this larger group, deliberately highlighting their ignorance of the poet's status as an Englishman in provincial Ireland.

In the same way, asking who does not know Colin Clout operates to separate those who knew Spenser's earlier career and adoption of this particular persona from those who had not read his work; those who were aware of *their* English literary history from those who either were not or thought they were (but were not). Given Spenser's bitter comments on his life in

Ireland recorded in *Colin Clouts Come Home Againe* (see below), it seems that those who could answer the question would have known how alienated the author had declared himself from the centres of power and the rewards distributed therefrom. If one really knew who Colin Clout was (assuming that Spenser did), one would know that what was being heard was an aggressive oppositional voice directed against the court in the name of a common people.[4] To put it another way, the posing of the question at a key point in the narrative of *The Faerie Queene* – the only appearance of Colin Clout in the poem – could be taken to denote the author's sense of his own obscurity rather than his popularity.

In *Colin Clout*, Skelton appears to have turned to the London commons as an audience to replace his lost patronage at court.[5] They are refigured as a national community, directly addressed towards the end of the poem by the poet, who adopts the first person plural to draw in his audience and set them against the aristocratic clerical figure of Wolsey:

> He sayes that we are recheles,
> And full of wylfulness,
> Shameles, and mercyles,
> Incorrigible and insatiate;
> And after this rate
> Agaynst us doth prate ...
> Howe we wyll rule all at wyll
> Without good reason or skyll;
> And say howe that we be
> Full of parcyallyte;
> And howe at a pronge
> We tourne ryght into wronge ...
>
> Howe may we thus endure?
> Wherfore we make you sure,
> Ye prechers shall be yawde [cut down].
>   (lines 1176–1204)

Spenser, writing in Ireland and acutely conscious of his distance from the court, was also aware of the different audiences who might read his work and who might be addressed by the poet. His questions, unlike Skelton's, deliberately divide reading communities rather than appealing to one against another. The Latin epitaph to *Colin Clout* reasserts a unified national identity the appeal to which actually serves to construct and hold together the figure of the poet:

> Lingua nocere parat, quia, quanquam rustica canto,
> Undique cantabor tamen et celebrator ubique,
> Inclina dum maneat gens Anglica. Lauris honoris,
> Quondam regnorum regina et gloria regum,
> Heu, modo marcesit, tabescit, languida torpet!
> Ah, pudet! Ah miseret! Vetor hic ego pandere plura
> Pro gemitu et lacrimis; prestet peto premia pena.
>
> (lines 5–11)

Although the envious tongue is prepared to injure me, because, although I sing rustic songs, nevertheless, I shall be sung and celebrated everywhere while the famous English race remains. At one time the laurel crown of honour, the queen of realms, and the glory of kings; alas, how feeble it grows, how it wastes away, how sluggishly it becomes inert. Ah, how shameful! Ah, how deplorable! I can expound no more of these things here because of sighing and tears; I pray that the rewards may justify the pain.

In this illocutionary act, *Colin Clout* resembles the *Laurel*; but the implied readership is different.[6] Spenser's acknowledgement of an audience split between those who know and those who do not, can be taken as paradigmatic of many developments between the lives of the two men; a recognition that a unified national community was no longer possible after the Reformation (ironically, an event often regarded by historians as a necessary cause of the rise of nationalism);[7] an understanding that an attempt to rule over a 'multiple kingdom' meant that Elizabeth, 'the Faerie Queene' referred to at the start of the poem in the letter to Raleigh published in the first edition, would possess subjects with fiercely divided loyalties; a realisation that a colonial official in Ireland was no longer simply 'mere' English.[8] If Spenser did become a national laureate, his legacy is even more complex than Skelton's and demonstrates the simultaneous existence and overlap of different interpretative communities. To some readers Spenser was part of the mainstream of an English literary tradition which rivalled the ancients and included Sidney, Daniel, Jonson, Drayton and Marlowe; to others he represented a politically radical Protestant tradition whose poetry – if read correctly – contained the possibility of resistance and hints for effective action; in Ireland he was reviled as part of an oppressive class by many yet his writings also helped to forge the identity of the 'New' English (English colonists and administrators who went to Ireland in the sixteenth century).[9]

Spenser's position had not always been so problematic and his audiences so conspicuously fragmented. His first two literary experiments were far more confident performances. *The Shepheardes Calender* succeeded in inaugurating 'a revolution in English poetry'.[10] Its physical form, the poem accompanied with a whole panoply of explanations, glosses and commentary so that it appeared as 'a fictional imitation of a humanist edition of classical texts', suggested that this was a deliberate ploy.[11] Simultaneously, Spenser and Gabriel Harvey published their two editions of letters to highlight the iconoclastic force and literary designs of those connected with the Earl of Leicester.[12] In essence they were designed as self-promotional manifestos.[13]

Much of the discussion contained in the letters concerns the reform of English metre and the possibility of writing English verse in classical hexameters with Harvey and Spenser both commenting on each other's literary innovations and experiments.[14] Spenser praises Harvey's hexameters which, he judges, 'neither so harde, nor so harshe, that it will easily and fairely, yeelde it selfe to oure Mother Tongue'.[15] He states that the real obstacle to the adoption of such classical syllabic forms in English is not the result of an intrinsic linguistic incompatibility, the ancient language stubbornly resisting translation into the modern, but rather, owing to a faulty accent, 'whyche sometime gapeth, and as it were yawneth ilfavouredly, comming shorte of that it should, and sometime exceeding the measure of the Number'. The passage concludes, 'it is to be wonne with Custome, and rough words must be subdued with Use. For, why a Gods name may not we, as else the Greekes, have the kingdome of oure owne Language, and measure our Accentes, by the sounde, reserving the Quantitie to the Verse' (p.611).

This is an extraordinarily ambitious analysis for a poet who, as yet, had only published translations of Petrarch and Du Bellay in Jan Van Der Noot's *A Theatre for Voluptuous Worldlings* (1569) whilst still at school (although we do not know what circulated in manuscript). Spenser equates his and Harvey's experiments with government over '*oure* owne language' (mother tongue); the metaphor of regal power ('kingedome') explicitly equates his role as poet with that of the secular monarch, a divided notion of authority which was to shadow his whole career.[16] The humanist project outlined here – modelling a contemporary vernacular on a classical language – reduces the resistance of the native medium to a minimal series of customs which can be eradicated without difficulty so that English can be made to resemble Greek if transformed by a sufficiently powerful poetic authority.[17]

However, it would appear that *The Shepheardes Calender* contradicts this project of rendering English effectively invisible and reducing it to a window through which to gain access to Greek culture. The typographical layout of the poem was startlingly innovative in that no original English poetry had ever appeared before 'as the central element in a tripartite unit of verse, scholarly apparatus and freshly designed woodcuts' and it is hard to believe that E. K.'s glosses – whatever their inadequacies as interpretations of the poem – were not designed as integral elements of the 'literary artefact'.[18] E. K.'s prefatory letter to Harvey and glosses resemble the form and style of the published Spenser-Harvey correspondence which serves to mark out both texts as products of a literary avant-garde.[19] Yet each can be read as representative of the two mutually contradictory impulses resulting from a humanist education.[20] Whilst the letters emphasise the transparency of English as a medium and its ability to ventriloquise Greek, the *Calender* roots its sense of the past in a vernacular now lost from sight in current English:

For in my opinion it is one special prayse, of many whych are dew to this Poete, that he hath laboured to restore, as to theyr rightfull heritage such good and naturall English words, as have ben long time out of use and almost clene disherited ... Other some not so wel seene

in the English tonge as perhaps in other languages, if they happen to
here an olde word albeit very naturall and significant, crye out streight
way, that we speak no English, but gibbrish, or rather such, as in olde
time Evanders mother spake. Whose first shame is, that they are not
ashamed, in their own mother tonge straungers to be counted and
alienes. (p.417).[21]

In the poem, classical examples are always placed at least one
remove from the present the text signifies.[22] The presence of
Chaucer underpins and surrounds the work, framing the year in
which the text exists and gesturing towards a historical time
scale which is essentially English. E. K. points out at the start of
his letter that 'our Colin Clout' calls Chaucer, Tityrus, 'the god
of shepherds' in his last eclogue, 'comparing him to the
worthines of the Roman Tityrus, Virgile' (p.416). Spenser,
whom E. K. claims 'secretly shadoweth himself' as Colin Clout
in his first eclogue, is announcing a desire to be the great poet of
English nation building through the invocation of the figure
who unites both classical Rome and the matter of Britain and
who started his career with humble pastorals.[23] The reliance
upon a distinct vernacular serves to emphasise the distance and
difference from Virgil's Rome as well as acknowledging a
model. E. K.'s rather sly joke – as if Spenser did not want his
ambitions to be declared and had intended the allegory to
escape all readers – is perhaps another imitation of Chaucer
who often distanced himself from the Italian humanist culture
of Dante, Boccaccio and Petrarch by means of deliberately
incongruous pastiche.[24]

However, in the January eclogue the figure adopted, Colin
Clout, is shown to be in a state of deep dejection over his
frustrated suit for Rosalinde, which hardly suggests a tri-
umphant inauguration into an arrogant literary career. In his
gloss E. K. observes that Colin Clout 'is a name not greatly used
and yet have I sene a Poesie of M. Skelton's under that title'.
Again, it is quite probable that this comment is not without its
ironic humour: readers who were familiar with Skelton's works
would have known that the invocation of Colin Clout signalled
an oppositional voice of national identity divorced from the life
of the court. Given the co-option of Skelton by radical

Protestant writers from the middle of the sixteenth century onwards, enough textual signs are given to mark out the *Calender* as a work of aggressive polemical intent: it was dedicated to Sir Philip Sidney, well known by this time as a leading Protestant courtier in favour of a more interventionist foreign policy, a severe critic of the queen's proposed marriage to Alençon and obviously sought out by writers of a like persuasion as Gosson's *Schoole of Abuse*, published in the same year as the *Calender*, illustrates; E. K.'s letter to Harvey and the references to him in the glosses further cement this political allegiance to the Leicester circle (to say nothing of the *Letters*); the poem bore the imprint of Hugh Singleton, famous as a printer of radical Protestant propaganda who had first flourished under the protectorship of Somerset and whose most recent and notorious venture had been to publish John Stubbs's attack on the projected Alençon marriage, *Discoverie of a Gaping Gulf* (1579), for which act he had only just avoided the severing of the right hand meted out to Stubbs.[25] The text, having instructed the reader to regard Spenser as the English Virgil, immediately casts him as a disaffected and disillusioned shepherd paralysed by his 'unfortunate love'. Although Colin's lady is called Rosalinde, 'a countrey lasse', the reader is encouraged to interpret allegorically by E. K.'s gloss: 'Rosalinde is also a feigned name, which being wel ordered, wil bewray the very name of hys love and mistresse, whom by that name he coloureth' (pp.422–3). E. K. then furnishes a list of classical and contemporary examples of this practice: Ovid called his love Coryanna, possibly Julia, daughter of Augustus; in Statius' 'Epithalamium', Violantilla is called Lady Astens and Ianthis; 'the famous Paragone of Italy, Madonna Coelia' called herself Zima in her letters and (the unidentified) Petrona called herself Bellochia.[26] E. K.'s refusal or inability to provide an allegorical identification whilst drawing the reader's attention to the existence of one (a common feature of his glosses), the national ambitions announced in his letter to Harvey and the widespread currency of such conventions as a courtly game of flattery signifying the relationship between the queen and a suitor, alert the reader to the possibility that Rosalinde stands for Elizabeth and that her rejection of him has caused his melancholy.[27] The provision of an interpretative framework which appears to be independent of the author – but could hardly have occurred without his sanction – enables Spenser to distance himself from such readings whilst clearly inviting them. This particular gloss highlights Ovid and his relationship to Augustus; whereas Virgil became the national poet of the Roman Empire, his younger contemporary was exiled by Augustus. The *Calender* thus invokes these two opposing classical authorities and situates itself in relation to both of them. Spenser's ambition may be Virgilian but his situation is Ovidian.[28] In the woodcut accompanying the eclogue (figure 1) Colin is depicted heading away from a city towards which he casts a wistful glance, his sheep in disarray behind him. The last lines describe his weary journey *home*:

> By that, the welked *Phoebus* gan availe,
> His weary waine, and nowe the frosty *Night*
> Her mantle black through heaven gan overhaile
> Which seene, the pensive boy halfe in despight
> Arose, and homeward drove his sonned sheepe,
> Whose hanging heads did seeme his carefull case to weepe.
>
> (lines 73–8)

Throughout the eclogue clues are provided to support a reading which emphasises that Colin's despair may not be due simply to an unsuccessful love suit. The narrator describes him as 'pale and wanne ... / May seeme he lovd, or els some care he tooke' (lines 8–9), which signals that just as the names of the characters are often disguised so may be their actions. Later, Colin directly addresses his flock to apologise for his neglect:

> Thou feeble flocke, whose fleece is rough and rent,
> Whose knees are weake through fast and evill fare:
> Mayst witnesse well by thy ill government,
> Thy maysters mind is overcome with care.
> Thou weake, I wanne: thou leane, I quite forlorne:
> With mourning pyne I, you with pyning mourne.
>
> (lines 43–8)

We have to ask what is figurative and what is literal in this stanza. Does the use of the word 'government' serve as a

. IANVARIE.

Edmund Spenser, *The Shepheardes Calender*, woodcut accompanying 'January eclogue', in *Works* (1611).

metonymic detail within a metaphoric (allegorical) discourse, sustaining the fictional nature of the shepherd's world which really refers to the frustrated courtship of Rosalinde's hidden identity? Or, does it return us to a discourse of the real, ironically reversing the metaphor of the shepherd in love and thus shattering the illusion of the fictional world? Ultimately, the ill government of the sheep is the result of Rosalinde's treatment of Colin and no Elizabethan reader could possibly have been ignorant of the use of sheep in pastoral poetry as a metaphor for the ordinary people whether as church-goers, citizens or both, which would lead us to the second reading.[29] A further clue might be rather obliquely provided in E. K.'s gloss on the word 'couthe', which he defines as derived from the verb 'Conne', meaning 'to know or to have skill' and comments that this interpretation is made by 'the worthy Sir Tho. Smith in his booke of government: wherof I have a perfect copie in writing, lent me by his kinesman, and my verye singular good freend, M.

Gabriel Harvey: as also of some other his most grave and excellent wrytings' (p.422). The gloss refers to the line 'Well couth he tune his pipe, and frame his stile' (line 10), which therefore provides an explicit link between the art of poetry and the art of government, suggesting that Spenser as Colin can teach the reader both arts through his poetry in the *Calender*. Smith was yet another member of the Leicester circle, so an informed reader would have expected Colin's political judgements to be Protestant and critical of Elizabeth; the work referred to here, *De Republica Anglorum*, written in the 1560s but not published until 1583, was a political anatomy of England which circulated widely in manuscript.[30] E. K. is possibly hinting that the *Calender* is its literary counterpart.

Colin significantly complains that his poetry is not approved of by Rosalinde:

> I love thilke lasse, (alas why doe I love?)
> And am forlorne, (alas why am I lorne?)
> Shee deignes not my good will, but does reprove,
> And of my rurall musick holdeth scorne.
> Shepheardes devise she hateth as the snake,
> And laughes the songes, that *Colin Clout* doth make.
>
> (lines 61–6)

Why does Rosalinde scorn the rural music and the 'Shepheardes devise'? Is it because she does not think it is interesting or competent poetry (a literal reading)? Or, is it because she is afraid of the devices of pastoral poetry, its veiled political references and frequently oppositional stance (an allegorical reading)?[31] Yet again, the reader has to negotiate between what is fictional or allegorical and what is literal.

Colin ends the eclogue deciding to give up poetry and breaks his pipe because although it pleases Pan, it 'pleaseth not, where most I would' (line 68). Various interpretations of this act have been provided; what is clear is that the pseudo-decision to cease writing poetry – for Colin ends the cycle just as he began it (something E. K. notes in his summary of the argument to the December eclogue) – signals the exile of Colin Clout from the favours of Rosalinde.[32] The poem reverses the situation of the

first eclogue of Virgil, thus inaugurating an Ovidian motif as I
have already noted. There, Tityrus, happy in his Arcadian
pastoral, is confronted by Meliboeus who has been ousted from
his farm and forced into exile by the Roman authorities. Whilst
Tityrus can, according to Meliboeus, 'lie there at ease under the
awning of a spreading beech and practise country songs on a
light shepherds pipe ... teaching the woods to echo back the
charms of Amaryllis', Meliboeus tells his goats that 'There will
be no more songs from me.'[33] Tityrus is free because he had the
good fortune to travel to Rome and purchase his freedom from
serfdom; his old love Galatea, under whose sway he had felt no
desire to alter his status, had thrown him over and he had given
his heart to the more forceful Amaryllis.

In Spenser's eclogue it is Colin himself who is exiled; whilst
Tityrus is saved by his romantic attachments, Colin is ruined by
his; whilst Tityrus continues to play his songs, Colin abandons
his; whilst Tityrus is at home and at ease enough to offer his
departing neighbour a bed for the night and a meal from his
home-grown produce, Colin abuses the gifts of kids, biscuits and
fruit from his male suitor, Hobbinol, to further his own hopeless
suit with Rosalinde. Both poems acknowledge that the place of
the poet in the pastoral scene depends upon the game of
patronage played out in the city; Virgil's in the journey Tityrus
makes to Rome, a city which 'stands out above all other cities
as the cypress soars above the drooping undergrowth', Spenser's
in Colin's disastrous visit:

> A thousand sithes I curse that carefull hower,
> Wherein I longd the neighbour towne to see:
> And eke tenne thousand sithes I blesse the stoure,
> Wherein I sawe so fayre a sight, as shee.
> Yet all for naught: such sight hath bred my bane.
> Ah God, that love should breede both joy and payne.
>
> (lines 49–54)

Tityrus's visit enables him to stay where he is whereas Colin's
makes him want to change places: the turned head of the
shepherd in the accompanying woodcut as he sets off in the
opposite direction signifies his frustrated desire. The one journey

serves to prevent exile and to preserve a home, the other leads to the perception that home is exile.

Virgil's *Eclogues*, like Spenser's, demand to be read within a paradigm of nationalist discourse. Meliboeus provides a long list of the benefits accruing to him who stays within the boundaries of state and Tityrus responds with a series of hyperbolic and absurd negative comparisons to emphasise his gratitude to the patron who sold him his land: 'stags must take wing and feed in the upper air; the sea roll back and leave her fishes high and dry; nations go wandering across each other's lands, and Germans drink in exile from the Tigris, or Parthians from the Saône – before the memory of my patron's gracious look could vanish from my heart' (p.23). Tityrus's cultural memory emphatically inscribes him as a patriot, a lover of local knowledge; the images of the chaos which would follow a change of state include both the breaking-up of nations and their transformation into nomadic peoples, and the barbarian (German) invasion of Italy. Meliboeus realises that he has to face the anarchy Tityrus has cleverly avoided: 'meanwhile the rest of us are off; some to foregather with the Africans and share their thirst; others to Scythia, and out to where the Oxus rolls the chalk along; others to join the Britons, cut off as they are by the whole width of the world' (p.23). He explicitly links the establishment of 'home' to the continuity of the nation in his lament that he may never see his 'little *realm*' (my emphasis) again and is painfully aware of the reason for the harsh reality of his exile: 'Is some blaspheming soldier to own these acres I have broken up and tilled so well – a foreigner to reap these splendid fields of corn? Look at the misery to which we have sunk since Romans took to fighting one another. To think that *we* have sown for men like that to reap!' (pp.23–4; my emphasis).[34]

No reader of Virgil in the light of Spenser's January eclogue could have failed to respond to the ironic reversal of Britain from the periphery of exile to the centre of 'home', but the same anxiety underlies each eclogue and thus serves as a starting point for both poetic sequences: the fear of the disintegration of the nation. Much criticism of the *Calender* has dealt with these

APRILL.

Aegloga quarta.

Edmund Spenser, *The Shepheardes Calender*, woodcut accompanying 'April
eclogue', in *Works* (1611).

conflicts – especially analyses of the 'moral eclogues' in terms of
the puritan challenge for control of the Church of England –
without situating the work within a discursive framework of nationhood.[35]
Yet, I would argue, the poem continually demands that it be
read that way. The most conspicuous example is the April
eclogue which is headed by a woodcut depicting a musical
ensemble of courtly ladies surrounding a central figure (figure
2). Her dress and demeanour mark her out as the queen, the
addressee of the eclogue singled out in E. K.'s summary of the
argument: 'This Aeclogue is intended to the honor and prayse
of our most gracious sovereigne, Queen Elizabeth' (p.431). The
shepherd piping in the left-hand corner of the picture is
presumably Colin, the composer of the lay referred to by E. K.

There are many disconcerting features in this eclogue which
prevent a straightforwardly patriotic reading of the relationship
between ruler and ruled – as was the case with Virgil's first
eclogue. The visual dynamic of the woodcut leads the viewer's

eye towards the centre of the picture and away from the
diminutive piping shepherd, whose music of praise appears to
be drowned by the ladies' ensemble so that Colin seems not only
subordinate in his task of praising and thereby representing the
monarch, but actually unable to function as a poet. The
indifference of the shepherds in the background to the royal visit
further indicates the lack of communication between the court
and the pastoral world. Colin himself does not appear in the
poem – the two speakers are Hobbinol and Thenot – so that the
reader is given the illusion that Colin is represented as a figure
equal in importance but opposite to the queen.[36] E. K.'s
argument returns the focus to Colin, so that it forms a balance
to the woodcut:

The two speakers herein be Hobbinoll and Thenott, two shepherdes:
the which Hobbinoll being before mentioned, greatly to have loved
Colin, is here set forth more largely, complayning him of that boyes
great misadventure in Love, whereby his mynd was alienate and with
drawen not onely from him, who moste loved him, but also from all
former delightes and studies, aswell in pleasaunt pyping, as conning
ryming and singing, and other laudable exercises. Whereby he taketh
occasion, for proofe of his more excellencie and skill in poetrie, to
recorde a songe, which the sayd Colin sometime made in honor of her
Majestie, whom abruptely he termeth Elysa. (p.431)

As in the January eclogue, Colin is unable to produce his poetry
because of the malign effect of love. It is possible to read his
silence as the direct result of the queen's displeasure: the eclogue
stresses the unhappiness and speechlessness of Colin owing to his
rejection, yet reproduces a poem he had written in praise of the
queen. The time when Colin composed this song is left
indeterminate through the use of a vague construction: 'which
the sayd Colin sometime made in honor of her Majestie'. The
reader cannot know, which, given the emphasis on Colin's
miserable present and the antagonism between court and
country throughout the eclogue, encourages the assumption
that Colin has fallen from grace. Hobbinol's response to
Thenot's prompting that he sing one of Colin's songs provides
no further clues: 'then will I singe his laye/ Of fayre *Eliza*,
Queene of shepheardes all:/ Which once he made, as by a

spring he laye' (lines 33–5). The eclogue hints at a time when
the poem recited was true, but points towards a present in
which such harmony has disappeared. Just as the letter to
Harvey referred to a pure English which had now become
corrupted, so the eclogue refers to a time when Elizabeth and
her subjects existed within mutually beneficial social relations
which have now gone sour. Eliza may be described as 'the
Queen of shepherds', but in the woodcut only one of them pays
any attention to her: his musical means are clearly swamped by
hers and, whilst he turns his head towards her, she stares
straight ahead. Thenot's opening speech could hardly be more
ominous and foreboding:

> Tell me good Hobbinoll, what garres thee greete?
> What? hath some Wolfe thy tender Lambes ytorne?
> Or is thy bagpype broke, that soundes so sweete?
> Or art thou of thy loved lasse forlorne?
>
> (lines 1–4)

Such lines hardly seem appropriate as the beginning of a poem
'*purposely intended* to the honor and prayse of our most gracious
sovereigne, Queene Elizabeth' (my emphasis). If all is well in
Elizabeth's dominions, why are her loyal subjects so unhappy?
The second line employs the ubiquitous iconography of Reformation debates – which looks forward to the May eclogue
and the debate between Piers and Palinode, 'two formes of
pastoures or Ministers, or the protestant and the Catholique'
(p.435) – illustrating that religious disharmony within the
realm is one of the first assumptions of any observer and that the
presence of the queen is not sufficiently authoritative to disperse
the Catholic wolves who threaten the body politic.[37] Lines three
and four are correct identifications of Colin's troubles, so the use
of such commonplace religious imagery in association with
what the reader learns to be true from the literal surface of the
poem, implies that although it has not been stated, he fears that
wolves exist within the hierarchy of the church.[38]

The eclogue announces its critical stance in no uncertain
terms (although exactly what Spenser's/ Colin's criticisms are is
less easy to decipher). Colin's hymn of praise to Elizabeth can be
read in at least two ways: either as an elegy for a desired state of

affairs which has now passed away (ie, analagous to a reading of the death of Dido in the November eclogue as an elegy for Elizabeth's projected religious death via her impending marriage to Alençon),[39] or as a strategy demanding that the queen attempt to read the series of tropes which represent her and examine the role she plays in the formation of the state. This involves moving from the fictional allegory of the eclogue to the 'real' allegory of political power and a scrupulous co-operation in reading the metaphors which form the literal structure of the imagined nation.[40] The poem focuses particularly on Elizabeth's status as the virgin queen. Stanza 1 summons the 'dayntye Nymphs' from the brooks where Colin is composing his song and the 'Virgins' who dwell on Mount Parnassus, asking them to 'Help me to Blaze/ Her worthy praise,/ Which in her sexe doth all excell' (lines 43–5). Stanza 2 describes the queen as 'The flowre of Virgins, may shee flourish long,/ In princely plight' and claims that 'So sprong her grace/ Of heavenly race,/ No mortall blemishe may her blott' (lines 52–4). Stanza 3 directs attention to the physical presence of the queen and describes her appearance noting that she is 'yclad in Scarlot like a mayden Queene'.

Many aspects of these opening verses make them as disturbing a beginning as the initial stanzas of the eclogue. Given the recent interest in the Alençon marriage suit and the *Calender*'s very deliberate association with factions hostile to the match (see above, p.177), the stress placed upon the queen's virginity is pointed and manipulative. It is implied that Elizabeth excels her sex in her virginity, which is why only virgins are summoned by the poet to praise her; that her status as queen depends upon her flourishing as 'The flowre of Virgins' and refusing to be mortal and stained with the concupiscence of carnality ('No mortall blemishe may her blott'). The use of a comparison in the third stanza draws the reader's attention to the possibility that this may all be an elaborate game of role-playing: is Elizabeth really a virgin queen or is she merely pretending to be one for reasons of state? The monarchy depends upon this confusion of the two bodies – private and public – for its very existence, a fiction Colin's encomium exposes as we are invited to examine the clothes the queen wears, strip them away and see what remains.[41] All that can be seen is Elizabeth's face:

> Tell me, have you seen her angelick face,
> Like *Phoebe* fayre?
> Her heavenly havoeur, her princely grace
> can you well compare?
> The Redde rose medled with the White yfere,
> In either cheeke depeincten lively chere.
> Her modest eye,
> Her Majestie,
> Where have you seene the like, but there?
>
> (lines 64–72)

E. K. glosses 'yfere' as 'together' and argues that the line contains a historical allegory:

By the mingling of the Red rose and the White, is meant the uniting of the two principal houses of Lancaster and York: by whose long *discord* this realm many years was sore travailed, and almost clean decayed. Till the famous Henry the seventh, of the line of Lancaster, taking to wife the most virtuous princess Elizabeth, daughter to the fourth Edward of the house of York, begat the most royal Henry the eight aforesaid, in whom was the first union of the White rose, and the Red. (p.434; my emphasis)

The reference to the foundation of the Tudor dynasty, begun by a 'virtuous Elizabeth', is surely pointed. Whilst the encomiastic verse praises virginity, the gloss undermines the virtue and warns of the possibility of civil war if the succession is not secured: if the nation once 'decayed', it could, of course, do so again, either through Elizabeth not following her grandmother into marriage, or through a discordant match, unacceptable to patriotic subjects (ie, Alençon). Just as the Red and White roses were united in the figure of Henry VIII, so can they be torn asunder in the body of Elizabeth. The disguised metaphors of the fiction within a fiction – the poem within the eclogue – in fact connote a discourse of the 'real'. The colours in Elizabeth's cheeks tell a contemporary history.[42]

The *Calender* ends on a note of defeat in the December eclogue. Colin reiterates his decision to hang up his pipe and in the winter season he says farewell to Rosalinde and prepares for his death. He next appears, again as the disciple of Tityrus, in the 'simple Pastoral', *Colin Clouts Come Home Againe*, written in 1591 and published in 1595.[43] Two very important developments separate the figure of Colin in this later work from his earlier incarnation. Firstly, the shepherds in the *Calender* were never clearly defined as a group, even when their allegorical tales dealt with matters of national importance as in the 'moral eclogues'.[44] At the start of *Colin Clouts Come Home Againe*, Hobbinol tells Colin 'how great a loss/ Had all the *shepherds nation* by thy lack!' (lines 16–17; my emphasis). Secondly, it is clear from the short letter dedicating the poem to Sir Walter Raleigh and the references to their journey to England earlier that year, that Colin's 'home' is no longer in England.[45] Spenser advertises the fact that he wrote the poem 'From my house of Kilcolman'; Colin, his fictionalised *alter ego*, has returned to the 'shepherds nation', ie, Ireland. Pastoral, as a genre of protest literature, is located quite clearly within the community of the 'New' English in Ireland and the poem serves to define their identity and speak with their voice.[46]

In the April eclogue, Elizabeth was referred to as 'the Queen of shepherds', but in *Colin Clouts Come Home Againe*, Colin has to cross the ocean to reach 'Cynthia's land' (line 288). The difference between the two nations is emphasised: Cuddy asks '"What is that land thou meanst ... / And is there other than whereon we stand?"' (lines 289–90). Cuddy is ridiculed by Colin for his ignorance; however, the poem has drawn the reader's attention to the vast distance between the queen and one group of her subjects (the first edition of Spenser's works was dedicated to 'Elizabeth, by the grace of God, Queen of England, France, and Ireland, and of Virginia').[47] Elizabeth's English representatives in Ireland obviously have difficulty in knowing who she is. Such a gulf leads to two crucial tenets of an English identity in Ireland: such subjects are neglected and thus likely to be unsafe and impoverished, but they also have more freedom.[48]

Colin does indeed praise Cynthia's land in extravagant terms and to the detriment of their life in Ireland:

> Both heaven and heavenly graces do much more
> (Quoth he) abound in that same land than this.

> For there all happy peace and plenteous store
> Conspire in one to make contented bliss:
> No wailing there nor wretchedness is heard,
> No bloody issues nor no leprosies,
> No grisely famine, nor no raging sweard,
> No nightly bodrags, nor no hue and cries;
> The shepherds there abroad may safely lie,
> On hills and downs, withouten dread or danger:
> No ravenous wolves the good man's hope destroy,
> Nor outlaws fell affray the forest ranger.
>
> (lines 308–19)[49]

He also praises the poets at court (lines 376–455), when asked by 'a lovely lass, hight Lucinda' (line 456), the ladies (lines 464–583), and Cynthia herself (lines 590–647). Eventually, Thestylis asks the obvious question:

> Why Colin, since thou foundest such grace
> With Cynthia and all her noble crew;
> Why didst thou ever leave that happy place,
> In which such wealth might unto thee accrue;
> And back returnedst to this barren soil,
> Where cold and care and penury do dwell,
> Here to keep sheep, with hunger and with toil?
> Most wretched he that is and cannot tell?
>
> (lines 652–9)

Colin explains that he is not suited to the corrupt life at court, being a rude shepherd, and that he 'rather chose back to my sheep to turn' (line 672) because he 'Durst not adventure such unknowen ways,/ Nor trust the guile of fortune's blandishment' (lines 670–1).

The poem clearly signals an alternative Englishness in Ireland, an aggressive satirical style which laments its exile but is also acutely conscious of its unwillingness to compromise.[50] Colin states that the court provides 'no sort of life' for young shepherds; it is a place where 'each one seeks with malice and with strife/ To thrust down other into foul disgrace,/ Himself to raise' (lines 690–2). The 'New' English, as the 'shepherdes nation', are cast in the role of the guardians of a tradition of English public poetry which is able to stand outside and by-pass the constraints of a purely courtly culture. It is they, the poem suggests, who are able to maintain the relatively unfettered speech community of the public sphere at the expense of enjoying a harmonious pastoral existence. Instead, their way of life is constantly under siege from the native Irish and the neglect and suspicion of the metropolitan authorities leaves them unprotected.[51] *Colin Cloutes Come Home Againe* is a colonial poem of hybrid identity; Colin can preserve his English voice only at the cost of choosing exile and no longer being recognisably English, having to define himself against both hostile natives and the central culture of the court.[52]

When Colin Clout appears for the third and final time in Spenser's poetry, he is again placed in direct opposition to the representative of the court. In *The Faerie Queene*, VI, X, Colin is shown conjuring up the Graces with his pipe on the top of mount Acidale.[53] Instead of the usual three, four appear. As the knight of courtesy, Calidore, stumbles into the scene, the Graces disappear and Colin, yet again, breaks his pipe. Calidore apologises and asks Colin who the naked ladies were. Colin explains that they only appear to those whom they favour and that they are almost certainly gone forever:

> Whom by no means thou canst recall againe;
> For, being gone, none can them bring in place,
> But whom they of themselves list to grace.
>
> (VI, X, 20)

He further explains that the Graces actually represent the virtue Calidore was searching for:

> These three on men all gracious gifts bestow,
> Which deck the body or adorn the mind,
> To make them lovely or well-favour'd show;
> As comely carriage, entertainment kind,
> Sweet semblance, friendly offices that bind,
> And all the complements of courtesy:
> They teach us, how to each degree and kind
> We should ourselves demean, to low, to high,
> To friends, to foes: which skill men call civility.
>
> (VI, X, 23)

As if this were not enough, Calidore is told that the fourth figure *should* represent Gloriana, the Faerie Queene (but actually represents Spenser's wife, for which impertinence he apologises (VI, X, 25–8)).

The ironies abound in this episode. Calidore, the supposed representative of courtesy has actually been the unwitting agent who makes its manifestation disappear. Calidore cannot ever find courtesy because it is clear that it will never appear to him as he has not been graced, unlike Colin. True courtesy belongs to humble shepherds such as Colin, who, as has been argued in this chapter, signal a public voice of opposition to the court. Furthermore, in depicting the fourth Grace as a substitute for Gloriana – who, as every reader of *The Faerie Queene* would have known from the Letter to Raleigh attached to the first edition of the poem, stood for both 'Glory' and 'the most excellent and glorious person of our sovereign the Queen' (p.407) – Spenser undercuts the supposed project of the Book of Courtesy in two ways. Firstly, he implies that Calidore is not the one who can truly represent the virtue of courtesy to the queen when he arrives at her court, because courtesy, despite its etymology, is at odds with the values of the court, a problem raised in the proem and first stanza of canto i.[54] There Spenser states that 'true courtesy' has become 'nought but forgery,/ Fashion'd to please the eyes of them that pass' and that it really exists 'deep within the mind,/ And not in outward shows but inward thoughts defined' (VI, proem, 5). He claims that the only properly courteous figure who can rival those of antiquity before the virtue decayed, is the Queen. But the praise is double-edged; Elizabeth's 'pure mind' is described as 'a mirror sheen' which 'with her brightness doth inflame/ The eyes of all which thereon fixed been' (6). A mirror reflects what is put in front of it, revealing only what the subject shows. The metaphor serves to empower that subject's ability to represent rather than the inherent control of the monarch who is thus meaningless and powerless without her subjects.[55] Colin, the poet, is the one who truly reveals the essence of the Queen, her virtue and the court, and not her ostensible servant, Calidore.[56]

Secondly, and more fundamentally still, Gloriana/Elizabeth is actually excluded from the composite representation of courtesy conjured up by Colin's pipe: she is made conspicuous by her absence. Even if Colin were to be invited to the court of Gloriana instead of Calidore, he would not be able to represent her as the embodiment of courtesy because another figure now stands in her place. The subject who can show her the image of herself in all her glory – the poet – has become so alienated from the supposed centre of power that he can only reveal her inner mind, her courteous conscience, as detached from her. Courtesy confronts the monarch as an alien virtue, severed from its imagined etymology and present only in opposition. The revealed essence of the queen proves to be a public criticism of her lost (political) honour.

The Book ends with Calidore's failure to subdue the Blatant Beast (just as he failed to protect the pastoral world within which he took refuge from the exhausting rigours of his quest in canto ix), the perpetrator of falsehoods, significantly cast as the obverse of courtesy and serving to define it as 'truth'.[57] The uncompleted *Faerie Queene* published in Spenser's lifetime, ends on a note of serious self-reflection. The narrator laments that the Blatant Beast 'rangeth through the world again,/ ... Barking and biting all that him do bate,/ Albe they worthy blame, or clear of crime'; but he only mentions one specific set of targets: 'Ne spareth he most learned wits to rate,/ Ne spareth he the gentle poet's rhyme' (VI, xii, 40). The last stanza refers directly to *The Faerie Queene* itself:

> Ne may this homely verse, of many meanest,
> Hope to escape his venemous despite,
> More than my former writs, all were they cleanest
> From blameful blot, and free from all that wite,
> With which some wicked tongues did it backbite,
> And bring into a mighty peer's displeasure,
> That never so deserved to indite.
> Therefore do you, my rhymes, keep better measure,
> And seek to please; that now is counted wise men's
> treasure.
>
> (VI, xii, 41)

These bitter lines bring the reader abruptly from Faerieland back to a contemporary political world. The description of the epic poem as a 'homely verse' deliberately links it to the pastoral world of the *Calender* and *Colin Clouts Come Home Againe* and their mode of disguised but nonetheless public criticism. The beast which threatens the poem is the attempt to stifle its freedom to articulate the 'truths' it has to tell. Spenser does not claim that poetry has to be free from error in its role as a forum for debate: the Blatant Beast is shown to attack wit and poetry which are both true and false. In the same way he claims that his own work, although condemned not just in terms of its truth value but in terms of its very right to be uttered, is clean and innocent and hence undeserving of its fate. The last two lines sarcastically demonstrate the alternative way of writing poetry; base flattery. The Book ends as it began, condemning those who want a servile poetics like the executors of Collingborne (see above, chapter 3). Whilst they want courtesy to be no more than 'forgery', *The Faerie Queene* claims to represent the true but hidden definition of the word in attempting to open up a space where the truth can be properly considered. Only then can Colin Clout take up his pipe again and speak to the nation as he should be allowed.

Within the text of the poem any hope for a coherent and stable body politic remains at the level of prophecy, longed-for events which the mirror of the poem seeks to impose upon the queen. The marriage between the Thames and the Medway in IV, xi, which unites all the British rivers (including the Irish ones) precedes the marriage of Marinell and Florimell. If Florimell is read as another manifestation of Elizabeth, then the emphasis is placed upon the need for Elizabeth to marry in order for her to unite her kingdoms and secure a succession.[58] The fact that the marriage of the rivers takes place in the hall of Proteus, the god of change, helps to undercut the security of the union and provides a direct link to the representation of Elizabeth in the 'Cantos of Mutabilitie' (see p.200). The union of the kingdoms is a wish-fulfilment or an urge to action, and cannot be read as unproblematic praise of Elizabeth.[59]

Similarly, Spenser's treatment of the matter of Britain, introduced in Book II, x, and continued in Book III, iii and ix, eventually undermines what it seems to affirm at first. If such a reading is correct, then the first edition of *The Faerie Queene*, far from giving Elizabeth glowing praise, later to be qualified and undermined in the second edition containing Books IV–VI, as some commentators have argued, illustrates that from the very beginning Spenser's epic contained warning signs for careful readers.[60]

At the end of Book II, x, Sir Guyon, the knight of Temperance, finds a chronicle entitled *Antiquity of Faery Land* in the House of Temperance. This is read out in canto xi and the head-verse directs the reader to the deliberate blend of fact and fiction which the canto provides:

> A chronicle of Briton kings,
> From Brute to Uther's reign;
> And rolls of Elfin emperors,
> Till time of Gloriane.

The narrator steps out of the fiction to address Elizabeth directly:

> Thy name, O sovereign Queen, the realm, and race,
> From this renowned prince [Jove] descended are,
> Who mightily upheld that royal mace
> Which now thou bears't, to thee descended far
> From mighty kings and conquerors in war.
>
> (II, x, 4)

The reader is confronted with the problem of sorting out what is fact and what is fiction. Is the statement that Elizabeth is descended from Jove a piece of flattery, an allegory or a myth?

Many commentators have pointed out that the treatment of Briton kings and Elfin emperors differs significantly. Whereas the Britons 'came by suffering to knowledge and by sin to salvation', 'Elfin Man' is shown from the start to possess 'Excellence, harmony and power'.[61] The Briton Chronicle contains few changes to the original material adapted (directly or indirectly) from Geoffrey of Monmouth. It presents a tortuous and difficult chart of progress containing numerous setbacks – in fact one of the few additions to his sources occurs in the exaggeration of the defeats suffered by Boadicea, a historical episode not derived from Geoffrey (54–6).[62] For example, the well-known episode of the usurper Vortigern's reliance upon the Saxon princes Hengist and Horsa to fight his civil war is told exactly as it is in the *Historia Regum Britanniae*, the defeat of the surreptitious invaders occurring only after they become reconciled to Vortigern and the land needs to be purged of both its false native prince and his foreign cohorts (64–7). During these wars three hundred British lords are slain, 'Whose doleful monuments who list to rew,/ Th'eternall markes of treason may at Stonheng vew' (66). A true British line is restored through Aurelius who 'peaceably did rayne' (67).[63] Uther Pendragon succeeds him and the chronicle breaks off, 'As if the rest some wicked hand did rend,/ Or th'Author selfe could not at least attend/ To finish it' (68). Guyon, 'ravisht with delight', celebrates the unity and cohesion of his native land (Guyon is a Briton) and the familial bond between ruler and soil:

> Deare countrey, O how dearely deare
> Ought thy remembraunce, and perpetuall band
> Be to thy foster Childe, that from thy hand
> Did commun breath and nouriture receave?
>
> (II, x, 69)

The chronicle continually points towards the future and the continuation of this line of British kings. Although the Romans plague the Britons after Caesar's defeat of Nennius, demanding and receiving tribute, the narrator declares that they will only have to obey until 'Arthur all that reckoning defrayed' (49). But we do not reach down as far as Arthur because the chronicle is incomplete and the narrator suggests that this may be due to hostile action. A clear warning is given that just as a book can be torn so can a dynasty if it is not looked after properly, a message that could also have been applied to contemporary events by the Elizabethan reader. A supposed history of unity is violently truncated – but we should be aware that it is authentic history told within a fictional narrative, which may serve to transport the reader from a discourse of myth to one of fact. Certainly many educated Elizabethan readers would have recognised the matter of Britain incorporated into the poem and have been forced to answer the question of its truth value and status within the poem.[64] The canto concludes with Guyon reading another history of the Elfs, descended from a man created by Prometheus. The last in the line of these is Gloriana or Tanaquill, unequivocally identifiable as Elizabeth:

> He [Oberon] dying left the fairest Tanaquill,
> Him to succeede therein, by his last will:
> Fairer and nobler liveth none this howre,
> Ne like in grace, ne like in learned skill;
> Therefore they Glorian call that glorious flowre,
> Long mayst thou Glorian live, in glory and great powre.
>
> (II, x, 26)

These lines express a hope not a certainty; the succession is clearly not secure. In referring to Elizabeth as an Elfin ruler alongside the British material, there is also a suggestion that the two dynasties may be separate and the allegorical portrait of Elizabeth in *The Faerie Queene* is fictionalised in a different way from that of a real British history. The line of the British kings may or may not lead to Gloriana as she is portrayed in the poem; she might turn out to be one of her other fictional manifestations: Britomart, Florimell, or even Radigund. Britomart is the ostensible reader of this chronicle and she serves as a counterpart to Elizabeth, being, in Faerieland, her ancestor.[65]

This sense of unease is repeated when Merlin reveals to Britomart the genealogical line which will result from her union with Artegall – unlike Elizabeth, she gets married and thus serves as a challenge to the queen, not just a flattering portrait.[66] The chronicle stresses over and again the eventual release of the land from civil war which will occur:

> Renowned kings, and sacred Emperours,
> Thy fruitfull Ofspring, shall from thee descend;
> Brave Captaines, and most mighty warriours,
> That shall their decayed kingdomes shall amend:
> The feeble Britons, broken with long warre,
> They shall upreare, and mightily defend
> Against their forrein foe, that comes from farre,
> Till universall peace compound all civill jarre.
>
> (III, iii, 23)

This prophecy seems to be fulfilled in Elizabeth. Merlin reveals that the exile of the Britons shall end with the birth of a leader on the isle of Mona, where Henry VII was born: 'So shall the Briton bloud their crowne againe reclame' (48). At last the Britons shall be united and at peace:

> Thenceforth eternall union shall be made
> Betweene the nations different afore,
> And sacred Peace shall lovingly perswade
> The warlike minds, to learne her goodly lore,
> And civile armes to exercise no more:
> Then shall a royall virgin raigne, which shall
> Stretch her white rod over the Belgicke shore,
> And the great Castle smite so sore with all,
> That it shall make him shake, and shortly learne to fall.
>
> (III, iii, 49)

The vision is undercut in two ways; firstly, although Book V does contain an allegorical representation of the victories in the Netherlands in cantos x and xi, it ends on a note of discord and disunity. Artegall's quest is to rescue Irena (Ireland) from the clutches of Grantorto (on one level Philip II of Spain). He does indeed vanquish Grantorto and starts 'to reforme that ragged common-weale' (v, xii, 26), but is called away prematurely to the Faerie Court, 'that of necessity/ His course of Justice he was forst to stay' (27). The book is thus framed by a logic which shows Elizabeth hindering rather than promoting the establishment of justice and leaving one of her kingdoms in a state of unrest. Artegall's fate bears close resemblance to the recall of Spenser's erstwhile employer, Lord Grey de Wilton, in 1580, an event bitterly lamented by Irenius in Spenser's unpublished dialogue, *A View of the Present State of Ireland*.[67]

Secondly, as with the *Antiquity of Faery Land*, the visions conjured up by the mirror break off suddenly and disturbingly, hinting at a potentially troubled future such as that provided in Book v (the events of which had already taken place even though they were not represented until the second edition of the poem in 1596):

> But yet the end is not. There Merlin stayd,
> As overcomen of the sprites powre,

Or other ghastly spectacle dismayd,
That secretly he saw, yet note discoure:
Which suddein fit, and halfe extaick stoure
When the two fearfull women saw, they grew
Greatly confused in behavioure;
At last the fury past, to former hew
Hee turnd againe, and chearfull looks (as earst) did shew.

(iii, iii, 50)

Although the protagonists return to a lighter frame of mind and deem themselves 'well instructed' and able to begin planning how to effect the marriage of Britomart and Artegall, the 'ghastly spectacle' invites the reader to apply the vision of unity to a less than perfect present. Prophecy, as so often, serves as a radical and dangerous political discourse expressing current forebodings.[68] Merlin's mirror shows the queen the disquiet of one of her subjects as well as an image of how she *should* be, like the mirror which represents her mind in Book vi.

The final use of the matter of Britain occurs in iii, ix during the incidents at the Castle of Malbecco, a re-telling and re-fashioning of the events which led to the Trojan War.[69] Sir Paridell, the would-be ravisher of Malbecco's wife, Hellenore, is asked by her to tell the company gathered in the castle his lineage and worthy deeds. Possessing 'a kindly pryde/ Of gracious speach, and skill his wordes to frame' (32), he consents and informs them that he is, in fact, descended from Paris. Paridell is proud of his ancestor, referring to him without irony as 'Most famous Worthy of the world, by whome/ That warre was kindled, which did Troy inflame' because he 'From Lacedaemon fetcht the fairest Dame,/ That ever Greece did boast' (34). His own fate inverts the story of Paris, although he appears not to realise this: Paridell is condemned to leave his native soil – the destruction of which resulted from Paris' ravishment of Helen – and perform deeds of arms in order to win the love of ladies. His skilful telling of stories has only one aim: to seduce the lustful and weak Hellenore who cannot resist him: 'Which he perceiving, ever privily/ In speaking, many false belgardes at her let fly' (52).

Among the assembled company is Britomart, who is also

attracted to Paridell's words, but for a different reason. Her reaction to the story of the origins of the Trojan War takes a different form:

> She was empassioned at that piteous act,
> With zealous envy of Greekes cruell fact,
> Against that nation, from whose race of old
> She heard, that she was lineally extract:
> For noble Britons sprong from Trojans bold,
> And Troynovant was built of old Troyes ashes cold.
>
> (III, ix, 38)

The reactions of the two knights to the genealogies provides a crucial contrast and reminds the reader that origin stories are never simply fixed and interpreted. In the timeless world of Faerieland, Britomart has to confront a repetition of a moment from the establishment of her own origins. Paridell, the destructive, philandering wanderer is the antitype of Aeneas, who rejects the claims of false love (Dido) for the higher calling of the establishment of Rome and, for the audience of *The Faerie Queene*, Britain. Paris is the figure in the origin myth who threatens to undo the creation of the nation, a warning to Britomart that genealogies contain possibilities as well as certainties, not all of which are desirable. Aeneas' wanderings ultimately point towards stability; Paris' to instability and destruction (Paridell abandons Hellenore among a band of satyrs where she degenerates into an idol of lust). Britomart interrupts Paridell's narrative when he reaches the establishment of Rome by Aeneas and stresses that in founding Troynovant (London) on the Thames, 'Troy out of her dust was reard' (44). Paridell apologises and repeats a truncated form of the details contained in the chronicle of the Briton kings. But in doing so his motives are highlighted; not only does he try to smooth matters over in order to impress Hellenore (52), getting many details wrong, but also he confesses that he did not tell that part of the story because he had not remembered it: 'Pardon I pray my heedlesse oversight,/ Who had forgot, that whilome I heard tell/ From aged Mnemon; for my wits bene light' (47).

The episode illustrates that the matter of Britain can be put to various bad uses by unscrupulous narrators. It also warns the reader, yet again, that reading history and making prophecies is a double-edged process so that a secure present is by no means assured. British/English history does not necessarily demonstrate smooth and inevitable progress, just as looking into the future is not always a source of comfort. There are false roads that can be taken: if Troy was destroyed once – significantly through an ill-considered union – the second Troy could also suffer the same fate.[70]

It is hard not to regard *The Faerie Queene* in all its guises as a dark political work, searching for a space to articulate a critical voice. In the 'Cantos of Mutabilitie', not published until the first folio edition of 1617, long after the deaths of Spenser and Elizabeth, criticisms of the queen are open and direct. Mutability, at the end of her bid to persuade Nature that she not Jove rules the Universe, argues that kings like Jove think that they are in control but that really they are governed by her power. She turns directly to Cynthia, the goddess she first confronted on her ascent to challenge Jove:

> Even you faire Cynthia, whom so much ye make
> Joves dearest darling, she was bred and nurst
> On Cynthus hill, whence she her name did take:
> Then is she mortall borne, how-so ye crake;
> Besides, her face and countenance every day
> We changed see, and sundry forms partake,
> Now horned, now round, now bright, now brown and gray:
> So that *as changefull as the Moone* men use to say.
>
> (vii, vii, 50)

Cynthia is Elizabeth as the letter to Raleigh made clear. Her decaying body is subject to the wiles of time and her inconsistent behaviour and inability to provide for a succession have made this private body dominate the public office of the monarchy which it should have protected.[71] The fragmentation of the body politic of the nation it could have held together is imminent. Elizabeth's refusal to sanction a genuine public sphere, principally through the medium of poetry, has served to risk the destruction of the nation. There are many reasons why

The Faerie Queene itself remains a fragment, but undoubtedly it could not have been completed unless a political forum existed which could accept its strictures. To this extent, the unfinished poem mirrors the split body politic; *The Faerie Queene* stands and falls on the hope for a national public sphere.

Notes

EPIGRAPHS

1 Elie Kedourie, *Nationalism* (London: Hutchinson, 1960), p.9; Rebecca West, *The Meaning of Treason* (London: Macmillan, 1952), p.216; David Antin, 'Fine Furs', *Critical Inquiry* 19 (1992), 151–63, p.161.

PREFACE

1 My earliest reflections on the problematic nature of (Irish) national identity, written in 1988, appear as 'Anglo-Irish Literature: Definitions and (False) Origins', in Joseph McMinn, ed., *The Internationalism of Irish Literature and Drama* (Gerrard's Cross: Colin Smythe, 1992), pp.320–4.

2 W. J. McCormack, *The Battle of the Books* (Gigginstown, Mullingar: Lilliput, 1986), pp.78–80.

3 A. J. Ayer, *Language, Truth and Logic* (London: Gollancz, 1964, rpt of 1946), p.5.

INTRODUCTION

1 Richard Helgerson, *Forms of Nationhood: The Elizabethan Writing of England* (Chicago University Press, 1992); Benedict Anderson, *Imagined Communities: Reflections on the Origin and Spread of Nationalism* (London: Verso, 1990, rpt of 1983), p.15; Derek Attridge, *Peculiar Language: Literature as Difference from the Renaissance to James Joyce* (Ithaca, New York: Cornell University Press, 1988), 'Introduction: The Peculiar Language of Literature'; Stephen J. Greenblatt, *Renaissance Self-Fashioning: From More to Shakespeare* (Chicago University Press, 1980), 'Introduction'.

2 Elie Kedourie, *Nationalism* (London: Hutchinson, 1960), p.9. See also Eric J. Hobsbawm, *Nations and Nationalism Since 1780: Myth, Programme, Reality* (Cambridge University Press, second edn,

1992); Ernst Gellner, *Nations and Nationalism* (Oxford: Blackwell, 1983). More useful is the discussion in Anthony Giddens, *The Nation State and Violence: Volume Two of a Contemporary Critique of Historical Materialism* (Cambridge: Polity Press, 1985), chs. 1–4.

3 Anthony D. Smith, *National Identity* (Harmondsworth: Penguin, 1991), p.14.

4 Sir Thomas Smith, *De Republica Anglorum, A Discourse of the Commonwealth of England*, ed. L. Alston (Shannon: Irish Universities Press, 1972, rpt of 1906); Richard Helgerson, *Forms of Nationhood*, pp.151–5, 132–3.

5 John A. Armstrong, *Nations before Nationalism* (Chapel Hill: North Carolina University Press, 1982).

6 For an overview see Jonathan Goldberg, 'The Politics of Renaissance Literature: A Review Essay', *ELH* 15 (1982), 514–42. More specifically see Gary Waller, *English Poetry of the Sixteenth Century* (London: Longman, 1986), pp.79–80; David Norbrook, *Poetry and Politics in the English Renaissance* (London: RKP, 1984), pp.5–7.

7 See, for example, the assumptions made in Pat Rogers, ed., *The Oxford Illustrated History of English Literature* (Oxford University Press, 1987), 'Editor's Foreword'; Alistair Fowler, *A History of English Literature* (Oxford: Blackwell, rev. edn, 1989), 'Preface to First Edition'.

8 See, for example, Waller, *English Poetry of the Sixteenth Century*, pp.76–93.

9 Alice S. Miskimin, *The Renaissance Chaucer* (New Haven: Yale University Press, 1975), chs. 1, 8.

10 John N. King, *English Reformation Literature: The Tudor Origins of the Protestant Tradition* (Princeton University Press, 1982); *Tudor Royal Iconography: Literature and Art in an Age of Religious Crisis* (Princeton University Press, 1989); *Spenser's Poetry and the Reformation Tradition* (Princeton University Press, 1990).

11 C. S. Lewis, *English Literature in the Sixteenth Century, Excluding Drama* (Oxford University Press, 1973, rpt of 1954), Bk 2.

12 See Jan Hardy and Chris Vieler-Porter, 'Race, Schooling and the 1988 Education Reform Act' in Dawn Gill, Barbara Mayor and Maud Blair, eds., *Racism and Education: Structures and Strategies* (London: Sage, 1992), pp.101–14. I owe this reference to Alison Hadfield.

13 Jürgen Häbermas, 'The Public Sphere', *New German Critique* 3 (1974), 49–55. Häbermas's periodisation dates from Immanuel Kant's famous essay, 'An Answer to the Question: What is Enlightenment?', reprinted in *Kant: Political Writings*, ed. Hans Reiss (Cambridge University Press, 1991), pp.54–60. See also

Michel Foucault's riposte, 'What is Enlightenment?', trans. Catherine Porter, in Paul Rabinow, ed., *The Foucault Reader* (Harmondsworth: Penguin, 1986), pp.32–50.

14 See Stephen K. White, *The Recent Thought of Jürgen Habermas: Reason, Justice and Modernity* (Cambridge University Press, 1987), ch. 2; Christopher Norris, 'Deconstruction, Postmodernism and Philosophy: Habermas on Derrida', in David Wood, ed., *Derrida: A Critical Reader* (Oxford: Blackwell, 1992), pp.167–92.

15 For a criticism of the ethnocentric exclusions of the Enlightenment, see Henry Louis Gates, Jr, 'Editor's Introduction: Writing "Race" and the Difference it Makes'; and Houstan A. Baker, Jr, 'Caliban's Triple Play', both in Henry Louis Gates, Jr, ed., '*Race*', *Writing and Difference* (Chicago University Press, 1986), pp.1–20, pp.381–95; Kwame Anthony Appiah, 'Race', in Frank Lentricchia and Thomas McLaughlin, eds., *Critical Terms for Literary Study* (Chicago University Press, 1990), pp.274–87.

16 See R. and M. H. Dodds, *The Pilgrimage of Grace, 1536–7 and the Exeter Conspiracy, 1538*, 2 vols. (Cambridge University Press, 1915), I, p.280.

17 (London, 1573), STC 13602–3. For an analysis of the poem see A. G. Dickens, 'Wilfrid Holme of Huntington: Yorkshire's First Protestant Poet', *Yorkshire Archaeological Journal* 39 (1956–8), 119–35.

18 See R. and M. H. Dodds, *The Pilgrimage of Grace*, I, pp.12–13.

19 *Ibid.*, ch. 11.

20 See Philippa Berry, *Of Chastity and Power: Elizabethan Literature and the Unmarried Queen* (London: Routledge, 1989), ch. 5; Helgerson, *Forms of Nationhood*, pp.199–200, for some relevant analyses.

21 See Philip Edwards, *Threshold of a Nation: A Study in English and Irish Drama* (Cambridge University Press, 1979); Walter Cohen, *Drama of a Nation: Public Theatre in Renaissance England and Spain* (Ithaca, New York: Cornell University Press, 1984).

22 See, for example, Lesley Johnson, 'Commemorating the Past: A Critical Study of the Shaping of British and Arthurian History in Geoffrey of Monmouth's *Historia Regum Britanniae*, Wace's *Roman de Brut* and the Alliterative *Morte Arthure*', unpublished PhD thesis (King's College, London, 1990); Pearl M. Kean, *Chaucer and the Making of English Poetry*, 3 vols. (London: RKP, 1972); Frank Brownlow, 'George Herbert's "The British Church" and the Idea of a National Church', in Vincent Newey and Ann Thompson, eds., *Literature and Nationalism* (Liverpool University Press, 1991), pp.111–19; Peter Womack, *Ben Jonson* (Oxford: Blackwell, 1986), 'Conclusion'; Nicholas Von Maltzan, *Milton's 'History of Britain'*:

Republican Historiography in the English Revolution (Oxford University Press, 1991).

23 Hans Kohn, *The Idea of Nationalism: A Study in its Origins and Background* (Ithaca, New York: Cornell University Press, 1946), chs. 1–4.

24 *Ibid.*, chs. 1–4; Timothy Brennan, 'The National Longing for Form', in Homi Bhabha, ed., *Nation and Narration* (London: RKP, 1990), pp.44–70. See also J. G. A. Pocock, *The Ancient Constitution and the Feudal Law: A Study of English Historical Thought in the Seventeenth Century* (Cambridge University Press, 1987), ch. 1 for a description of an analogous process.

25 See, for example, Jonathan Dollimore, 'Introduction: Shakespeare, Cultural Materialism and the New Historicism', in Jonathan Dollimore and Alan Sinfield, eds., *Political Shakespeare: New Essays in Cultural Materialism* (Manchester University Press, 1985), pp.2–17; H. Aram Veeser, ed., *The New Historicism* (London: Routledge, 1989).

26 See D. M. Loades, 'The Theory and Practice of Censorship in Sixteenth Century England', *TRHS*, fifth series, 24 (1974), 141–57; Richard A. McCabe, 'Elizabethan Satire and the Bishops' Ban of 1599', *YES* 11 (1981), 188–93; John Feather, *A History of British Publishing* (London: Croom Helm, 1988), ch. 3; W. W. Greg, *Some Aspects and Problems of London Publishing between 1550 and 1650* (Oxford: Clarendon Press, 1956), ch. 1 et passim.

27 See, for example, Jonathan Goldberg, *James I and the Politics of Literature: Jonson, Shakespeare, Donne and Their Contemporaries* (Baltimore: Johns Hopkins University Press, 1983), p.9; David J. Baker, '"Some Quirk, Some Subtle Evasion": Legal Subversion in Spenser's *A View of the Present State of Ireland*', *Sp. St.* 6 (1986), 147–63, pp.151–2; Clark Hulse, 'Spenser and the Myth of Power', *SP* 85 (1988), 378–89, p.387.

28 See 'Briton and Scythian: Tudor Representations of Irish Origins', *IHS* 112 (1993), 390–408.

29 See Brendan Bradshaw, Andrew Hadfield and Willy Maley, eds., *Representing Ireland, 1534–1660: Literature and the Origins of Conflict* (Cambridge University Press, 1993).

30 See Michael Hechter, *Internal Colonialism: The Celtic Fringe in British National Development, 1536–1966* (Berkeley: California University Press, 1975).

31 See Geoffrey Bennington, 'Postal Politics and the Institution of the Nation', in Bhabha, ed., *Nation and Narration*, 121–37, p.123.

32 F. Smith Fussnser, *The Historical Revolution* (London: RKP, 1962); F. J. Levy, *Tudor Historical Thought* (San Marino: Huntington

Library Publications, 1967); Arthur B. Ferguson, *Clio Unbound: Perceptions of the Social and Cultural Past in Renaissance England* (Durham, N. Carolina: Duke University Press, 1979); Peter Burke, *The Renaissance Sense of the Past* (London: Arnold, 1969).

33 See Jean-François Lyotard, *The Postmodern Condition: A Report on Knowledge*, trans. Geoff Bennington and Brian Massumi (Manchester University Press, 1986); Terry Eagleton, 'Capitalism, Modernism and Postmodernism', *New Left Review* 152 (July, 1985), 60–73.

34 See, for example, Johnson, 'Commemorating the Past'; John Gillingham, 'The Concept and Purpose of Geoffrey of Monmouth's *History of the Kings of Britain*', in Marjorie Chibnall, ed., *Anglo-Norman Studies* 13 (Ipswich: Boydell, 1991), pp.99–118.

35 D. W. Robertson, *A Preface to Chaucer* (Princeton University Press, 1963), pp.51, 265, 501–2, cited in David Aers, 'Reflections on Current Histories of the Subject', *Literature and History*, second series, 2, ii (1991), 20–34, p.21. All subsequent references to this article in parentheses in the text.

36 Aers is quoting Brian Stock, *The Implications of Literacy* (Princeton University Press, 1983), p.85. See also Rodney Hilton, *Bond Men Made Free: Medieval Peasant Movements and the English Rising of 1381* (London: Routledge, 1973); Rodney Hilton, ed., *The Transition from Feudalism to Capitalism* (London: Verso, 1976).

37 T. S. Eliot, 'The Metaphysical Poets', 'Andrew Marvell', in *Selected Essays* (London: Faber, 1951), pp.281–91, 292–304; Q. D. Leavis, *Fiction and the Reading Public* (London: Chatto and Windus, 1939); F. R. Leavis, *Mass Civilization and Minority Culture* (Cambridge: Gordon Fraser, 1930); E. M. W. Tillyard, *The Elizabethan World Picture* (London: Chatto and Windus, 1943). For a critical overview see Louis A. Montrose, 'Professing the Renaissance: The Poetics and Politics of Culture', in Veeser, ed., *The New Historicism*, pp.15–36.

38 Aers is quoting Francis Barker, *The Tremulous Private Body: Essays on Subjection* (London: Methuen, 1984), p.31.

39 See Robert Young, 'The Jameson Raid' in *White Mythologies: Writing History and the West* (London: Routledge, 1990), pp.91–118.

40 Erwin Panofsky, *Renaissance and Renascences in Western Art* (Stockholm: Almquist and Wiksell, 1960). See also Arnold J. Toynbee, 'A Survey of Renaissances', in *A Study of History*, abridged by D. C. Somervell (Oxford University Press, 1960), pp.241–60; Jacob Burckhardt, *The Civilization of the Renaissance in Italy*, trans. S. G. A. Middlemore, rev. Irene Gordon (New York: Mentor, 1960),

pp.145–6; Christopher Brooke, *The Twelfth-Century Renaissance* (London: Thames and Hudson, 1969).

41 A. C. Spearing, *Medieval to Renaissance in English Poetry* (Cambridge University Press, 1985), p.1; Bennington, 'Postal Politics', pp. 122–3.

42 Spearing, *Medieval to Renaissance*, pp.1–2.

43 Two recent surveys are Pierre Chaunu, ed., *The Reformation* (Gloucester: Alan Sutton, 1989); Andrew Pettigree, ed., *The Early Reformation in Europe* (Cambridge University Press, 1992).

44 Waller, *English Poetry of the Sixteenth Century*, p.90; Alan Sinfield, *Literature in Protestant England* (London: Croom Helm, 1983), ch. 3.

45 Kenneth Parker, 'The Revelation of Caliban: "The Black Presence" in the Classroom', in Gill *et al.*, eds., *Racism and Education*, pp.284–302. See also Alan Sinfield, 'Shakespeare and Education', in Sinfield and Dollimore, eds., *Political Shakespeare*, pp.134–57; David Hornbrook, '"Go play, boy, play": Shakespeare and Educational Drama', in Graham Holderness, ed., *The Shakespeare Myth* (Manchester University Press, 1988), pp.145–59.

46 Cited in Edwards, *Threshold of a Nation*, p.1.

47 *Ibid.*, pp.242–4.

48 Terry Eagleton, *The Function of Criticism from ' The Spectator' to Post-Structuralism* (London: Verso, 1984); *Literary Theory: An Introduction* (Oxford: Blackwell, 1983); Chris Baldick, *The Social Mission of English Criticism, 1848–1932* (Oxford: Clarendon Press, 1983); Brian Doyle, *English and Englishness* (London: Routledge, 1989); Peter Widdowson, ed., *Re-Reading English* (London: Methuen, 1982). The first book cited here makes use of Häbermas's notion of the 'public sphere' with regard to the development of criticism in the eighteenth century.

49 For further comment, see my article, 'Writing the New World: More Invisible Bullets', *Literature and History*, second series, 2, ii (1991), 3–19, pp.9–10; and review of *Marvelous Possessions*, *TP* 7 (1993), 103–10. See also Goldberg, 'The Politics of Renaissance Literature'.

50 See, for example, Catherine Belsey, 'Towards Cultural History – In Theory and Practice', *TP* 3 (1989), 159–72; Alan Sinfield and Jonathan Dollimore, 'Culture and Textuality: Debating Cultural Materialism', *TP* 4 (1990), 91–100.

51 Hardin Craig, ' *The Geneva Bible* as a Political Document', *Pacific Historical Review* 7 (1938), 40–9; King, *English Reformation Literature*, pp.127–30.

52 See Jacques Derrida, 'From/Of the Supplement to the Source: The Theory of Writing', in *Of Grammatology*, trans. Gayatri

Chakravorty Spivak (Baltimore: Johns Hopkins University Press, 1976), pp.269–316.

53 See Lee Patterson, 'Literary History'; Louis A. Renza, 'Influence', in Lentricchia and McLaughlin, eds., *Critical Terms for Literary Study*, pp.250–62, 186–202.

54 See my review, 'English Spenser', *English* 166 (1991), 69–73.

55 For relevant discussions of this problem, see Hayden White, *Metahistory: The Historical Imagination in Nineteenth-Century Europe* (Baltimore: Johns Hopkins University Press, 1973), 'Introduction'; Robert Young, 'Post-Structuralism: An Introduction', in Robert Young, ed., *Untying the Text: A Post-Structuralist Reader* (London: RKP, 1980), pp.1–28; Jonathan Culler, 'Beyond Interpretation', in *The Pursuit of Signs: Semiotics, Literature, Deconstruction* (London: RKP, 1981), pp.3–17.

56 See Patterson, 'Literary History'.

57 'The past is a foreign country: they do things differently there'; L. P. Hartley, *The Go-Between* (Harmondsworth: Penguin, 1980, rpt of 1953), p.7.

58 See Christopher Norris, *The Contest of Faculties: Philosophy and Theory after Deconstruction*, ch. 2 (London: Methuen, 1985); Eagleton, *Literary Theory*, p.vi.

59 Roland Barthes, *S/Z: An Essay*, trans. Richard Miller (New York: Hill and Wang, 1987, rpt of 1974), pp.20–1.

60 See Stanley Fish, *Is There a Text in this Class? The Authority of Interpretative Communities* (Cambridge, Mass.: Harvard University Press, 1980); Jonathan Culler, *On Deconstruction: Theory and Criticism after Structuralism* (London: RKP, 1983), ch. 1.

1 A SKELTON IN THE CLOSET

1 Stephen Jay Gould, *Wonderful Life: The Burgess Shale and the Nature of History* (London: Hutchinson, 1989), p.197. All subsequent references to this work in parentheses.

2 See J. J. Scarisbrick, *The Reformation and the English People* (Oxford: Basil Blackwell, 1984).

3 *A Skeltonicall Salutation ... of the Spanish Nation* (1589), *STC* 22619, lines 1–12. See Anthony Edwards, *Skelton: The Critical Heritage* (London: RKP, 1981), p.9. According to Alistair Fox, Garnesche's poem was written by Alexander Barclay; *Politics and Literature in the Reigns of Henry VII and Henry VIII* (Oxford: Basil Blackwell, 1989), p.44. For another example of the posthumous use of Skelton, see the 1624 edition of *The Tunning of Eleanor Rumming*, *STC* 22614, where a prefatory poem envisages 'Skelton's ghost' wandering the streets of Jacobean London.

4 George Puttenham, *The Arte of English Poesie* (1589), ed. R. C. Alston (Menston: Scolar Press, 1968), p.50.
5 Edwards, *Critical Heritage*, pp.10–14.
6 E. J. L. Scott, ed., *The Letter-Book of Gabriel Harvey, AD 1573–1580* (London: Camden Society, 1884), p.57.
7 STC 22593–22620. See also the list in Alexander Dyce, ed., *The Poetical Works of John Skelton*, 2 vols. (London: Thomas Rodd, 1843), I, xci–ciii.
8 John Skelton, *The Complete English Poems*, ed. John Scattergood (Harmondsworth: Penguin, 1983). All subsequent references to this edition. On Horatian and Juvenalian satire, see Alvin B. Kernan, *The Cankered Muse: Satire of the English Renaissance* (New Haven: Yale University Press, 1959), chs. 1 and 2; John Peter, *Complaint and Satire in Early English Literature* (Oxford: Clarendon Press, 1956), passim. On Skelton as a satirist, see A. R. Heiserman, *Skelton and Satire* (Chicago University Press, 1961).
9 See King, *English Reformation Literature*, pp. 254–6 et passim; William Nelson, *John Skelton, Laureate* (New York: Russell and Russell, 1964), pp.231–3.
10 See also Thomas Campion, 'Ad Thamesin', in Walter R. Davies, ed., *The Works of Thomas Campion* (London: Faber, 1969), pp.362–77; Spenser, *Faerie Queene*, v, xi, 1–35. For commentary on Spenser's representation of the Armada victory, see Michael O'Connell, *The Mirror and the Veil: The Historical Dimension of Spenser's 'Faerie Queene'* (N. Carolina University Press, 1978), pp.148–9 et passim; Thomas H. Cain, *Praise in 'The Faerie Queene'* (Nebraska University Press, 1978), p.51; James Norhnberg, *The Analogy of 'The Faerie Queene'* (Princeton University Press, 1976), pp.420–1 et passim. Spenser cannot, of course, be seen as simply 'officially sanctioned', but the contrast to the linguistic register of the imitation-Skeltonic should be noted.
11 Published by Richard Facques (Fawkes) in 1523, *STC* 22610. See the list of works published in Skelton's lifetime in Maurice Pollet, *John Skelton, Poet of Tudor England*, trans. John Warrington (London: Dent, 1971), p. 264.
12 *STC* 22608. For Stow's role, see William Ringler, 'John Stow's Edition of Skelton's *Workes* and of *Certaine Worthye Manuscript Poems*', *Studies in Bibliography* 8 (1956), 215–17. This edition remained the standard until Dyce's edition of 1843.
13 See A. C. Spearing, *Medieval Dream Poetry* (Cambridge University Press, 1976), pp.211–18.
14 See Ernest Robert Curtius, *European Literature and the Latin Middle Ages*, trans. Willard R. Trask (London: RKP, 1979, rpt of 1953), pp.83–5.

15 Greg Walker, *John Skelton and the Politics of the 1520s* (Cambridge University Press, 1988), p.56; Stanley Fish, *John Skelton's Poetry* (New Haven: Yale University Press, 1965), p.230.
16 Walker, *John Skelton*, p.57; Fish, *John Skelton*, p.232.
17 John Skelton, *The Book of the Laurel*, ed. F. W. Brownlow (Newark: Delaware University Press, 1990), pp. 30–6.
18 F. M. Salter, 'Skelton's *Speculum Principis*', *Speculum* 9 (1934), 25–7, pp.31–3; Pollet, *John Skelton*, ch.2; Walker, *John Skelton*, ch.2.
19 Pollet, *John Skelton*, chs. 7–8; Walker, *John Skelton*, ch.6, especially p.191.
20 For a list of Facques's works, see *STC*, III, p.61.
21 On the symbolism of the oak, see David A. Loewenstein, 'Skelton's Triumph: *The Garland of Laurel* and Literary Fame', *Neophilologus* 68 (1984), 611–22, p.612. Galtres forest surrounds Sherrif Hutton, owned by the Howard family. On the Skelton–Howard links, see Walker, *John Skelton*, ch.1, especially pp.8–13; Arthur F. Kinney, *John Skelton: Priest as Poet* (Chapel Hill: North Carolina University Press, 1987), pp.191–4; Fox, *Politics and Literature*, pp.147–55, 191–5.
22 See Goldberg, *James I and the Politics of Literature*, especially ch.1; Jonathan Dollimore, *Radical Tragedy: Religion, Ideology and Power in the Drama of Shakespeare and his Contemporaries* (London: Harvester, second edn, 1989). See also, with particular reference to Skelton, Fish, *John Skelton*, especially 'Introduction'.
23 An example of type one might be *A Ballad of the Scottish Kynge*, or the unpublished 'A Lawde and Prayse Made for Our Sovereigne Lord the Kyng'; type two, *Colin Clout*; type three, *Speke Parrot*. See below for discussion.
24 The source is Ovid, *Metamorphoses*, trans. Mary M. Innes (Harmondsworth: Penguin, 1979, rpt of 1955), pp.41–4. Phoebus claims Daphne's laurels for victorious generals; Skelton transfers the honour to poets.
25 John Scattergood, 'Skelton's *Garlande of Laurell* and the Chaucerian tradition', in Ruth Morse and Barry Windeatt, eds., *Chaucerian Traditions: Studies in Honour of Derek Brewer* (Cambridge University Press, 1990), pp.122–38, p.123. Scattergood's analysis of Skelton's debt to *The House of Fame* and the theme of national identity in the *Garland* in many ways parallels mine. On the logic of the 'supplement', which 'trangresses' and 'respects' what goes before, see Jacques Derrida, '"That Dangerous Supplement"', *Of Grammatology*, pp.141–64.
26 When Gower in the *Garland* asks Skelton to 'encrese and amplyfy/ The bruttid Britons of Brutus Albion' (lines 404–5), he is, in effect,

asking him to complete the story of Aeneas' lineage. Lydgate, who finally conveys Skelton into the Palace of Fame, had written the massive *The Troy Book* (1412–20), ed. H. Bergen, 4 vols. (EETS, Oxford University Press, 1906–35).

27 *The Riverside Chaucer*, ed. Larry D. Benson (Boston: Houghton Mifflin, 1987). All subsequent references to this edition.

28 John Skelton, *The Bibliotheca Historia of Diodorus Sicilius*, ed. F. M. Salter and H. L. R. Edwards, 2 vols. (EETS, Oxford University Press, 1971, rpt of 1957), I, p.38, line 12. *OED* cites Chaucer as the first user of the term.

29 As Alice Miskimin claims was the wont of Renaissance readers; *Renaissance Chaucer*, especially pp.30–4.

30 On *The House of Fame*, see J. A. W. Bennett, *Chaucer's Book of Fame: An Exposition of 'The House of Fame'* (Oxford: Clarendon Press, 1957); Spearing, *Medieval Dream-Poetry*, pp.73–89.

31 Vincent Gillespie, 'Justification by Good Works: Skelton's *The Garland of Laurel*', *Reading Medieval Studies* 7 (1981), 19–31, p.25. Derek Pearsall, *John Lydgate* (London: RKP, 1970), ch.6.

32 Miskimin, *Renaissance Chaucer*, omits a discussion of the *Garland of Laurel* in her comments on the influence of *The House of Fame*, pp.67–80; but see her remarks on *Phyllyp Sparrowe*, pp.134–5.

33 Harold Bloom, *The Anxiety of Influence: A Theory of Poetry* (Oxford University Press, 1973), p.11.

34 Bloom, *Anxiety of Influence*, p.19.

35 Lewis, *English Literature of the Sixteenth Century*, p.135. See also Stanley J. Kozikowski, 'Allegorical Meanings in Skelton's *The Bowge of Court*', *PQ* 61 (1982), 305–15; Paul D. Psilos, '"Dulle" Drede and the Limits of Prudential Knowledge in Skelton's *The Bowge of Court*', *JMRS* 6 (1976), 297–317.

36 See Michael West, 'Skelton and the Renaissance Theme of Folly', *PQ* 50 (1971), 23–35; Alexander Barclay, *The Ship of Fools*, ed. T. H. Jamieson (Edinburgh, 1874).

37 For another representation of England as 'Anglia', see Holme, *The Fall and Evill Successe of Rebellion*. For comment see A. D. Hadfield, 'The Art of Fiction: Poetry and Politics in Reformation England', *Leeds Studies in English*, NS 23 (1992), 127–56, pp.144–6.

38 See Skelton, *Complete English Poems*, pp.501–2, for translation and comment. See also Brownlow, ed., *The Book of the Laurel*, p.183.

39 The moon, associated with Diana, was often a symbol of mutability; see Spenser, *Faerie Queene*, VII.

40 Iopas was the Carthagian poet who sang before Aeneas; *Aeneidos*, I, lines 740–7, in Publius Virgili Maronis, *Opera*, ed. R. A. B. Mynors (Oxford: Clarendon Press, 1969).

41 See John Scott Colley, 'John Skelton's Ironic Apologia: the Medieval Sciences, Wolsey, and *The Garlande of Laurell*', *Te.SLL* 18 (1973), 19–32, p.31.

42 'Against Dundas', lines 1–10; 'Agenst Garnesche', (iii) line 20, (v) line 129; 'Against Venemous Tongues', lines 79–82.

43 See David Lawton, 'Skelton's Use of Persona', *EIC* 30 (1980), 9–28; Heirsman, *Skelton and Satire*.

44 On the identity of the women, see M. J. Tucker, 'The Ladies in Skelton's *The Garland of Laurel*', *RQ* 22 (1969), 333–45.

45 Bernard Sharratt, 'John Skelton: Finding a Voice – Notes after Bakhtin', in David Aers, ed., *Medieval Literature: Criticism, Ideology and History* (Brighton: Harvester, 1986), pp.192–222, p.196; M. M. Bakhtin, *The Dialogic Imagination: Four Essays*, trans. C. Emerson and M. Holquist (Austin: Texas University Press, 1981), p.67.

46 Susan Schibanoff, 'Taking Jane's Cue: *Phyllyp Sparowe* as a Primer for Women Readers', *PMLA* 101 (1986), 832–44. Other readings of the poem can be found in Kinney, *John Skelton*, pp.98–116; F. W. Brownlow, '"The Boke of Phyllyp Sparowe" and the Liturgy', *ELR* 9 (1979), 5–20.

47 See Colley, 'John Skelton's Ironic Apologia'; Fish, *John Skelton*, pp.225–39.

48 Deliberately so, according to Stanley Fish, *John Skelton*, pp.225–39.

49 *Colin Clout*, lines 922–68; *Diodorus Sicilius*, p.359. On the 'laureateship', see Gordon Kipling, 'John Skelton and Burgundian Letters', in Jan Van Dorsten, ed., *Ten Studies in Anglo-Dutch Relations* (Leiden: Sir Thomas Browne Institute, G. S. 5, 1974), pp.1–29, pp.10–13; Gillespie, 'Justification by Good Works'.

50 Virgil, *Opera*, IX, line 525. On Calliope, see the entry 'Musae' in William Smith, ed., *A Dictionary of Greek and Roman Biography and Mythography*, 3 vols. (London: Murray, 1980), II, pp. 1124–6; Curtius, *Latin Literature*, ch.13. See also Spenser, *Faerie Queene*, VII, vi, 37, where Calliope is summoned to help the poet narrate his 'brief epic' of Mutability.

51 See T. D. Kendrick, *British Antiquity* (London: Methuen, 1950).

52 Brownlow, '"The Boke of Phyllyp Sparowe"', p.12; Schibanoff, 'Taking Jane's Cue', pp.839–42.

53 See the comments in Schibanoff, 'Taking Jane's Cue', pp.835–7, 841.

54 *Ibid.*, p.844.

55 See Quentin Skinner, *The Foundations of Modern Political Thought*, 2 vols. (Cambridge University Press, 1978).

56 See John Scattergood, 'Skelton and Heresy', in Daniel Williams, ed., *Early Tudor England: Proceedings of the 1987 Harlaxton Symposium*

(Woodbridge: Boydell, 1989), pp.157–70; Pollet, *John Skelton*, p.156; Walker, *John Skelton*, pp. 58–9, 188.

57 Nelson, *John Skelton*, p.126. See also Scattergood, 'Skelton and Heresy', p.161.

58 *STC* 18084 (1529).

59 Sharratt, 'John Skelton', p.196; Bakhtin, *The Dialogic Imagination*, p.324.

60 See Nelson, *John Skelton*, pp.155, 174; Walker, *John Skelton*, pp.63–7. For interpretations of this notoriously difficult poem, see Nathaniel Owen Wallace, 'The Responsibilities of Madness: John Skelton, "Speke Parrot", and Homeopathic Satire', *SP* 82 (1985), 60–80; F. W. Brownlow, '"The Boke Compiled by Maister Skelton, Poet Laureate, Called Speake Parrot"', *ELR* 1 (1971), 3–26.

61 See J. K. McConica, *English Humanists and Reformation Politics* (Oxford University Press, 1965); W. Gordon Zeeveld, *Foundations of Tudor Polity* (Cambridge, Mass.: Harvard University Press, 1948); Maria Dowling, *Humanism in the Age of Henry VIII* (London: Croom Helm, 1986).

62 See D. G. Hale, *The Body Politic: A Political Metaphor in Renaissance English Literature* (The Hague: Mouton, 1971).

63 Fish, *John Skelton*, p.249.

64 Peter Green, *John Skelton* (London: Longman, 1978), p.39. See also Richard Halpern, 'John Skelton and the Poetics of Primitive Accumulation', in Patricia Parker and David Quint, eds., *Literary Theory/ Renaissance Texts* (Baltimore: Johns Hopkins University Press, 1986), pp.225–56, pp.225–7.

65 Kipling, 'John Skelton and Burgundian Letters', p.3.

66 See also Nan Cooke Carpenter, *John Skelton* (New York: Twayne, 1967), p.36.

67 Kipling, 'John Skelton and Burgundian Letters', p.13.

68 For alternative literary genealogies, see R. S. Kinsman, 'Skelton's "Uppon a Dedmans Hed": New Light on the Origin of the Skeltonic', *SP* 50 (1953), 101–9; John Norton-Smith, 'The Origins of the Skeltonic', *EIC* 23 (1973), 57–62; Fitzroy Pyle, 'The Origin of the Skeltonic: A Note', *N. and Q.* 171 (1936), 362–4.

69 See Frances A. Yates, 'The Spirit of Chivalry', in *Ideas and Ideals in the North European Renaissance*, vol. III of *Collected Essays* (London: RKP, 1984), pp.24–7; Gillespie, 'Justification by Good Works', p.22. On the influence of Burgundian culture on the English Renaissance, see also Gordon Kipling, *The Triumph of Honour: Burgundian Origins of the Elizabethan Renaissance* (Leiden: Sir Thomas Browne Institute, G. S. 6, 1977); 'Henry VII and the Origins of Tudor Patronage', in Guy Finch Lytle and Stephen Orgel, eds.,

Patronage in the Renaissance (Princeton University Press, 1981), pp.117–64; J. H. Hexter, 'The Education of the Aristocracy in the Renaissance', *The Journal of Modern History* 22 (1950), 1–20.

70 On the use of 'homologies' and 'analogies', see Stephen Greenblatt, *Shakespearian Negotiations: The Circulation of Social Energy in Renaissance England* (Oxford: Clarendon Press, 1990, rpt of 1988), ch. 1, especially p.11; Gould, *Wonderful Life*, pp.213–14.

71 On the dominance of Bernard André at court, see Nelson, *John Skelton*, ch. 1; Walker, *John Skelton*, pp.36–9; Pollet, *John Skelton*, ch. 2.; Kipling, *Triumph of Honour*, ch. 1.

72 Edwards, *Critical Heritage*, pp.43–4; Nelson, *John Skelton*, p.34; Walker, *John Skelton*, pp.40–1.

73 Walker, *John Skelton*, p.38.

74 See Beatrice White, ed., *The Eclogues of Alexander Barclay* (EETS, Oxford University Press, 1960, rpt of 1928), 'Introduction', xxvi–xxx; Fox, *Politics and Literature*, pp.42–5, 52–3. One should also note that Barclay was probably Scottish and that Skelton was the major anti-Scots poet at court.

75 See Walker, *John Skelton*, pp.63–6; Pollet, *John Skelton*, pp.113–18.

76 See *Magnificence*, ed. Paula Neuss (Manchester University Press, 1980); William O. Harris, *Skelton's 'Magnificence' and the Cardinal Virtue Tradition* (Chapel Hill: N. Carolina University Press, 1965).

77 See A. D. Hadfield, 'Translating the Reformation: John Bale's *Vocacyon*', in Bradshaw, Hadfield and Maley, eds., *Representing Ireland*, pp.43–59.

78 John Bale, *Scriptorum Illustrium Majoris Brytanniae* (Basle, 1557), p.651, translated in Edwards, *Critical Heritage*, pp.54–5. The Latin 'blateronimus' from the verb 'blatero', means to 'babble or talk foolishly', so Bale may be responding to Skelton's distinctions between 'true' and 'false' speech, although Bale's own separation of 'truth' and 'falsehood' clearly differs from Skelton's.

79 See Erasmus, *Tyrannicida*, in *Collected Works*, 29, ed. and trans. E. Farntham and E. Rummel (Toronto University Press, 1989), pp.71–123; Thomas More, *Translations of Lucian*, ed. Craig R. Thompson, vol. III of *The Complete Works of Saint Thomas More* (New Haven: Yale University Press, 1974).

80 Miskimin, *Renaissance Chaucer*, ch. 8; King, *English Reformation Literature*, pp.50–2.

81 See Dyce, ed., *Poetical Works*, II, pp.400–47 for the texts.

82 Walker, *John Skelton*, p.38. The text of Thomas Colwell's *Merie Tales* (1566), *STC* 22618, plus variants, is printed in Dyce, ed., *Poetical Works*, I, 'Introduction', Appendix I, liii–lxxvii.

83 Dyce, ed., *Poetical Works*, lxxx.

84 Walker, *John Skelton*, p.32.

85 King, *English Reformation Literature*, pp.254–6; Edwards, *Critical Heritage*, pp.64–6.

86 See R. S. Kinsman, 'John Skelton' in A. C. Hamilton, ed., *The Spenser Encyclopedia* (London: RKP, 1990), pp. 659–60.

87 See Virginia F. Stern, 'Gabriel Harvey' and David R. Shore, 'Colin Clout' in Hamilton ed., *Spenser Encyclopedia*, pp.347–8, 172–3; Paul E. McLane, 'Skelton's *Colyn Cloute* and Spenser's *Shepherd's Calender*', *SP* 70 (1973), 141–59; *Spenser's 'Shepherdes Calender': A Study in Elizabethan Allegory* (Notre Dame University Press, 1968, rpt of 1961), pp. 37–9 et passim.

88 See Annabel Patterson, *Pastoral and Ideology: Virgil to Valéry* (London: Longman, 1977), especially ch. 2; Helen Cooper, *Pastoral: Medieval Into Renaissance* (Ipswich: Brewer, 1977), passim.

89 See Spenser's letter to Raleigh, *Faerie Queene*, ed. A. C. Hamilton (London: Longman, 1977), pp.737–8; Edwin A. Greenlaw, *Studies in Spenser's Historical Allegory* (Baltimore: Johns Hopkins University Press, 1932), ch. 4; Cain, *Praise in 'The Faerie Queene'*, passim; Robin Hedlam Wells, *Spenser's 'Faerie Queene' and the Cult of Elizabeth* (London: Croom Helm, 1983), ch. 1.

90 King, *English Reformation Literature*, p.255. On Churchyard, see *DNB* entry; Michael Brennan, *Literary Patronage in the English Renaissance: The Pembroke Family* (London: Croom Helm, 1988), passim.

91 Edwards, *Critical Heritage*, p.73.

92 King, *English Reformation Literature*, p.256.

93 William Webbe, *A Discourse of English Poetry* (1586), ed. Edward Arber (London: Bloomsbury, 1870), p.33.

94 Puttenham, *Arte of English Poesie*, p.69.

95 Henry Peacham, *The Compleat Gentleman* (London, 1622), *STC* 19502, p.95.

96 G. S. Fraser, cited in Edwards, *Critical Heritage*, p.188.

97 Lewis, *English Literature in the Sixteenth Century*, p.143.

98 J. Huizinga, *The Waning of the Middle Ages: A Study of Life, Thought, and Art in France and the Netherlands in the Fourteenth and Fifteenth Centuries*, trans. F. Hopman (Harmondsworth: Penguin, 1982, rpt of 1955); see also Kipling, *The Triumph of Honour*, pp.1–3.

99 Walker, *John Skelton*, ch. 1. See also John Scattergood, 'The London Manuscripts of John Skelton's Poems', in Felicity Riddy, ed., *Regionalism in Late Medieval Manuscripts and Texts: Essays Celebrating the Publication of 'A Linguistic Atlas of Late Medieval England'* (Cambridge: D. S. Brewer, 1991), pp.171–82.

100 Walker, *John Skelton*, chs. 3–4.

101 See Nancy A. Gutierrez, 'John Skelton: Courtly Poet/ Popular Maker', *JRMMRS* 4 (1983), 59–76. For differing assessments of

Skelton's relationship to Wolsey, see Fox, *Politics and Literature*, part III, 'The Cardinal'; Walker, *John Skelton*, chs. 5 and 6.

102 Walker, *John Skelton*, p.192.

103 Gutierrez, 'John Skelton: Courtly Poet', p.72; Lowenstein, 'Skelton's Triumph', pp.619–20.

104 See Jill Mann, *Chaucer and Medieval Estates Satire: The Literature of Social Classes and the General Prologue to 'The Canterbury Tales'* (Cambridge University Press, 1973).

105 See Paul E. McLane, 'Wolsey's Forced Loans and the Dating of Skelton's *Colyn Cloute*', *ELN* 10 (1972), 85–9.

106 Burgundian and Spanish soldiers, on behalf of the Emperor Charles V, fought alongside the English in France; see Skelton, *Complete English Poems*, ed. Scattergood, p. 486. On Henry VIII's wars with France, see J. J. Scarisbrick, *Henry VIII* (London: Methuen, 1988, rpt of 1968), chs. 4–6.

107 Gutierrez, 'John Skelton: Courtly Poet', p.76.

108 Sharratt, 'John Skelton: Finding a Voice', p.193.

109 William Caxton, *Eneydos* (London, c.1490), *STC* 24796, 'Prologue'.

110 Sharratt, 'John Skelton: Finding a Voice', p.194. See also Elizabeth Eisenstein, *The Printing Press as an Agent of Change* (Cambridge University Press, 1979); L. Febvre and H. J. Martin, *The Coming of the Book: The Impact of Printing, 1450–1800* (London: Verso, 1976, rpt of 1958).

111 Sharratt, 'John Skelton: Finding a Voice', p.194.

112 Roy Foster Jones, *The Triumph of the English Language: A Survey of Opinions Concerning the Vernacular from the Introduction of the Printing Press to the Restoration* (Stanford University Press, 1966, rpt of 1953).

113 See John Scattergood, 'John Skelton's Lyrics: Tradition and Innovation', *The Fifteenth Century*, *Acta* 12 (1985), 19–39; 'Skelton's *Garlande of Laurell*', pp.131–2.

114 N. F. Blake, *Non-Standard Language in English Literature* (London: André Deutsch, 1981), pp.40–6.

115 See Waller, *English Poetry of the Sixteenth Century*, pp.27–8; C. S. Lewis, *English Literature in the Sixteenth Century*, pp.133–43; Fowler, *A History of English Literature*, pp.39–40.

116 Young, *White Mythologies*, p.22.

117 Gould, *Wonderful Life*, ch.5.

2 JOHN BALE AND THE TIME OF THE NATION

1 See John Arden, 'Rug-Headed Irish Kerns and British Poets', *New Statesman*, 13 July 1979, pp.56–7.

2 See Franklin Le Van Baumer, *The Early Tudor Theory of Kingship* (New Haven: Yale University Press, 1940), ch. 4.

3 On Bodin, see Julian H. Franklin, *Jean Bodin and the Rise of Absolutist Theory* (Cambridge University Press, 1975); Skinner, *Foundations of Modern Political Thought*, II, pp.284–301; George Sabine, *A History of Political Theory* (Hinsdale, Illinois: Dryden Press, fourth edn, 1973), ch. 21.

4 *The Pagent of Popes*, trans. John Studeley (1574), *STC* 1304, 'To the Reader'.

5 *A Brief Chronicle Concerning the Examination and Death of Sir John Oldcastle, the Lord Cobham* (1544), reprinted in H. Christmas, ed., *Select Works of John Bale* (Cambridge: Parker Society, 1849), p.56. See also *Yet a Course at the Romysh Foxe* (1543), *STC* 1309, fo. 28; *Pagent of Popes*, fo. 102; *King Johan*, lines 2597–600 in *Complete Plays of John Bale*, 2 vols., ed. Peter Happé (Cambridge: Boydell and Brewer, 1985), I, p.96. For general information see Helen C. White, *Tudor Books of Saints and Martyrs* (Madison: Wisconsin University Press, 1963), ch. 3.

6 On Bale's use of rhetorical devices, see Rainer Pineas, 'Some Polemical Techniques in the Nondramatic Works of John Bale', *Bibliothèque d'Humanisme et Renaissance* 24 (1962), 583–8; Thora Balsler Blatt, *The Plays of John Bale: A Study of Ideas, Technique and Style* (Copenhagen: G. E. C. Gad, 1968), ch. 6. On Bale's distinctions between true and false martyrs, see *The Examinations of Anne Askew* in Christmas, ed., *Select Works*, pp.188, 238; *Romysh Foxe*, fos. 4, 18, 42; *The Actes of the English Votaries* (1546), *STC* 1270, fos. 5, 10.

7 Martin Luther, *An Appeal to the Ruling Class of German Nationality as to the Amelioration of the State of Christendom* (1520), in John Dillenberger, ed., *Martin Luther: Selections from his Writings* (New York: Doubleday, 1961), pp.409–10. See also W. Cargill-Thompson, 'Martin Luther and the "Two Kingdoms"' in David Thompson, ed., *Political Ideas* (Harmondsworth: Penguin, 1969), pp.34–52; Skinner, *Foundations of Modern Political Thought*, II, pp.196–200; Sabine, *History of Political Theory*, pp.336–9.

8 W. T. Davies, 'A Bibliography of John Bale', *Proceedings and Papers of the Oxford Bibliographical Society* 5 (1940), 201–79, p.226.

9 See A. G. Dickens, *The English Reformation* (London: Fontana, rev. edn, 1986, rpt of 1967), chs. 11–12; Sabine, *History of Political Theory*, pp.343–6; Skinner, *Foundations of Modern Political Thought*, II, pp.210–11, 223–4, 234–5.

10 Christopher Goodman, *How Superior Powers Ought to be Obeyed* (Geneva, 1558), *STC* 12020, p.183; John Knox, *The First Blast of the Trumpet against the Monstrous Regiment of Women* (1558), reprinted

in David Lang, ed., *Works*, IV (Edinburgh: Johnstone and Hunter, 1855), pp.403–4, 415–18; John Ponet, *A Shorte Treatise of Politike Power* (1556), *STC* 20178, pp.58–9, 98–9.

11 Goodman, *Superior Powers*, pp.44, 60; Knox, *First Blast*, p.416; 'A Homily against Disobedience and Wilful Rebellion', in *Certain Sermons: Appointed by the Queen's Majesty (1574)*, ed. G. E. Corrie (Cambridge University Press, 1850), pp.551–601. On Wyatt's rebellion, see Anthony Fletcher, *Tudor Rebellions* (London: Longman, third edn, 1983), ch. 7.

12 Ponet, *Politike Power*, p.33.

13 Rainer Pineas, 'William Tyndale's Influence on John Bale's Polemical Use of History', *Archiv für Reformationgeschichte* 53 (1962), 79–96; Stephen Ellis, 'John Bale, Bishop of Ossory, 1552–3', *Journal of the Butler Society* 3 (1984), 280–93, p.289; Norbrook, *Poetry and Politics*, p.40.

14 Patrick Collinson, *The Birthpangs of Protestant England: Religious and Cultural Change in the Sixteenth and Seventeenth Centuries* (London: Macmillan, 1988), p.27. See also Dickens, *English Reformation*, pp.394–417; William Haller, *Foxe's Book of Martyrs and the Elect Nation* (London: Cape, 1963), ch. 3.

15 Skinner, *Foundations of Modern Political Thought*, II; Michael Walzer, *The Revolution of the Saints* (London: Weidenfeld and Nicolson, 1966), especially chs. 2–3; M. M. Knappen, *Tudor Puritanism: A Chapter in the History of Idealism* (Chicago University Press, 1939), part II; H. C. Porter, ed., *Puritanism in Tudor England* (London: Macmillan, 1970).

16 Lawrence Stone, *The Causes of the English Revolution, 1529–1642* (London: RKP, 1972), pp.91–117; D. M. Loades, *Politics and the Nation, 1450–1660: Obedience, Resistance and Public Order* (London: Fontana, 1974, rpt of 1973), chs. 12, 15; Collinson, *Birthpangs of Protestant England*, ch. 1; John Morrill, 'The Church in England, 1642–9', in John Morrill, ed., *Reactions to the English Civil War* (London: Macmillan, 1986), pp.89–114.

17 The classic study is Ernst Kantorowicz, *The King's Two Bodies: A Study in Medieval Political Theology* (Princeton University Press, 1957). See also Marie Axton, *The Queen's Two Bodies: Drama and the Elizabethan Succession* (London: Royal Historical Society, 1977); Jacques Derrida, 'Given Time: The Time of the King', *Critical Inquiry* 18 (1992), 161–87.

18 See Roman Jakobson, 'Two Aspects of Language and two Types of Aphasic Disturbances', in *Selected Writings*, II (The Hague: Mouton, 1971), pp.239–59.

19 The best life of Bale remains, Davies, 'John Bale'; for more recent

work, see Peter Happé, 'Recent Studies in John Bale', *ELR* 17 (1987), 103–13.

20 Dickens, *English Reformation*, p.237.

21 On these, see Zeeveld, *Foundations of Tudor Polity*; McConica, *English Humanists and Reformation Politics*; T. F. Mayer, *Thomas Starkey and the Commonweal: Humanist Politics and Religion in the Reign of Henry VIII* (Cambridge University Press, 1989).

22 Dickens, *The English Reformation*, p. 237; *Letters and Papers of Henry VIII*, 14 (1), ed. James Gairdner and R. H. Brodie (London: Eyre and Spottiswoode, 1894), no. 47, pp.22–3.

23 King, *English Reformation Literature*, p. 293; Fairfield, '*The Vocacyon of John Bale*', pp. 328–9.

24 King, *English Reformation Literature*, pp.66–71; Collinson, *Birthpangs of Protestant England*, pp.99–115.

25 See Scarisbrick, *Henry VIII*, pp.375–83; C. S. L. Davies, *Peace, Print and Protestantism, 1450–1558* (London: Paladin, 1990, rpt of 1977), pp.210–13.

26 See Davies, 'John Bale', pp.248–9, 252–4, for bibliographical details. See also Haller, *Foxe's Book of Martyrs*, pp.61–72; King, *English Reformation Literature*, pp.422–4.

27 See Honor McCusker, *John Bale, Dramatist and Antiquary* (Bryn Mawr University Press, 1942), especially ch. 2; Caroline Brett, 'John Leland, Wales, and Early British History', *The Welsh History Review* 15 (1990), 169–82.

28 *Illustrium Majoris, STC* 1295. See also *Index Britanniae Scriptorum*, ed. R. L. Poole and Mary Bateson (Oxford: Clarendon Press, 1902). For commentary, see L. P. Fairfield, *John Bale: Mythmaker for the English Reformation* (Indiana: Purdue University Press, 1976), chs. 4–6; Jessie W. Harris, *John Bale, A Study in the Minor Literature of the Reformation* (Urbana: Illinois University Press, 1940), chs. 6, 9, 17.

29 See Katherine R. Firth, *The Apocalyptic Tradition in Reformation Britain, 1530–1645* (Oxford University Press, 1979), ch. 2; Richard Baukham, *Tudor Apocalypse, from John Bale to John Foxe and Thomas Brightman* (Oxford: Sutton Courtnay Press, 1978), pp.21–33, 68–76; Florence Sandler, '*The Faerie Queene*: an Elizabethan Apocalypse', in C. A. Patrides and Joseph Wittreich, eds., *The Apocalypse in English Renaissance Thought and Literature: Patterns, Antecedents and Repercussions* (Manchester University Press, 1984), pp.148–74; pp.157–8.

30 See Haller, *Foxe's Book of Martyrs*, pp.68–71; J. F. Mozeley, *John Foxe and his Book* (London: SPCK, 1940), pp.29–30, 51; Fairfield, *John Bale: Mythmaker*, pp.71–96, 106. For a more sceptical view of Bale's alleged influence, see V. Norskov Olsen, *John Foxe and the*

Elizabethan Church (Berkeley: California University Press, 1973), pp.39–45, 74–5.

31 Davies, 'John Bale', p.226.

32 E. J. Baskeville, 'John Ponet in Exile: A Ponet Letter to John Bale', *JEH* 37 (1986), 442–7, p.447. On Bale and Ponet in exile, see Christina H. Garrett, *The Marian Exiles: A Study in the Origins of Elizabethan Puritanism* (Cambridge University Press, 1966, rpt of 1938), pp.77–8, 253–8.

33 Davies, 'John Bale', p.227; John Foxe, *The Acts and Monuments of the Christian Church*, ed. Josiah Pratt, 8 vols. (London: Religious Trust Society, 1853–70), VIII, p.112.

34 See Honor McCusker, 'Books and Manuscripts formerly in the Possession of John Bale', *The Library*, fourth series, 16 (1935), 144–65.

35 See Conrad Russell, 'The British Background to the Irish Rebellion of 1641', *Historical Research* 61 (1988), 166–82; 'The British Problem and the English Civil War', *History* 73 (1988), 395–415. For evidence of Milton's plans, see 'Mansus' (1639), lines 80–4; 'Epitaphum Damonis' (1639), lines 162–71, in John Carey, ed., *Milton: Complete Shorter Poems* (London: Longmans, 1968), pp.264–5, 275–6. I owe these last references to David Fairer.

36 Davies, 'John Bale', p.230.

37 Blatt, *The Plays of John Bale*, pp.54–5; Pineas, 'Some Polemical Techniques'.

38 Davies, 'John Bale', p.230; Barnaby Googe, *Eclogues, Epitaphs, and Sonnets* (1563), ed. Judith M. Kennedy (Toronto University Press, 1989), pp.84–5.

39 Collinson, *Birthpangs of Protestant England*, p.14. See also Baukham, *Tudor Apocalypse*, pp.12–13, 71, 86; Firth, *Apocalyptic Tradition*, pp.106–9; Olsen, *John Foxe*, pp.36–47; Carol Z. Weiner, 'The Beleaguered Isle: A Study of Elizabethan and Early Jacobean Anti-Catholicism', *P. & P.* 51 (1971), 27–62; Bernard Capp, 'The Political Dimension of Apocalyptic Thought', in Patrides and Wittreich, eds., *The Apocalypse in English Renaissance*, pp.93–124; pp.95–6.

40 Haller, *Foxe's Book of Martyrs*, p.69.

41 Firth, *Apocalyptic Tradition*, pp.88–110. See also Olsen, *John Foxe*, pp.43–4; Baukham, *Tudor Apocalypse*, pp.86–8; Mozeley, *John Foxe*, pp.113–17.

42 Firth, *Apocalyptic Tradition*, p.109.

43 Norbrook, *Poetry and Politics*, p.44; Haller, *Foxe's Book of Martyrs*, ch. 2; Mozeley, *John Foxe*, ch. 5; Helen White, *Tudor Books of Saints and Martyrs*, ch. 5; *DNB* entry on John Foxe; A. D. Hadfield, 'The

English Conception of Ireland, c.1540–c.1600, with Special Reference to the Works of Edmund Spenser', unpublished PhD thesis (University of Ulster at Coleraine, 1988), pp.109–10.

44 Firth, *Apocalyptic Tradition*, p.68.

45 Cited in Mozeley, *John Foxe*, p.143.

46 Richard Hakluyt, *The Principal Navigations, Voyages, Traffiques and Discoveries of the English Nation*, 8 vols. (London: Dent, 1907), I, 'The Preface to the Second Edition, 1598', p.19. See also Catherine Belsey, 'The Illusion of Empire: Elizabethan Expansionism and Shakespeare's Second Tetralogy', *Literature and History*, second series, 1:2 (Autumn 1990), 13–21.

47 Homi K. Bhabha, 'DissemiNation: Time, Narrative, and the Margins of the Modern Nation', in Bhabha, ed., *Nation and Narration*, pp.297–302; Michel Foucault, *Discipline and Punish: The Birth of the Prison*, trans. Alan Sheridan (Harmondsworth: Penguin, 1986, rpt of 1977), pp.160–2, 190–1.

48 See Homi K. Bhabha, 'DissemiNation', pp.291–324, p.297.

49 Compare Raphael Holinshed, *Chronicles of England, Scotland and Ireland*, 6 vols. (London, 1809), II, pp.341–8; III, pp.136–56, 276–9; Edward Hall, *Chronicle Containing the History of England* (London, 1809), pp.114–16, 257–8; Richard Grafton, *Chronicle, or History of England, 1189–1588*, 2 vols. (London, 1809), I, pp.247–8, 549–61; II, pp.1–2.

50 *Expostulation, STC* 1294, fo. 50.

51 See King, *Tudor Royal Iconography*, pp.73–93.

52 *Epistel Exhortatorye STC* 1291; fo. 23.

53 *Ibid.*, fos. 13, 25.

54 *Ibid.*, fos. 27–8.

55 *Ibid.*, fo. 6.

56 See Foucault, *Discipline and Punish*, pp.79–80.

57 See Davies, 'John Bale', pp.250–1, 265–7, 270–2, for bibliographical details.

58 *Pagent of Popes*, fos. 23, 67, 193; *Lord Cobham*, pp.8–9; Fairfield, *John Bale, Mythmaker*, pp.126–7; Harris, *John Bale*, p.116. On the divided reactions to Polydore Vergil in the sixteenth century, see Polydore Vergil, *Anglia Historia, Bks 24–7*, ed. and trans. Denys Hay (London: Royal Historical Society, 1950), Camden Society, third series, 74, 'Introduction', especially, xxxiv–v; Cl. Hooper, 'Queen Katherine Parr, Polydore Vergil', *N. and Q.*, second series, 4 (1857), 67; Kendrick, *British Antiquity*, Chs. 6–7; Levy, *Tudor Historical Thought*, ch. 2.

59 *Votaries*, fo. 25; Polydore Vergil, *English History, Containing the First Eight Books, from an Early Translation*, ed. Sir Henry Ellis (London:

Royal Historical Society, 1840), Camden Society, second series, XXXVI, pp.129–30; Geoffrey of Monmouth, *The History of the Kings of Britain*, trans. Lewis Thorpe (Harmondsworth: Penguin, 1980, rpt of 1966), pp.124–6; Ranulph Higden, *Polychronicon*, ed. Churchill Babington and Joseph R. Lumby, 9 vols. (London: Longman, 1865–6), v, pp.28–34.

60 *Votaries*, fo. 23. See also, *Pagent of Popes*, 'Bale to the Reader'; Rainer Pineas, 'John Bale's Nondramatic Works of Religious Controversy', *Studies in the Renaissance* 9 (1962), 218–33, p.226. Peter Happé speculated that Bale's obsession possibly resulted from 'a sexual shock' whilst he was a Carmelite; *Complete Plays*, I, pp.2–3.

61 *Votaries*, fos. 28–30.

62 *Votaries*, fo. 24. See also *Scriptorum Illustrium Majoris Brytanniae*, I, 'Praefatio', pp.19–20.

63 *Pagent of Popes*, fo. 35.

64 See *Pagent of Popes*, fo. 57; *Anne Askew*, pp.235–7; *Vocacyon*, STC 1307, reprinted in *Harlean Miscellany*, 10 vols. (1813), X, pp.437–64, pp.446–7, 452; *Illustrium Scriptorum*, I, pp.64–6; Pineas, 'John Bale's Nondramatic Works', p.230; Fairfield, *John Bale: Mythmaker*, p.38.

65 Firth, *Apocalyptic Tradition*, pp.51–2; Baukham, *Tudor Apocalypse*, p.59.

66 *Pagent of Popes*, fo. 36; *Anne Askew*, p.188; Firth, *Apocalyptic Tradition*, p.83; Olsen, *John Foxe*, p.116. See also, Foxe, *Acts and Monuments*, I, pp.328–41. Foxe praises Gregory as a barrier against Roman perversions of the faith and blames Boniface II, his successor, for destroying the British church.

67 *Pagent of Popes*, Bk 5; Firth, *Apocalyptic Tradition*, pp.51–2, 83; Haller, *Foxe's Book of Martyrs*, pp.137, 171; Olsen, *John Foxe*, pp.70, 179, 189; Frances A. Yates, *Astrea: The Imperial Theme in the Sixteenth Century* (London: RKP, 1985, rpt of 1975), p.44; Fairfield, *John Bale: Mythmaker*, ch. 4; Foxe, *Acts and Monuments*, II, pp.116–34.

68 *Lord Cobham*, p.8.

69 Bhabha, 'DissemiNation', pp.312–14; Edward W. Said, 'An Ideology of Difference' in Gates, Jr., ed., '*Race*', *Writing, and Difference*, pp.38–58.

70 *Lord Cobham*, pp.15–18.

71 Goodman, *Superior Powers*, pp.44, 60. See also, Kantorowicz, *King's Two Bodies*, p.506; Sabine, *History of Political Theory*, ch. 20; Skinner, *Foundations of Modern Political Thought*, II, ch. 4.

72 Harris, *John Bale*, p.30. Cobham was not, of course, a dramatist or

a priest, but he did, according to Bale, deny 'real' presence in the sacraments and was, like Bale, a follower of Wycliffe; see *Lord Cobham*, pp.31, 50; Margaret Aston, 'John Wycliffe's Reformation Reputation', *P. & P.* 30 (1965), 23–51, pp.24–7.

73 *Anne Askew*, pp.188–9.

74 King, *English Reformation Literature*, p.61; Kohn, *The Idea of Nationalism*, pp.5, 8, 110, 114; Hadfield, 'Translating the Reformation', p.47.

75 King, *English Reformation Literature*, p.61; Firth, *Apocalyptic Tradition*, ch. 7.

76 King, *English Reformation Literature*, pp.61, 429; Firth, *Apocalyptic Tradition*, ch. 7. Fairfield, *John Bale: Mythmaker*, pp.100–3 shows how Bale's view of history altered between *The Pagent of Popes* and the *Image of Both Churches*; Olsen, *John Foxe*, pp.83, 141, points out how Foxe did not follow Bale's periodisation slavishly, but made alterations.

77 See Fairfield, *John Bale: Mythmaker*, ch. 4; Baukham, *Tudor Apocalypse*, pp.21–36, 66, 80–90; Firth, *Apocalyptic Tradition*, ch. 2; King, *English Reformation Tradition*, pp. 61–4, 128–9, 448–9.

78 King, *English Reformation Literature*, p.62.

79 *Image of Both Churches*, p.254.

80 See Robert C. Holub, *Reception Theory: A Critical Introduction* (London: Methuen, 1984), ch. 5, for a summary of contemporary debates on the problems of reading.

81 See chapter 1, footnote 25.

82 *Image of Both Churches*, pp.260–1.

83 King, *English Reformation Literature*, p.62.

84 *Image of Both Churches*, p.389.

85 *Ibid.*, pp.497, 605.

86 Roland Barthes, *S/Z: An Essay*, trans. Richard Miller (New York: Hill and Wang, 1987, rpt of 1974), p.20.

87 Michel Foucault, *The Order of Things: An Archaeology of the Human Sciences* (London: Tavistock, 1986, rpt of 1970), pp.42–3.

88 See also Walter J. Ong, *Ramus, Method and the Decay of Dialogue: From the Art of Discourse to the Art of Reason* (Cambridge, Mass.: Harvard University Press, 1958); Gerald Graff, 'Co-option', in Veeser, ed., *The New Historicism*, pp.168–81, pp.171–2; Barthes, *S/Z*, pp.3–4.

89 *Image of Both Churches*, p.350.

90 See Hadfield, 'English Conception of Ireland', pp.71–5. On enunciation, see Julia Kristeva, 'The Speaking Subject', in Marshall Blonsky, ed., *On Signs: A Semiotics Reader* (Oxford: Basil Blackwell, 1985), pp.210–21.

91 See Michel Foucault, 'The Eye of Power', in *Power/Knowledge: Selected Interviews and Other Writings, 1972–1977*, ed. Colin Gordon (New York: Pantheon, 1980), pp.146–65.

92 Collinson, *Birthpangs of Protestant England*, pp.4–7; Haller, *Foxe's Book of Martyrs*, p.87; Skinner, *Foundations of Modern Political Thought*, II, pp.106–7. See also Keith Dockray, 'Patriotism, Pride and Paranoia: England and the English in the Fifteenth Century', *The Ricardian: Journal of the Richard III Society*, 8, No. 110 (1990), 430–42; John W. McKenna, 'How God Became an Englishman', in Delloyd G. Guth and John W. McKenna, *Tudor Rule and Revolution: Essays for G. R. Elton from his American Friends* (Cambridge University Press, 1982), pp.25–44.

93 King, *English Reformation Literature*, p.69.

94 See Hadfield, 'Translating the Reformation'; Ellis, 'John Bale'.

95 George Sampson, *The Concise Cambridge History of English Literature*, rev. R. C. Churchill (Cambridge University Press, 1979, rpt of 1972); Fowler, *A History of English Literature*.

96 *Lord Cobham*, 'Preface', pp.5–14; *Anne Askew*, 'Preface', pp.137–44; *Image of Both Churches*, passim; *Scriptorum Illustrium*, passim.

97 Harris, *John Bale*, p.118.

98 King, *English Reformation Tradition*, pp.69–70.

99 See Terrance Cave, *The Cornucopian Text: Problems of Writing in the French Renaissance* (Oxford: Clarendon Press, 1979); Attridge, *Peculiar Language*, ch. 1.

100 *Expostulation*, STC 1274; fo. 18.

101 *Papystycall Exhortacyon*, fo. 1.

102 *Ibid.*, fo. 5. See also the frontispiece to the *Vocacyon* (not reprinted in *Harlean Miscellany*).

103 *Papystycall Exhortacyon*, fo. 6.

104 On this, see Barbara Kiefer Lewalski, *Protestant Poetics and the Seventeenth Century Religious Lyric* (Princeton University Press, 1979); John N. King and Robin Smith, 'Recent Studies in Protestant Poetics', *ELR* 21 (1991), 283–307, pp.283–5.

105 See Ruth H. Blackburn, *Biblical Drama under the Tudors* (The Hague: Mouton, 1971), ch. 2, for analysis and discussion of Bale's dramatic output.

106 See Jürgen Häbermas, *Legitimation Crisis*, trans. Thomas McCarthy (Oxford: Polity Press, 1988, rpt of 1976), pp.117–30; A. D. Nuttall, *Overheard by God: Fiction and Prayer in Herbert, Milton, Dante and St John* (London: Methuen, 1980), ch. 1.

107 L. P. Fairfield, '*The Vocacyon of Johan Bale* and early English Autobiography', *RQ* 24 (1971), 327–40, p.339.

108 *Vocacyon*, p.439.

109 Bale's assertion was by no means obvious to all students of the Constitution and many argued that Ireland was a country ruled by the English king but with its own separate legislature and executive; see Hans Pawlisch, *Sir John Davies and the Conquest of Ireland: A Study in Legal Imperialism* (Cambridge University Press, 1985), chs. 3, 6; R. Dudley Edwards and T. W. Moody, 'The History of Poynings' Law, 1494–1615', *IHS* 2 (1941), 415–24.

110 See Ellis, 'John Bale', pp. 285–8; Brendan Bradshaw, 'George Browne, First Reformation Archbishop of Dublin, 1536–54', *JEH* 21 (1970), 301–26.

111 See Fairfield, '*The Vocacyon of Johan Bale*', p. 331; King, *English Reformation Literature*, p. 419.

112 On 'disguisings', see Glynn Wickham, *Early English Stages*, 3 vols. (London: RKP, 1966), I, chs. 5, 6. The implication may also be that Catholic plays are disguised and 'dark conceits', whereas Bale's Protestant dramas are clear and 'true'.

113 *The Temptation of Our Lord*, in Happé, ed., *Complete Plays of John Bale*, II, p.61.

114 Sidney, *Apology for Poetry*, pp.99–100, 123. See also Paul Ricoeur, *The Rule of Metaphor: Multi-Disciplinary Studies in the Creation of Meaning in Language*, trans. Robert Czerny *et al* (Toronto University Press, 1984, rpt of 1977), 'Introduction'.

115 David Bevington, *Tudor Drama and Politics: A Critical Approach to Topical Meaning* (Cambridge, Mass.: Harvard University Press, 1968), p.98. See also note 22 above.

116 See *King Johan*, ed. Barry B. Adams (San Marino: Huntington Library, 1969), 'Introduction', pp.1–25; Peter Happé, 'Sedition in *King Johan*: Bale's Development of a Vice', *Medieval English Theatre* 3. 1 (1981), 3–6, pp.3–4; Happé, ed., *Complete Plays of John Bale*, I, pp.9–11; Greg Walker, *Plays of Persuasion: Drama and Politics at the Court of Henry VIII* (Cambridge University Press, 1991), pp.170–8; Davies, 'John Bale', pp.211–12, for more detail of the play's textual history.

117 Happé, 'Sedition in *King Johan*'; Clarence G. Cason, 'Additional Lines for Bale's *Kynge Johan*', *JEGP* 27 (1928), 42–50.

118 Adams, ed., *Kynge Johan*, 'Introduction', pp.23–4; Happé, ed., *Complete Plays of John Bale*, I, pp.11, 97.

119 Bevington, *Tudor Drama and Politics*, p.105.

120 See S. F. Johnson, 'The Tragic Hero in Early Elizabethan Drama', in Josephine W. Bennett *et al.*, eds., *Studies in English Renaissance Drama* (London: Peter Owen and Vision Press, 1959), pp.157–71; J. M. R. Margeson, *The Origins of English Tragedy* (Oxford: Clarendon Press, 1967), pp.47–50; Northrop Frye,

Anatomy of Criticism: Four Essays (Princeton University Press, 1973, rpt of 1957), pp.35–52.

121 See Blackburn, *Biblical Drama*, p.36; Blatt, *Plays of John Bale*, p.23; May Mattsson, *Five Plays about King John* (Uppsala: Almquist & Wiksell International, 1977), p.130; Paul Whitfield White, *Theatre and Reformation: Protestantism, Patronage, and Playing in Tudor England* (Cambridge University Press, 1993), p.28. Becket is attacked in *King John*, lines 2589–92.

122 See Peter Womack, 'Imagining Communities: Theatre and the English Nation in the Sixteenth Century', in David Aers, ed., *Culture and History, 1350–1600: Essays on English Communities, Identities and Writing* (Hassocks: Harvester, 1992), pp.91–145, p.116.

123 *King John*, line 28. Future references in parentheses. See also Edwin Shepherd Miller, 'The Roman Rite in Bale's *King John*', *PMLA* 64 (1949), 802–22.

124 See Mattsson, *Five Plays about King John*, p.95; Blatt, *Plays of John Bale*, p.128.

125 Happé, 'Sedition in *King Johan*'; Mattsson, *Five Plays about King John*, pp.122–30; Blatt, *Plays of John Bale*, p.125; White, *Theatre and Reformation*, p.36.

126 The change takes place after line 1782; see David Bevington, *From Mankind to Marlowe: Growth of Structure in the Popular Drama of Tudor England* (Cambridge, Mass.: Harvard University Press, 1962), p.132; Irving Ribner, *The English History Play in the Age of Shakespeare* (London: Methuen, 1965, rpt of 1957), p.34. On Langton, see *DNB* entry.

127 Womack, 'Imagining Communities', p.117.

128 See Mattsson, *Five Plays about King John*, pp.21–7; Ribner, *English History Play*, p.34; Blatt, *Plays of John Bale*, p.106; Walker, *Plays of Persuasion*, p.183.

129 Mattsson, *Five Plays about King John*, p.123.

130 Womack, 'Imagining Communities', pp.116–19.

131 See Hayden White, *Metahistory*, pp.31–8; Fredric Jameson, *The Political Unconscious: Narrative as Socially Symbolic Act* (London: Methuen, 1986, rpt of 1981), p.102.

132 Lines 2194–5; see note 58 above.

133 Bevington, *Tudor Drama and Politics*, p.100; M. H. and R. Dodds, *The Pilgrimage of Grace*, II, chs. 19–20; Mary Bateson, ed., 'Aske's Narrative of the Pilgrimage of Grace', *EHR* 5 (1890), 330–45.

134 See Ribner, *English History Play*, p.36; Blatt, *Plays of John Bale*, pp.123–5; Haller, *Foxe's Book of Martyrs*, pp.85–6. For an elaborate analytical account of the contemporary events and their significance for Bale's position as a reformer, see Walker,

Plays of Persuasion, pp.210–21; see also Louis Montrose, 'The Elizabethan Subject and the Spenserian Text', in Parker and Quint, eds., *Literary Theory/Renaissance Texts*, 303–40, p.322.

135 Karl Marx, *The Eighteenth Brumaire of Louis Napoleon*, in *Surveys From Exile*, ed. David Fernbach (Harmondsworth: Penguin, 1973), pp.143–249, p.146.

136 On the Elizabethan church settlement, see William P. Haugaard, *Elizabeth and the English Reformation: The Struggle for a Stable Settlement of Religion* (Cambridge University Press, 1968). On Bale's influence, see King, *English Reformation Literature*, pp.56–61, 96–8; Baukham, *Tudor Apocalypse*, ch. 11.

137 See Capp, 'The Political Dimension of Apocalyptic Thought'; Firth, *Apocalyptic Tradition*, 'Conclusion'.

3 LITERATURE AND HISTORY

1 A. M. Kinghorn, *The Chorus of History: Literary–Historical Relations in Renaissance Britain, 1485–1558* (London: Batsford, 1971), pp. 266–9; Waller, *English Poetry of the Sixteenth Century*, pp.40–1; Evans, *English Poetry in the Sixteenth Century*, pp.124–8; E. M. W. Tillyard, *A Mirror for Magistrates* revisited', in Herbert Davies and Helen Gardner, eds., *Elizabethan and Jacobean Studies Presented to Frank Percy Wilson in Honour of his Seventieth Birthday* (Oxford: Clarendon Press, 1959), 1–16, pp. 8–10; Lily B. Campbell, *Tudor Conceptions of History and Providence in 'A Mirror for Magistrates'* (Berkeley: California University Press, 1936), pp. 7–8, 13–14, 24–5. For the *Homilies* see 'An Homily against Disobedience and Wilful Rebellion' in *Certain Sermons Appointed by the Queen's Magesty* (1574), ed. G. E. Corrie (Cambridge: Parker Society, 1850), pp.551–601.

2 See Willard Farnham, *The Medieval Heritage of Elizabethan Tragedy* (Oxford: Basil Blackwell, 1956, rpt of 1936), ch. 7; Frederick Kiefer, 'Fortune and Providence in the *Mirror for Magistrates*', *SP* 74 (1977), 146–64; Campbell, *Tudor Conceptions of History and Tragedy*, pp.18–19.

3 Jerry Leath Mills, 'Recent Studies in *A Mirror for Magistrates*', *ELR* 9 (1979), 343–54, p.349 and the list on pp.351–2. See also E. M. W. Tillyard, *Shakespeare's History Plays* (London: Chatto and Windus, 1969, rpt of 1944), pp.83–8; Lily B. Campbell, *Shakespeare's Histories: Mirrors of Elizabethan Policy* (San Marino: Huntington Library Publications, 1947), passim.

4 See L. C. Knights, 'How Many Children Had Lady Macbeth?' in *Explorations: Essays in Criticism Mainly on the Literature of the Seventeenth Century* (London: Chatto and Windus, 1963), pp.1–39.

5 Sir Philip Sidney, *An Apologie for Poetry*, ed. Geoffrey Shepherd (Manchester University Press, rpt of 1965), p.133. All subsequent references to this edition in parentheses.

6 *A Mirror for Magistrates*, ed. Lily B. Campbell (Cambridge University Press, 1938), p.198, lines 22–35. All subsequent references to this edition in parentheses. See also Homer Nearing, *English Historical Poetry, 1599–1641* (Philadelphia: University of Pennsylvania Press, 1945), p.34. Alwin Thaler discusses parallels between the *Mirror* and the *Apologie* in 'Literary Criticism in *A Mirror for Magistrates*', *JEGP* 49 (1950), 1–13.

7 See Lily B. Campbell, 'The Suppressed Edition of *A Mirror for Magistrates*', *Huntington Library Bulletin* 6 (1934), 1–16. On Wayland see *STC*, III, p.179.

8 Campbell, *Tudor Conceptions of History and Tragedy*, p.9.

9 John Bale, *Scriptorum Illustrium*, II, p.108, cited in Campbell, ed., *Mirror*, 'Introduction', p.21. On Baldwin's life, see Eveline I. Feasey, 'William Baldwin', *MLR* 20 (1925), 407–18; Stephen Gresham, 'William Baldwin: Literary Voice of the Reign of Edward VI', *HLQ* 44 (1980–1), 101–16; *DNB* entry; Campbell, ed., *Mirror*, 'Introduction', pp.21–5.

10 Campbell, *Tudor Conceptions of History and Tragedy*, p.10.

11 Thomas Warton claimed that Thomas Sackville was the originator of the plan for the *Mirror*, which he intended to be a Dantesque descent into hell where 'all the illustrious but unfortunate characters of the English history, from the conquest to the end of the fourteenth century, were to pass in review before the poet'. This had been scotched when he was called away on important matters of state with only the famous 'Induction' completed and he passed responsibility on to Baldwin and Ferrars; *The History of English Poetry* (London, 1781), p.38. Warton cites no source for such a history of the text and Campbell (ed., *Mirror*, p.38) was unable to find any evidence to support his contentions ('that he was the "primary inventor" of the design ... there is certainly not the faintest suggestion'), although she believes 'Sackville must ... have been cognizant of events connected with the suppressed edition, and he may have been one of the group who undertook to write the account of the unfortunate English princes.'

12 See Campbell, ed., *Mirror*, pp.25–31; *DNB* entry.

13 Campbell, ed., *Mirror*, p.10. However there is a single extant leaf of the suppressed edition which identifies two other contributors, Thomas Phaer (author of 'The Tragedy of Owen Glendower') and Thomas Chaloner (author of 'The Tragedy of Richard II'). For details, see pp.31–4. Later contributors included Thomas

Churchyard (author of 'The Tragedy of Jane Shore'), Thomas Sackville (author of the 'Induction' and 'The Tragedy of Henry, Duke of Buckingham'), and John Dolman (author of 'The Tragedy of Hastings'). For details of the lives, see Campbell, ed., *Mirror*, pp.21–48.

14 Prose links 4 and 24 in the *Mirror*, pp.110–11, 371–2. Edmund Halle, *Chronicle, Containing the History of England* (London, 1809); Richard Grafton, *Chronicle, or History of England*, 2 vols. (London, 1809); Thomas More, *History of King Richard III, Complete Works of Saint Thomas More*, vol. II, ed. R. S. Sylvester (Yale University Press, 1963).

15 Campbell, 'Suppressed Edition', pp.10–11.

16 The printer was Thomas Marsh; Edward Arber, ed., *A Transcript of the Registers of the Company of the Stationers of London, 1554–1640*, 5 vols. (London, 1875), I, p.33. On Marsh's work see *STC*, III, p.115.

17 Campbell, ed., *Mirror*, pp.3–20; Lily B. Campbell, ed., *Parts Added to 'The Mirror for Magistrates'* (Cambridge University Press, 1946), pp.8–10. All subsequent references to this edition.

18 On the numerous editions of the various guises of the *Mirror* which appeared between 1559 and 1610, see *STC*, I, pp.57–8, 585–6. On the progeny of the *Mirror* see Nearing, *English Historical Poetry*, chs. 2–4; Farnham, *Medieval Heritage*, ch.8.

19 John Lydgate, *The Fall of Princes*, 4 vols., ed. H. Bergen (EETS: Oxford University Press, 1967, rpt of 1924–27), I, 'Introduction', p.x. All subsequent references to this edition.

20 Derek Pearsall, *John Lydgate* (London: RKP, 1970), p.224; Herbert G. Wright, *Boccaccio in England from Chaucer to Tennyson* (London: Athlone Press, 1957), pp.5–7. On Humphrey Plantaganet, Duke of Gloucester, see *DNB* entry; V. J. Scattergood, *Politics and Poetry in the Fifteenth Century* (London: Blandford, 1971), pp.137–60; Roberto Weiss, *Humanism in the Fifteenth Century* (Oxford: Basil Blackwell, 1941), chs. 3, 4.

21 On Richard Pynson, see *STC*, III, pp.140–1.

22 For details of the textual history see Bergin, ed., *Fall*, IV, pp.3–124; Pearsall, *John Lydgate*, pp.250–1; Wright, *Boccaccio in England*, p.21; Farnham, *Medieval Heritage*, pp.277–9.

23 Farnham, *Medieval Heritage*, pp.78–9. See also D. W. Robertson Jr, 'Chaucerian Tragedy', *ELH* 19 (1952), 1–37; Howard R. Patch, *The Goddess Fortuna in Medieval Literature* (Cambridge, Mass.: Harvard University Press, 1927), ch. 2. Both these studies suggest that the problem is more complex than Farnham alleges here.

24 Farnham, *Medieval Heritage*, p.168.

25 Kiefer, 'Fortune and Providence in the *Mirror*', p.150.

26 Farnham, *Medieval Heritage*, pp.280–1.
27 Robertson, 'Chaucerian Tragedy', p.37; Farnham, *Medieval Heritage*, ch. 3 et passim. See also Raymond Williams, *Modern Tragedy* (London: Verso, 1979, rpt of 1966), pp.19–23.
28 Campbell, *Tudor Conceptions of History and Tragedy*, p.9; see also Farnham, *Medieval Heritage*, pp.155–6; Tillyard, *Shakespeare's History Plays*, pp.71–2.
29 Pearsall, *John Lydgate*, p.235.
30 William Peery, 'Tragic Retribution in the 1559 *Mirror for Magistrates*', *SP* 46 (1949), 113–30, pp.128–9.
31 See Roger Howell, *Sir Philip Sidney: The Shepherd Knight* (London: Hutchinson, 1968), ch. 6.
32 On humanism in England before the 'Renaissance', see Weiss, *Humanism in England*.
33 See Pearsall, *John Lydgate*, especially chs. 4, 8; Weiss, *Humanism in England*, especially chs. 3–7.
34 Scattergood, *Poetry and Politics*, pp.43–4. For a more comprehensive analysis of Lydgate's alterations, see Wright, *Boccaccio in England*, pp.5–16.
35 On the re-establishment of English in the fourteenth century, see A. C. Baugh, *A History of the English Language* (London: RKP, 1959), pp.171–88.
36 See Ralph A. Griffiths, *The Reign of King Henry VI: The Exercise of Royal Authority, 1422–1461* (London: Ernest Benn, 1981), part 1.
37 Bakhtin, *Dialogic Imagination*, pp.84–85.
38 See Rosalie L. Colie, *The Resources of Kind: Genre-Theory in the Renaissance*, ed. Barbara K. Lewlaski (Berkeley: California University Press, 1973). For an intelligent application of genre-theory to the *Mirror*, see S. Clark Hulse, 'The Elizabethan Minor Epic: Toward a Definition of Genre', *SP* 73 (1976), 302–19.
39 Bakhtin, *Dialogic Imagination*, p.273; see also *Rabelais and his World*, trans. Hélène Iswolsky (Bloomington: Indiana University Press, 1984), especially ch.1 and the review by Frances Yates reprinted as 'The Last Laugh' in *Ideas and Ideals*, pp.153–63.
40 See Henry Chadwick, *The Early Church* (Harmondsworth: Penguin, 1976, rpt of 1967), ch. 12, 'The Ascetic Movement'.
41 For the relevant historical background, see Peter Heath, *Church and Realm, 1272–1461* (London: Fontana, 1988).
42 Bakhtin, *Dialogic Imagination*, pp. 285–6. See also Anthony Easthope, *Poetry as Discourse* (London: Methuen, 1983).
43 L. D. Green, 'Modes of Perception in the *Mirror for Magistrates*', *HLQ* 44 (1980–1), 117–33, pp.123–4.
44 See the comments in Wright, *Boccaccio in England*, p.23.

45 On Tresilian, see *DNB* entry; Anthony Steel, *Richard II* (Cambridge University Press, 1941), pp.89–90, 149–56 et passim.
46 Grafton, *Chronicle*, I, pp.412–73. Halle's *Chronicle* only begins with the reign of Henry IV.
47 See Skinner, *Modern Political Thought*, II, ch. 7. On Richard's reign, see F. R. H. Du Boulay and C. M. Barron, eds., *The Reign of Richard II, Essays in Honour of May McKitrick* (London: Athlone Press, 1971); Steel, *Richard II*.
48 G. B. Harrison, *The Life and Death of Robert Devereux, Earl of Essex* (London: Cassell, 1937), pp.281–2.
49 Skinner, *Foundations of Modern Political Thought*, II, chs. 7–9.
50 See Walzer, *The Revolution of the Saints*; Lawrence Stone, *The Causes of the English Revolution, 1529–1642* (London: RKP, 1972); Sabine, *A History of Political Theory*, pp.339–44.
51 On the Mortimers, see *DNB* entries; Steel, *Richard II*, pp.230–46 et passim; J. H. Harvey, 'Richard II and York', in Du Boulay and Barron, eds., *The Reign of Richard II*, pp.202–17, 212–14.
52 On Woodstock, see *DNB* entry; Steel, *Richard II*, pp.117–18, 147–57, chs. 7–8.
53 Eveline Iris Feasey, 'The Licensing of the *Mirror For Magistrates*', *The Library*, fourth series, III (123), 177–93.
54 Feasey, 'The Licensing of the *Mirror*', p.181. On Edward Seymour, see W. K. Jordan, *Edward VI, The Young King: The Protectorship of the Duke of Somerset* (Cambridge, Mass.: Harvard University Press, 1971).
55 Feasey, 'The Licensing of the *Mirror*', p.183; William Baldwin, *A Treatise of Morall Philosophie* (1548), *STC* 1253, 'Dedication'. On Seymour as a patron of letters, see King, *English Reformation Literature*, pp.113–22; McConica, *English Humanists and Reformation Politics*, ch. 8.
56 Feasey, 'The Licensing of the *Mirror*', p.181.
57 On Eleanor Cobham, see *DNB* entry for Humphrey Plantaganet, Duke of Gloucester; Bertram Wolfe, *Henry VI* (London: Methuen, 1981), pp.126–32.
58 On Suffolk, see *DNB* entry for Pole, William de la; Wolfe, *Henry VI*, passim.
59 See also Lily B. Campbell, 'Humphrey Duke of Gloucester and Eleanor Cobham His Wife in the *Mirror for Magistrates*', *Huntington Library Bulletin* 5 (1934), 119–55; John King, *English Reformation Literature*, pp.414–16. King's attempts to deny specific historical references in the *Mirror* are unconvincing. See also Benedicta J. H. Rowe, 'John, Duke of Bedford, in *A Mirror For Magistrates*, Tragedy 30', *N.and Q.* NS 22 (1975), 296–300.

60 See Jennifer Loach and Robert Tittler, eds., *The Mid-Tudor Polity*, *c*.1540–1560 (London: Macmillan, 1980).

61 Feasey, 'The Licensing of the *Mirror*', p.184. On Gardiner, see *DNB* entry; Wolfe, *Henry VI*, passim.

62 On Tiptoft, see *DNB* entry; Weiss, *Humanism in England in the Fifteenth Century*, pp.109–22.

63 On Jack Cade, see *DNB* entry; Wolfe, *Henry VI*, pp.231–8. On Glendower, see *DNB* entry; J. L. Kirby, *Henry IV of England* (London: Constable, 1970), pp.106–8 et passim.

64 See Kiefer, 'Fortune and Providence in the *Mirror*'.

65 Smith, *De Republica Anglorum*, p.46.

66 On prophecy in the English Renaissance, see Howard Dobin, *Merlin's Disciples: Prophecy, Poetry and Power in Renaissance England* (Stanford University Press, 1990); pp.157–61 deal with Owen Glendower. See also the discussion of the tragedy of George, Duke of Clarence in the *Mirror*, pp.61–75.

67 See Kendrick, *British Antiquity*; Levy, *Tudor Historical Thought*, pp.65–9; Greenlaw, *Studies in Spenser's Historical Allegory*, ch. 1; Charles Millican Bowie, *Spenser and the Table Round: A Study in the Contemporaneous Background for Spenser's Use of the Arthurian Legend* (London: Frank Cass, 1967, rpt of 1932).

68 Glendower is associated with Merlin (*Mirror*, p.123, line 53; p.127, line 158 et passim), the most ambiguous and dangerous British figure in Tudor England; see Dobin, *Merlin's Disciples*, ch.1.

69 On Norton, see *DNB* entry.

70 On Sackville, see Normand Berlin, *Thomas Sackville* (New York: Twayne, 1974); Fitzroy Pyle, 'Thomas Sackville and *A Mirror for Magistrates*', *RES* 14 (1938), 315–21.

71 See King, *English Reformation Literature*, pp.114, 369; Gresham, 'William Baldwin', pp.107–9.

72 See, for example, Sinfield, *Literature in Protestant England*, especially ch. 2; Virgil K. Whitaker, *The Religious Basis of Spenser's Thought* (Stanford University Press, 1950); Nuttall, *Overheard By God*, ch.1.

73 Martin Luther, *The Bondage of the Will* (1525), in *Works*, 33, ed. and trans. Philip S. Watson and Benjamin Drewery (Philadelphia: Fortress Press, 1972); Richard Hooker, *Of The Laws of Ecclesiastical Polity*, 2 vols. (London: Dent, 1968, rpt of 1907), II, pp.507–43. See also Dickens, *The English Reformation*.

74 Sabine, *A History of Political Theory*, pp.339–44. On Calvin, see François Wendel, *John Calvin: The Origins and Development of His Religious Thought*, trans. Philip Mairet (London: Fontana, 1978, rpt of 1963); T. H. L. Parker, *John Calvin* (Tring, Herts.: Lion, 1975).

75 Jean Calvin, *The Institution of the Christian Religion*, trans. Thomas Norton (1582), *STC* 4415. All subsequent references to this edition.

76 Baldwin, *Morall Philosophie*, Bk 3; Gresham, 'William Baldwin', p.104.

77 Feasey, 'William Baldwin', p.417.

78 Alan T. Bradford, 'Mirrors of Mutability: Winter Landscapes in Tudor Poetry', *ELR* 4 (1974), 3–39, pp.8–21; Berlin, *Thomas Sackville*, ch.4.

79 On Holinshed, see *DNB* entry.

80 Green, 'Modes of Perception in the *Mirror*', p.125.

81 Nearing, *English Historical Poetry*, chs. 2–4. See also Peter, *Complaint and Satire in Early English Literature*, a work which, curiously enough, fails to mention the *Mirror*.

82 For other versions of the tragedy of Wolsey, see Nearing, *English Historical Poetry*, pp.30–1, 50.

83 See Griffiths, *The Reign of King Henry VI*, pp.459–73, on the military history.

84 See Cave, *The Cornucopian Text*, part 2, ch. 1.

85 See Campbell, ed., *Mirror*, pp.11–15 on the 1563 edition. See also Feasey, 'The Licensing of the *Mirror*', pp.190–3; Thaler, 'Literary Criticism in *A Mirror*', pp.12–13; Annabel Patterson, *Censorship and Interpretation: The Conditions of Writing and Reading in Early Modern England* (Wisconsin University Press, 1984), pp.11–13.

86 See *DNB* entry; Rachael Horrox, *Richard III: A Study of Service* (Cambridge University Press, 1989), passim.

87 Sir Philip Sidney, *Astrophel and Stella*, sonnet 1, in Maurice Evans, ed., *Elizabethan Sonnets* (London: Dent, 1977), p.2; Dante, *La Vita Nuova*, trans. Beatrice Reynolds (Harmondsworth: Penguin, 1978, rpt of 1969), pp.31–3.

88 Feasey, 'The Licensing of the *Mirror*', p.191.

89 For details on William Collingborne's life and death, see K. Hillier, 'William Collingborne'; K. Hillier, P. Normark and P. W. Hammond, 'Collingborne's Rhyme' in J. Petrie, ed., *Richard III: Crown and People* (London: Ricardian Society, 1985), pp. 101–6, 107–8. Halle glosses the 'hogge' as 'the dreadful wilde bore which was the king's cognaisance', calls Catesby, 'his secret seducer' and Ratcliffe, 'his myschevous mynion', *Chronicle*, p.398. Grafton copied Halle; *Chronicle*, vol. II, pp.137–8. The poem was apparently nailed to the door of St Paul's Cathedral.

90 See Thaler, 'Literary Criticism in a *Mirror*', p.12. On executions, see John Bellamy, *The Tudor Law of Treason, an introduction* (London: RKP, 1979), ch.5.

91 See Rosamund Tuve, *Elizabethan and Metaphysical Imagery: Renaissance Poets and Twentieth Century Critics* (Chicago University Press, 1965, rpt. of 1947), ch. 2.

92 See Thomas More, *Utopia*, trans. Paul Turner (Harmondsworth: Penguin, 1980, rpt. of 1965), pp.57–68; Alistair Fox, *Thomas More: History and Providence* (Oxford: Basil Blackwell, 1982), ch. 2; R. S. Johnson, *More's 'Utopia': Ideal and Illusion* (New Haven: Yale University Press, 1969).

93 For brief recent discussions of this problem, see Annabel Patterson, 'Intention' and Stephen Mailloux, 'Interpretation', in Lentricchia and McLaughlin, eds., *Critical Terms for Literary Study*, pp.121–34, 135–46.

94 On the literature of the period, see King, *English Reformation Literature*, pp.407–25.

95 Tuve, *Elizabethan and Metaphysical Imagery*, ch. 14; Frances Yates, *The Occult Philosophy in the Elizabethan Age* (London: RKP, 1983, rpt. of 1979).

96 My interpretation of the *Mirror* suggests that it can be read analogously to those humanist texts analysed by Arthur F. Kinney, *Humanist Poetics: Thought, Rhetoric, and Fiction in Sixteenth-Century England* (Amherst: Massachusetts University Press, 1986).

97 Nearing, *English Historical Poetry*, pp.16, 20–1, 40–1.

4 RHETORIC AND LITERARY THEORY

1 Sir Thomas Wilson, *The Arte of Rhetorique*, ed. G. H. Mair (Oxford: Clarendon Press, 1909), p.181. All subsequent references to this edition in parentheses.

2 On this distinction see Ann Jefferson, 'Russian Formalism', in Ann Jefferson and David Robey, eds., *Modern Literary Theory: A Comparative Introduction* (London: Batsford, 1982), pp.31–2.

3 See Peter Trudgill, *Sociolinguistics: An Introduction to Language and Society* (Harmondsworth: Penguin, 1974), ch. 1; R. A. Hudson, *Sociolinguistics* (Cambridge University Press, 1980), pp.25–32.

4 One might compare, for example, the conflicting voices and audiences addressed in Hitler's *Mein Kampf*, trans. anon. (London: Hurst and Blackett, 1933).

5 On the Dudley family, see Barrett L. Beer, *Northumberland: The Political Career of John Dudley, Earl of Warwick and Duke of Northumberland* (Kent State University Press, 1973).

6 Generally, see Garrett, *Marian Exiles*. On English links with Italy see Dowling, *Humanism in the Age of Henry VIII*, ch. 5.

7 For details of Wilson's life see *DNB* entry.

8 In addition, two Latin poems, one by Nicholas Udall and one by Roberti Hilermii, were deleted. Despite the able help of Ken Rowe I have been unable to determine why or to trace the latter author.

9 On rhetoric and logic in the Renaissance, see Lawrence Manley, *Convention, 1500–1700* (Cambridge, Mass.: Harvard University Press, 1980), pp.137–58; Ong, *Ramus, Method and the Decay of Dialogue*; Wilbur H. Howell, *Logic and Rhetoric in England, 1500–1700* (Princeton University Press, 1965).

10 See Joan W. Scott, 'The Evidence of Experience', *Critical Inquiry* 17 (1991), 773–97, for a penetrating analysis of this manoeuvre.

11 See, for example, Tillyard, *The Elizabethan World Picture*, pp.96–9; Baumer, *Early Tudor Theory of Kingship*, chs. 3–4.

12 See Victoria Kahn, 'Humanism and the Resistance to Theory', in Parker and Quint, eds., *Literary Theory/Renaissance Texts*, pp.373–96; pp.384–5.

13 Technically, 'Interrogatio (Erotema)'; see Lee A. Sonnino, *A Handbook to Sixteenth-Century Rhetoric* (London: RKP, 1968), pp. 117–18.

14 Lewis, *English Literature in the Sixteenth Century*, p.291; Jones, *Triumph of the English Language*, pp.100–2. More generally see George Gregory Smith, ed., *Elizabethan Critical Essays*, 2 vols. (Oxford: Clarendon Press, 1904), I, lv–lx; Vere L. Rubel, *Poetic Diction in the English Renaissance: From Skelton through to Spenser* (New York: MLA, 1941).

15 Jones, *Triumph of the English Language*, p.102.

16 See Trudgill, 'Language and Nation', *Sociolinguistics*, ch. 5; *On Dialect: Social and Geographical Perspectives* (Oxford: Basil Blackwell, 1983), ch. 11.

17 For a relevant discussion of Wilson's views on usury and truth, see Barry Taylor, *Vagrant Writing: Social and Semiotic Disorders in the English Renaissance* (Hemel Hempstead: Harvester, 1991), ch. 2.

18 A problem which still haunts 'speech act' theory; see John Searle, *Speech Acts: An Essay in the Philosophy of Language* (Cambridge University Press, 1989, rpt of 1969), ch. 1; Mary Louise Pratt, *Towards a Speech Act Theory of Literary Discourse* (Bloomington: Indiana University Press, 1977).

19 The work went through eight editions before 1585 when it was superseded by, among other works, Puttenham's *Arte of English Poesie* (see below); *STC*, II, p.468. Warton praised Wilson highly; *History of English Poetry*, sec. LV.

20 Smith, ed., *Elizabethan Critical Essays*, I, vi. Smith notes Wilson's influence on later writers; xci.

21 See Sonnino, *Handbook to Sixteenth-Century Rhetoric*, pp.6–7.

22 See, for example, Abraham Fraunce, *The Arcadian Rhetoric* (1588), ed. R. C. Alston (Menston: Scolar Press, 1969); Henry Peacham, *The Garden of Eloquence*, ed. R. C. Alston (Menston: Scolar Press, 1971), fos. 2–6; Sonnino, *Handbook to Sixteenth-Century Rhetoric*, pp.181–4.

23 See Barthes, *Mythologies*, pp.111–17.

24 Richard Sherry, *A Treatise of Schemes and Tropes* (1550), *STC* 22428, fos. 4, 9–10. See also Sir John Harington, *A Brief Apology for Poetry* (1591), in Smith, ed., *Elizabethan Critical Essays*, II, p.196; Francis Meres, *Palladis Tamia* (1598), in Smith, ed., *Elizabethan Critical Essays*, II, pp.309–11; Fraunce, *Arcadian Rhetoric*, chs. 1, 6, 7; Peacham, *Garden of Eloquence*, 'Epistle to John Elmer'.

25 Arthur Kinney, ed., *Markets of Bawdrie: The Dramatic Criticism of Stephen Gosson* (Universitat Salzburg Press, 1974), pp.1–2, 28. All subsequent references to this edition. For further information on Gosson, see William Ringler, *Stephen Gosson: A Biographical and Critical Study* (Princeton University Press, 1942).

26 See also Russell Fraser, *The War Against Poetry* (Princeton University Press, 1970), ch. 1; Ernest B. Gilman, *Iconoclasm and Poetry in the English Reformation: Down went Dagon* (Chicago University Press, 1986); Alan Sinfield, 'The Cultural Politics of *The Defence of Poetry*', in Gary F. Waller and Michael D. Moore, eds., *Sir Philip Sidney and the Interpretation of Renaissance Culture: The Poet in His Time and Ours* (London: Croom Helm, 1984), pp.124–43, pp.127–8, 133–4. For Gosson's sources, see Plato, *The Republic*, trans. Desmond Lee (Harmondsworth: Penguin, 1980, rpt of 1955), Bk 10; Tertullian, *Spectacles* (*De Spectaculis*) in *Disciplinary, Moral and Ascetic Works*, trans. Rudolph Arbesmann *et al.* (Washington: Catholic University of America Press, 1977), pp.33–107.

27 Plato, *Gorgias*, trans. Walter Hamilton (Harmondsworth: Penguin, 1971), pp.42–8.

28 On Gosson's intellectual odyssey see Kinney, ed., *Markets of Bawdrie*, p.18. Gosson may well be looking back to an older intellectual tradition; see Walker, *Plays of Persuasion*, 'Introduction'; Kinney, *Humanist Poetics*, 'Introduction'.

29 Sallust, *Bellum Catilinae*, ed. J. T. Ramsey (Chico, California: Scholars Press, 1984), p.36.

30 Compare Spenser's comments on the Irish bards: *A View of the Present State of Ireland*, ed. W. L. Renwick (Oxford: Clarendon Press, 1970, rpt of 1934), pp.72–4.

31 See Stephen Greenblatt, 'Psychoanalysis and Renaissance Culture', in Parker and Quint, eds., *Literary Theory/Renaissance Texts*, pp.210–24.

32 Taylor, *Vagrant Writing*, pp.71–3. More generally, see G. K. Hunter, 'Humanism and Courtship', in Paul Alpers, ed., *Elizabethan Poetry: Modern Essays in Criticism* (Oxford University Press, 1967), pp.3–40; Frank Whingham, *Ambition and Privilege: The Social Tropes of Elizabethan Courtesy Theory* (Berkeley: California University Press, 1984). On the figure of Boudicca in the English Renaissance, see Simon Shepherd, *Amazons and Warrior Women: Varieties of Feminism in Seventeenth-Century Drama* (Brighton: Harvester, 1981), ch. 10.

33 On the decline of Greece, see H. D. F. Kitto, 'The Decline of the Polis' in *The Greeks* (Harmondsworth: Penguin, 1951), pp.152–69.

34 See Denys Hay, *The Italian Renaissance in its Historical Background* (Cambridge University Press, 1977, rpt of 1960), ch. 5; Levy, *Tudor Historical Thought*, ch. 3.

35 See *The Trumpet of Warre* (1598), *STC* 12099. On 'ideological state apparatuses', see Louis Althusser, 'Ideology and the State', in *Lenin and Philosophy and Other Essays*, trans. Ben Brewster (London: Verso, 1969), pp.121–73.

36 Andrew Parker *et al.*, eds., *Nationalisms and Sexualities* (London: Routledge, 1992), 'Introduction'.

37 See Hiram Morgan, 'The Colonial Venture of Sir Thomas Smith in Ulster, 1571–5', *HJ* 28 (1985), 261–78; Nicholas Canny, 'The Permissive Frontier: Social Control in English Settlements in Ireland and Virginia, 1550–1650', in K. R. Andrews *et al.*, eds., *The Westward Enterprise: English Activities in Ireland, the Atlantic and America, 1480–1650* (Liverpool University Press, 1978), pp.17–44.

38 Sidney, to whom *The Schoole of Abuse* was dedicated, was clearly revising this conception of poetry in *The Apologie for Poetry*; see ch. 5 below and Arthur F. Kinney, 'The Significance of Sidney's *Defense of Poesie* as Parody', *SEL* 12 (1972), 1–20.

39 Puttenham's authorship of *The Arte of English Poesie* has been disputed; see *DNB* entry; *The Arte of English Poesie*, ed. Gladys Doidge Willcock and Alice Walker (Cambridge University Press, 1936), 'introduction'.

40 See Arthur B. Ferguson, 'Circumstances and the Sense of History in Tudor England: The Coming of the Historical Revolution', *Medieval and Renaissance Studies* 3 (1967), 170–205; Herbert Weisinger, 'Ideas of History during the Renaissance', in Paul O. Kristeller and Philip P. Weiner, eds., *Renaissance Essays from the Journal of the History of Ideas* (New York: Harper and Row, 1968), pp.74–94.

41 George Puttenham, *The Arte of English Poesie* (1589), ed. R. C. Alston (Menston: Scolar Press, 1968), p.63. All subsequent references to this edition in parentheses.

42 See Louis Adrian Montrose, 'Of Gentlemen and Shepherds: The Politics of Elizabethan Pastoral Form', *ELH* 50 (1983), 415–59, pp.427–8, 435–7.

43 Lewis, *Literature in the Sixteenth Century*, Bk 3; Waller, *English Poetry of the Sixteenth Century*, p.29; Evans, *English Poetry of the Sixteenth Century*, ch. 2; Elizabeth Story Donno, ed., *The Renaissance, Excluding Drama* (London: Macmillan, 1983), p.1; V. De Sola Pinto, ed., *The English Renaissance, 1510–1688* (London: Cresset Press, 1966, rpt of 1938), pp.10–13.

44 William Webbe, *A Discourse of English Poesie*, in Smith, ed., *Elizabethan Critical Essays*, I, pp.226–302, pp.234, 297, 278–9, 239; Puttenham, *Arte of English Poesie*, pp.3–4, 48. See also Norbrook, *Poetry and Politics*, pp.77–9.

45 Webbe, *Discourse of English Poesie*, pp.242, 262–8; Puttenham, *Arte of English Poesie*, pp.19–21, 120–1, 34–5.

46 On this logic of time, see Claude Lévi-Strauss, 'Race and History', in *Structural Anthropology*, trans. Monique Layton, 2 vols. (Harmondsworth: Penguin, 1987, rpt of 1976), II, pp.323–62; Peter Hulme, *Colonial Encounters: Europe and the Native Caribbean, 1492–1797* (London: Methuen, 1986), ch. 2.

47 The two main Elizabethan texts dealing with the question of rhyme and poetry are Thomas Campion, *Observations on the Art of English Poesie* (1602) and Samuel Daniel, *A Defence of Rhyme* (1603), reprinted in Smith, ed., *Elizabethan Critical Essays*, II, pp.327–55; 356–84. For a lucid discussion of poetics and national identity, see Richard Helgerson, '"Barbarous Tongues": The Ideology of Poetic Form in Renaissance England', in Heather Dubrow and Richard Strier, eds., *The Historical Renaissance: New Essays on Tudor and Stuart Literature and Culture* (Chicago University Press, 1988), pp.273–92.

48 Manley, *Convention*, pp.17–18.

49 See Haller, *Foxe's Book of Martyrs*, pp.85–6 and ch. 6 above.

50 See Barry Taylor, '"The Instrument of Ornament": George Puttenham's *Arte of English Poesie*', in *Vagrant Writing*, ch. 4.

51 Montrose, 'Of Gentlemen and Shepherds', p.438. See also Daniel Javitch, *Poetry and Courtliness in Renaissance England* (Princeton University Press, 1978), ch. 2.

52 See Stephen Orgel, *The Illusion of Power: Political Theatre in the English Renaissance* (Berkeley: California University Press, 1975); David Lindley, ed., *The Court Masque* (Manchester University Press, 1984), 'Introduction'.

53 Taylor, *Vagrant Writing*, pp.137–40.

54 See Roger Kuin, 'Sir Philip Sidney: The Courtier and the Text', *ELR* 19 (1981), 249–71.

55 For related discussions, see Derek Attridge, 'Nature, Art and the Supplement in Renaissance Literary Theory: Puttenham's Poetics of Decorum', in *Peculiar Language*, pp.17–45; Taylor, *Vagrant Writing*, pp.138, 144–6.

56 See Hilton, *Bond Men Made Free*; Barrett L. Beer, *Rebellion and Riot: Popular Disorder in England during the Reign of Edward VI* (Kent State University Press, 1973).

57 For alternative interpretations, see Jonathan V. Crewe, 'The Hegemonic Theatre of George Puttenham', *ELR* 16 (1986), 71–85; Montrose, 'Of Gentlemen and Shepherds', pp.433–40.

58 Hence Puttenham's attacks on Skelton as a 'rude, rayling rimer' (see above, p.44).

59 See Lewis, *English Literature in the Sixteenth Century*, p.431; Tuve, *Elizabethan and Metaphysical Imagery*, pp.146–8, 391–3; Lauro Martines, *Society and History in English Renaissance Verse* (Oxford: Basil Blackwell, 1985), p.26; A. C. Partridge, *The Language of Renaissance Poetry: Spenser, Shakespeare, Donne, Milton* (London: André Deutsch, 1971), p.41.

60 See Derek Attridge, *Well-Weighed Syllables: Elizabethan Verse in Classical Metres* (Cambridge University Press, 1974); Helgerson, '"Barbarous Tongues"'.

61 See King, *English Reformation Literature*, pp.411–15, for a description of the effects of Edward's death on literary output.

62 An unhistorical faith and desire to homogenise which bedevils much 'New Historicism'; in addition to the articles by Crewe and Montrose cited above, see Greenblatt, *Renaissance Self-Fashioning*, p.136.

5 SIR PHILIP SIDNEY, THE NATION AND THE PUBLIC

1 See, for example, Alan Sinfield, 'The Cultural Politics of *Astrophil and Stella*'; S. K. Heninger, Jr, 'Speaking Pictures: Sidney's Rapprochement between Poetry and Painting' in Waller and Moore, eds., *Sir Philip Sidney and the Interpretation of Renaissance Culture*, pp.3–16.

2 Sidney, *Apologie for Poetry*, ed. Shepherd. All references to this edition; the divisions referred to are reproduced in *A Defence of Poetry*, ed. J. A. Van Dorsten (Oxford University Press, 1978, rpt of 1973).

3 O. B. Hardison, Jr, 'The Two Voices of Sidney's *Apology for Poetry*', *ELR* 2 (1972), 83–99, p.93. Subsequent references in parentheses.

4 Arthur K. Amos, Jr, *Time, Space and Value: The Narrative Structure*

of the New Arcadia (London: Associated Universities Press, 1977), p.14. On manuscript and print see below, notes 116 and 117.

5 On Sidney's use of rhetoric see Kenneth Myrick, *Sir Philip Sidney as a Literary Craftsman* (Lincoln: Nebraska University Press, rev. edn, 1965), ch. 3.

6 See Forrest G. Robinson, *The Shape of Things Known: Sidney's Apology in its Philosophical Tradition* (Cambridge, Mass.: Harvard University Press, 1972), ch. 3; Ong, *Ramus, Method and the Decay of Dialogue*, pp.38, 308–14.

7 See, for example, A. C. Hamilton, 'Sidney's Idea of the "Right Poet"', *CL* 9 (1957), 51–9; John P. McIntyre, S J, 'Sidney's "Golden World"', *CL* 14 (1962), 356–65; Ronald Levao, 'Sidney's Feigned *Apology*', *PMLA* 94 (1979), 223–33.

8 On this problem, see Chicago Cultural Studies Group, 'Critical Multiculturalism', *Critical Inquiry* 18 (1992), 530–55; Victor P. Pecora, 'The Limits of Local Knowledge' in Veeser, ed., *The New Historicism*, pp.243–76.

9 Anthony Miller, 'Sidney's *Apology for Poetry* and Plutarch's *Moralia*', *ELR* 17 (1987), 259–76; Cornell March Dowlin, 'Sidney's Two Definitions of Poetry', *MLQ* 3 (1942), 573–81; D. H. Craig, 'A Hybrid Growth: Sidney's Theory of Poetry in *An Apology for Poetry*', *ELR* 10 (1980), 183–201.

10 Foucault, *Power/Knowledge*, p.133. For other assessments of Sidney's attitudes see F. J. Levy, 'Sir Philip Sidney and the Idea of History', *Bibliothèque d'Humanisme et Renaissance* 26 (1964), 608–17; Elizabeth Story Donno, 'Old Mouse-eaten Records: History in Sidney's *Apology*', *SP* 72 (1975) 275–98; Levao, 'Sidney's Feigned *Apology*', pp.225–8.

11 Linus was the tutor of Orpheus; see *Apologie*, ed., Shepherd, p.146.

12 D. P. Walker, 'Orpheus the Theologian and Renaissance Platonism', *JWCI* 16 (1953), 100–20.

13 See William R. Parker, 'The Sonnets in "Tottel's Miscellany"', *PMLA* 54 (1939), 669–77; and above, p.143.

14 See Germaine Warkentin, 'The Meeting of Muses: Sidney and the Mid-Tudor Poets', in Waller and Moore, eds., *Sidney and the Interpretation of Renaissance Culture*, pp.17–33, p.29; Arthur F. Marotti, '"Love is not Love": Elizabethan Sonnet Sequences and the Social Order', *ELH* 49 (1982), 396–428, pp.396–400.

15 John C. Ulreich, Jr, '"The Poets Only Deliver": Sidney's Conception of Mimesis', *S. Litt. I.* 15 (1982), pp.67–84.

16 See David Beers Quinn, *The Elizabethans and the Irish* (New York: Cornell University Press, 1966); Hadfield, 'The English Conception of Ireland', ch. 4; Hechter, *Internal Colonialism*; Charles Hughes, ed., *Shakespeare's Europe* (London: Sherrat and Hughes,

1903), pp.1–71. For Sidney's views, see 'Discourse on Irish Affairs', in *Miscellaneous Prose of Sir Philip Sidney*, ed. Katherine Duncan-Jones and Jan Van Dorsten (Oxford: Clarendon Press, 1973), pp.4–12.

17 See Robinson, *The Shape of Things Known*; King, *Spenser's Poetry and the Reformation Tradition*, ch. 2; Gilman, *Iconoclasm and Poetry in the English Reformation*; Stephen Gosson, *The Schoole of Abuse* (London, 1579), *STC* 12097.

18 But see Myrick, *Philip Sidney*, ch. 2; Edward Berry, 'Sidney's "Poor Painter": Nationalism and Social Class' in Newey and Thompson, eds., *Literature and Nationalism*, pp.1–10, p.1.

19 See Martin Bernal, *Black Athena: The Afroasiatic Roots of Classical Civilization*, vol. 1, *The Fabrication of Ancient Greece* (London: Free Association Books, 1987), for a recent analysis of Western assumptions.

20 See Derek Attridge, 'Language as History/ History as Language: Saussure and the Romance of Etymology' in *Peculiar Language*, pp.90–126; E. H. Curtius, 'Etymology as a Category of Thought' in *European Literature*, pp.495–500.

21 Jonathan Culler, 'The Call of the Phoneme: Introduction' in Jonathan Culler, ed., *On Puns: The Foundation of Letters* (Oxford: Basil Blackwell, 1988), pp.1–16, pp.2–3.

22 See Easthope, *Poetry as Discourse*.

23 Sidney assumes that poetry is male. For a relevant recent discussion see Julia Kristeva, *Revolution in Poetic Language*, trans. Margaret Waller (New York: Cornell University Press, 1984); Calvin Bedient, 'Kristeva and Poetry as Shattered Signification', *Critical Inquiry* 16 (1990), 807–29.

24 See Michael Hamburger, *The Truth of Poetry: Tensions in Modern Poetry from Baudelaire to the 1960s* (London: Weidenfeld and Nicolson, 1969). Hamburger's discussion, particularly of national identity versus internationalism, Utopianism and politics, mirrors that of Sidney.

25 Greenblatt, *Renaissance Self-Fashioning*, ch. 4.

26 See Culler, 'The Call of the Phoneme', p.16; Samuel Beckett, *Murphy* (London: Picador, 1982), p.41; Marguerite Alexander, *Flights From Realism* (London: Arnold, 1990), ch. 1. I owe this last reference to Richard Brown.

27 Aristotle, *On the Art of Poetry* in *Classical Literary Criticism*, trans. T. S. Dorsch (Harmondsworth: Penguin, 1965), ch. 9.

28 Craig, 'A Hybrid Growth', pp.193–4; John Hunt, 'The Allusive Coherence in Sidney's *Apology for Poetry*', *SEL* 27 (1987), 1–16, pp.8–13.

29 Sidney visited Hungary in 1573; see *Apologie*, ed. Shepherd, p.191.

30 See Pecora, 'The Limits of Local Knowledge'; Brendan Bradshaw, 'Nationalism and Historical Scholarship in Modern Ireland', *IHS* 104 (1989), 329–51, pp.350–1.

31 See *Apologie*, ed. Shepherd, p.193; J. A. Van Dorsten, 'The Arts of Memory and Poetry', *ES* 48 (1967), 419–25; Frances A. Yates, *The Art of Memory* (Harmondsworth: Penguin, 1978, rpt of 1969), pp.274–6.

32 Although elsewhere Sidney wrote against the foolishness of the Brute legend: see Levy, 'Sidney and the Idea of History', p.616.

33 Witness Sidney's letter to the queen urging her not to marry the Duke of Alençon; see Howell, *Sir Philip Sidney, The Shepherd Knight*, ch. 2. See also Roger Kuin, 'Sir Philip Sidney: The Courtier and the Text', *ELR* 19 (1989), 249–71, for a discussion of the relationship between Sidney's life and art.

34 Edward Berry, 'The Poet as Warrior in Sidney's *Defence of Poetry*', *SEL* 29 (1989), 21–34, p.30.

35 Sir Fulke Greville, *The Life of Sir Philip Sidney* (1652), ed. Nowell Smith (Oxford: Clarendon Press, 1907); Andrew Mousley, 'The Making of the Self: Life Writing in the English Renaissance' (unpublished PhD thesis, University of Kent, 1990), ch. 4; Richard Helgerson, *Self-Crowned Laureates: Spenser, Jonson, Milton and the Literary System* (Berkeley: California University Press, 1983), p.64.

36 Berry, 'Poet as Warrior', p.31; more generally see Andrew Parker *et al.*, eds., *Nationalisms and Sexualities*.

37 Hardison, 'The Two Voices of Sidney's *Apology*', p.93.

38 See Warkenten, 'The Meeting of the Muses', for evidence of Sidney's use of mid-sixteenth-century poetry. Jonson probably employed Sidney's phrase in the epigram, 'On Poet Ape'.

39 The only other work that Sidney praises is *A Mirror* as 'meetly furnished of beautiful parts'.

40 See Myrick, *Sir Philip Sidney*, p.53; *Apologie*, ed. Shepherd, pp.11–17.

41 See Paul Ricoeur, 'Between Rhetoric and Poetics: Aristotle' in *The Rule of Metaphor*, pp.9–43, on the relationship between poetry and rhetoric.

42 See Ulreich, '"The Poets only Deliver"'; Dowlin, 'Sidney's Two Definitions of Poetry'; Hunt, 'The Allusive Coherence in Sidney's *Apology*'.

43 See Elaine Y. L. Ho, 'The Rhetoric of the-"I"-witness in Fulke Greville's *The Life of Sir Philip Sidney*', *Literature and History*, second series, II, i (Spring, 1991), 17–26; Mousley, 'The Making of the Self', ch. 4.

44 On 'Aporia' see Culler, *On Deconstruction*, ch. 2.

45 See William A. Sessions, *Henry Howard, Earl of Surrey* (Boston: Twayne, 1986); Edwin Casedy, *Henry Howard, Earl of Surrey* (New York: MLA, 1938). For further reference see Ellen C. Caldwell, 'Recent Studies in Henry Howard, Earl of Surrey', *ELR* 19 (1989), 389–401.

46 Casedy, *Henry Howard*, ch. 9; D. M. Loades, *Two Tudor Conspiracies* (Cambridge University Press, 1985).

47 Sessions, *Henry Howard*, p.26; Norbrook, *Poetry and Politics*, pp. 126–8.

48 Sessions, *Henry Howard*, p.41; Puttenham, *Arte of English Poesie*, I, 31.

49 Hence I find it difficult to accept Andrew Weiner's arguments that Sidney can be read as a Protestant author *per se*; see 'Moving and Teaching: Sidney's *Defence of Poesie* as a Protestant Poetic', *JMRS* 2 (1971–2), 259–78; *Sir Philip Sidney and the Poetics of Protestantism: A Study of Contexts* (Minnesota University Press, 1978).

50 Sessions, *Henry Howard*, p.27.

51 Spearing, *Medieval to Renaissance in English Poetry*, pp.19–21, 30–5; Stephen Minta, *Petrarch and Petrarchanism: The English and French Traditions* (Manchester University Press, 1980), pp.150–1.

52 See also Surrey, *Poems*, ed. Emrys Jones (Oxford: Clarendon Press, 1973, rpt of 1964), pp.1–2.

53 On the lyric form see David Lindley, *The Lyric* (London: Methuen, 1985).

54 See Jonathan Culler, 'Apostrophe' in *The Pursuit of Signs*, pp.135–54.

55 Sessions, *Henry Howard*, pp.140–1.

56 Petrarch, *Canzioniere*, 140, reprinted in Minta, *Petrarch and Petrarchanism*, pp.61–2. See also the version of Surrey's sonnet in *Poems*, p.3.

57 Surrey, *Poems*, p.105; Virgil, *The Aeneid*, p.72.

58 Marotti, '"Love is Not Love"', p.397.

59 All references to William A. Ringler, Jr, ed., *The Poems of Sir Philip Sidney* (Oxford: Clarendon Press, 1962).

60 See David Kalstone, *Sidney's Poetry: Contexts and Interpretations* (Cambridge, Mass.: Harvard University Press, 1965), pp.126–7; J. G. Nicholls, *The Poetry of Sir Philip Sidney: An Interpretation in the Context of his Life and Times* (Liverpool University Press, 1974), pp.9–12.

61 Ann Rosalind Jones and Peter Stallybrass, 'The Politics of *Astrophil and Stella*', *SEL* 24 (1984), 53–68. For an opposing view see Nona Finenberg, 'The Emergence of Stella in *Astrophil and Stella*', *SEL* 25 (1985), 5–19.

62 Evans, ed., *Elizabethan Sonnets*, xvii.

63 Ringler, ed., *Poems*, pp.458–9.
64 See Ann Banfield, 'Ecriture, Narration and the Grammar of French', in Jeremy Hawthorn, ed., *Narrative: From Malory to Motion Pictures* (London: Arnold, 1985), pp.1–22.
65 Gary F. Waller, 'The Rewriting of Petrarch: Sidney and the Languages of Sixteenth-Century Poetry', in Waller and Moore, eds., *Sidney and the Interpretation of Renaissance Culture*, pp.69–83; Margreta De Grazia, 'Lost Potential in Grammar and Nature: Sidney's *Astrophil and Stella*', *SEL* 21 (1981), 21–35.
66 Marotti, '"Love is Not Love"', pp.399–400; Jones and Stallybrass, 'The Politics of *Astrophil and Stella*'; Waller, *English Poetry of the Sixteenth Century*, pp.140–56. See also Louis Adrian Montrose, 'Celebration and Insinuation: Sir Philip Sidney and the Motives of Elizabethan Courtship', *RD* 8 (1977), 3–35. For details of the extant manuscripts see *Poems*, ed. Ringler, pp.447–57.
67 As Ringler has lamented, 'A cooperative Sidney allusion book is much to be desired'; 'Sir Philip Sidney: The Myth and The Man', in Jan Van Dorsten *et al.*, eds., *Sir Philip Sidney: 1586 and the Creation of a Legend* (Brill/Leiden University Press, 1986), pp.3–15, p.15.
68 R. D. Bedford, *Dialogues with Convention: Readings in Renaissance Poetry* (Brighton: Harvester, 1989), p.30. See also Sidney, 'Discourse on Irish Affairs', pp.3–6; Katherine Duncan-Jones, *Sir Philip Sidney: Courtier Poet* (London: Hamish Hamilton, 1991), pp.108–12, 135–6.
69 Marotti, '"Love is Not Love"', p.401; Kalstone, *Sidney's Poetry*, p.156; Richard McCoy, *Sir Philip Sidney: Rebellion in Arcadia* (Brighton: Harvester, 1979), p.71; Fienberg, 'The Emergence of Stella', pp.9–10.
70 Kalstone, *Sidney's Poetry*, pp.172–5; A. C. Hamilton, *Sir Philip Sidney: A Study of his Life and Work* (Cambridge University Press, 1977), p.100; Jones and Stallybrass, 'The Politics of *Astrophil and Stella*', pp.58–9.
71 Ricoeur, *Rule of Metaphor*, pp.24–7; see also Kuin, 'The Courtier and the Text'.
72 John Donne, *The Complete English Poems*, ed. A. J. Smith (Harmondsworth: Penguin, 1971), pp.80–1.
73 See Patterson, *Censorship and Interpretation*, ch. 1; *Fables of Power: Aesopian Writing and Political History* (Durham: Duke University Press, 1991).
74 See Christopher Martin, 'Misdoubting His Estate: Dynastic Anxiety in Sidney's *Arcadia*', *ELR* 18 (1988), 369–88, pp.369–71; A. C. Hamilton, 'Sidney's *Arcadia* as Prose Fiction: Its Relation to its Sources', *ELR* 2 (1972), 29–60; Jon S. Lawry, *Sidney's Two*

Arcadias: Pattern and Proceeding (Ithaca, New York: Cornell University Press, 1972).

75 Sir Philip Sidney, *The Old Arcadia*, ed. Katherine Duncan-Jones (Oxford University Press, 1985), p.4. All subsequent references to this edition in parentheses.

76 See Johnson, *More's Utopia: Ideal and Illusion*; Lawry, *Sidney's Two Arcadias*, pp.16–17; William Dinsmore Briggs, 'Political Ideas in Sidney's "Arcadia"', *SP* 28 (1931), 137–61, p.140.

77 See Katherine Duncan-Jones, 'Sidney's Urania', *RES*, NS, 66 (1966), 123–32.

78 On Dametas see Lawry, *Sidney's Two Arcadias*, pp.57–8, 100–3; Robert E. Stillman, *Sidney's Poetic Justice: The Old Arcadia, its Eclogues, and Renaissance Pastoral Traditions* (London: Associated Universities Press, 1986), pp.133–6.

79 For differing interpretations see Martin N. Raitiere, *Faire Bitts: Sir Philip Sidney and Renaissance Political Theory* (Pittsburgh: Duquesne University Press, 1984); Briggs, 'Political Ideas in Sidney's *Arcadia*'; 'Sidney's Political Ideas', *SP* 29 (1932), 534–42; Irving Ribner, 'Machiavelli and Sidney: The *Arcadia* of 1590', *SP* 47 (1950), 152–72; 'Sir Philip Sidney and Civil Insurrection', *JHI* 13 (1952), 257–65; McCoy, *Rebellion in Arcadia*; Norbrook, *Poetry and Politics*, ch. 4; Alan Sinfield, 'Power and Ideology: An Outline Theory and Sidney's *Arcadia*', *ELH* 52 (1985), 259–77; Robert E. Stillman, 'The Politics of Sidney's Pastoral: Mystification and Mythology in *The Old Arcadia*', *ELH* 52 (1985), 795–814; Patterson, *Fables of Power*, pp.67–75.

80 On Sidney as Philisides see Raitiere, *Faire Bitts*, pp.57–8; Patterson, *Fables of Power*, p.67.

81 For an opposing view see Raitiere, *Faire Bitts*; Ribner, 'Sidney on Civil Insurrection'.

82 Speech at Tilbury, 8 August 1588; reprinted in part in J. E. Neale, *Queen Elizabeth* (London: Cape, 1934), pp.297–8.

83 On attitudes to women rulers in the sixteenth century see Constance Jordan, 'Woman's Rule in Sixteenth-Century British Political Thought', *RQ* 40 (1987), 421–51; Ian MacLean, *The Renaissance Notion of Woman: A Study in the Fortunes of Scholasticism and Medical Science in European Intellectual Life* (Cambridge University Press, 1980), ch. 4.

84 See Knox, *First Blast of the Trumpet*. On Sidney's connection with Scottish Calvinist circles see James E. Philips, 'George Buchanan and the Sidney Circle', *HLQ* 12 (1948–9), 23–55, p.39.

85 See Philippa Berry, *Of Chastity and Power*, 'Introduction', ch. 3; Yates, *Astrea*, part 1.

86 Sidney, 'A Letter to the Queen', in *Miscellaneous Prose*, pp.33–57;

W. Gordon Zeeveld, 'The Uprising of the Commons in Sidney's *Arcadia*', *MLN* 48 (1933), 209–17.

87 See J. G. A. Pocock, *The Ancient Constitution and the Feudal Law*, chs. 2, 3; Skinner, *Foundations of Modern Political Thought*, II, part 3.

88 Ribner, 'Machiavelli and Sidney'; Philips, 'George Buchanan and the Sidney circle'; Raitiere, *Faire Bitts*.

89 Stephen Greenblatt, 'Invisible Bullets', in *Shakespearian Negotiations*, pp.21–65, p.49; Edwards, *Threshold of a Nation*, ch. 4.

90 Aristotle, *The Politics*, trans. T. A. Sinclair (Harmondsworth: Penguin, 1962), bk. 3.

91 *The Old Arcadia*, ed. Katherine Duncan-Jones, p.374; see also Jean Robertson, ed., *The Old Arcadia* (Oxford: Clarendon Press, 1973), p.442.

92 See Conrad Russell, *The Crisis of Parliaments: English History, 1509–1660* (Oxford University Press, 1977, rpt of 1971), pp.232–3.

93 The entry of Dametas singing his 'ill-noised song' (p.116) adds to the humour; see Stillman, '*Sidney's Poetic Justice*', p.85.

94 *The New Arcadia*, ed. Victor Skretkowicz (Oxford: Clarendon Press, 1987), p.280. All subsequent references to this edition.

95 See John L. Sutton, Jr, 'A Historical Source for the Rebellion of the Commons in Sidney's *Arcadia*', *ELN* 23 (1986), 6–11.

96 Mario Praz, 'Sidney's Original *Arcadia*', *The London Mercury* 15 (1926–7), 507–14, pp.512–3.

97 Stephen Greenblatt, 'Murdering Peasants: Status, Genre and the Representation of Rebellion', *Representations* 1 (1983), 1–29, p.17.

98 Different explanations are provided by Peter Lindbaum, 'Sidney's *Arcadia*: The Endings of the Three Versions', *HLQ* 34 (1970–1), 205–18; Kenneth Thorpe Rowe, 'The Countess of Pembroke's Editorship of the *Arcadia*', *PMLA* 54 (1939), 122–38; Joan Rees, *Sir Philip Sidney and Arcadia* (London: Associated Universities Press, 1991), ch. 5.

99 Lawry, *Sidney's Two Arcadias*, pp.176–7.

100 Ribner, 'Sidney on Civil Insurrection', pp.259–60; Edwin A. Greenlaw, 'Sidney's *Arcadia* as an example of Elizabethan Allegory', *Anniversary Papers by Colleagues and Pupils of George Lyman Kittredge* (New York: Russell and Russell, 1967, rpt of 1913), pp.327–37. Raitiere's reading of the episode (*Faire Bitts*, ch. 3), informative though it is, also ignores the merging of class and national distinctions and the evidence of the *Old Arcadia*.

101 Cheke, *STC* 5109; on the *Homilies* see above, ch. 3, note 1.

102 But Victor Skretkowicz, 'Building Sidney's Reputation: Texts and Editors of the *Arcadia*', in Van Dorsten *et al.*, eds., *Philip Sidney: 1586*, pp.111–24, p.117 and Raitiere, *Faire Bitts*, pp.48–53,

demonstrate that Sidney probably intended to return to Sparta and comment further on the war had he lived to complete the *New Arcadia*.

103 See Rees, *Sidney and Arcadia*, pp.101–14.
104 For analysis see McCoy, *Rebellion in Arcadia*, ch. 5; Lawry, *Sidney's Two Arcadias*, pp.217–18, 212–14.
105 Kernan, *Cankered Muse*, ch. 3.
106 On the perilous position of the Sidneys see Duncan-Jones, *Sir Philip Sidney*, pp.46–7, 225–7.
107 He is slain by Musidorus having been overthrown by a popular rebellion.
108 Patterson, *Fables of Power*, p.72.
109 Possibly a reference to factionalism at Elizabeth's court; see Sinfield, 'Power and Ideology', pp.263–5; Montrose, 'Celebration and Insinuation'. See also Howell, *Sir Philip Sidney*, 'Introduction'; W. T. MacCaffrey, 'Place and Patronage in Elizabethan Politics', in S. T. Bindoff *et al.*, eds., *Elizabethan Government and Society* (London: Athlone Press, 1961), pp.95–126.
110 Patterson, *Censorship and Interpretation*, p.41. See also Raitiere, *Faire Bitts*, chs. 4–5 for a thorough, but erroneous analysis. Greville included the song in the First Eclogues in his version of the *New Arcadia*; see *Faire Bitts*, Appendix B.
111 Greenblatt, 'Murdering Peasants', p.18; Berry, 'Sidney's "Poor Painter"', pp.9, 6.
112 Ovid, *Metamorphoses*, pp.274–82.
113 Berry, 'Sidney's "Poor Painter"', p.9.
114 Greville, *Life of Sidney*, pp.15–16.
115 Sinfield, 'Power and Ideology', p.275.
116 John Danby, *Poets on Fortune's Hill: Studies in Sidney, Shakespeare, Beaumont and Fletcher* (London: Faber, 1952), pp.31–3; John Buxton, *Sir Philip Sidney and the English Renaissance* (London: Macmillan, 1966), pp.23–4; Nicholls, *The Poetry of Sidney*, pp.9–12; Helgerson, *Self-Crowned Laureates*, pp.34–5.
117 Christopher Hill, 'Censorship and English Literature' in *The Collected Essays of Christopher Hill* vol. I, *Writing and Revolution in Seventeenth-Century England* (Brighton: Harvester, 1985), pp.32–71; Harold Love, 'Scribal Publication in Seventeenth-Century England', *TCBS* 9 (1987), 130–54. I owe these references to Paul Hammond.
118 Ringer, 'Sidney: The Myth and the Man'; F. J. Levy, 'Sir Philip Sidney Reconsidered', *ELR* 2 (1972), 5–18.

6 THE PERMANENT EXILE OF EDMUND SPENSER

1 Helgerson, *Self-Crowned Laureates*, pp.12, 55–6, 61.

2 See 'Arlo Hill', *Spenser Encyclopedia*, p.60.

3 See Dan Sperber and Deirdre Wilson, 'Rhetoric and Reference', in John Bender and David E. Wellbery, eds., *The Ends of Rhetoric: History, Theory, Practice* (Stanford University Press, 1990), pp.140–55.

4 See Robert S. Kinsman, 'The Voices of Dissonance: Patterns in Skelton's *Colyn Cloute*', *HLQ* 26 (1963), 291–313.

5 See Walker, *John Skelton*, chs. 3–4.

6 See J. L. Austin, *How To Do Things With Words*, ed. J. O. Urmson and Marina Sbisa, second edn (Oxford University Press, 1975), ch. 8; Searle, *Speech Acts*.

7 See, for example, Kohn, *The Idea of Nationalism*, ch. 1.

8 Stephen Ellis, '"Not Mere English": The British Perspective, 1400–1650', *History Today* 28 (1988), pp.41–8.

9 See the comments by William Webbe, George Puttenham, Richard Carew, Francis Meres and others, reprinted in R. M. Cummings, ed., *Spenser: The Critical Heritage* (London: RKP, 1971); William B. Hunter, ed., *The English Spenserians: The Poetry of Giles Fletcher, George Wither, Michael Drayton, Phineas Fletcher and Henry More* (Salt Lake City: Utah University Press, 1977); Norbrook, *Poetry and Politics*, chs. 3 and 5; N. P. Canny, 'Edmund Spenser and the Development of an Anglo-Irish Identity', *YES* 13 (1983), 1–19; Pauline Henley, *Spenser in Ireland* (Cork University Press, 1928).

10 Norbrook, *Poetry and Politics*, p.59.

11 Michael McCanles, '*The Shepheardes Calender* as Document and Monument', *SEL* 22 (1982), 5–19, pp.6–7.

12 Eleanor Rosenberg, *Leicester, Patron of Letters* (New York: Columbia University Press, 1955). See also 'letter as genre', *Spenser Encyclopedia*, pp.433–4.

13 'Letters, Spenser's and Harvey's', *Spenser Encyclopedia*, pp.434–5.

14 See Helgerson, 'Barbarous Tongues'; Attridge, *Well-Weighed Syllables*, ch. 13.

15 *The Poetical Works of Edmund Spenser*, ed. J. C. Smith and A. De Selincourt (Oxford University Press, 1965, rpt. of 1912), p.611. All subsequent references to this edition unless stated.

16 See Cain, *Praise in 'the Faerie Queene'*; David Lee Miller, *The Poem's Two Bodies* (Princeton University Press, 1988).

17 Richard Mulcaster, *Positions* (London, 1581), ch. 5; Augusto Campana, 'The Origin of the Word "Humanist"', *JWCI* 9

(1946), 60–73; Vito R. Giustiniani, 'Homo, Humans, and the Meaning of "Humanism"', *JHI* 46 (1985), 167–85.

18 Norbrook, *Poetry and Politics*, p.74; McCanles, '*The Shepheardes Calender* as Document and Monument', p.6.

19 'Letters, Spenser's and Harvey's', *Spenser Encyclopedia*.

20 See John Pitcher, 'Tudor Literature (1485–1603)', in Pat Rogers, ed., *The Oxford Illustrated History of English Literature* (Oxford University Press, 1987), 59–111, pp.74–8; Victoria Kahn, 'Humanism and the Resistance to Theory'. On the development of 'humanist' educational ideas in England see Dowling, *Humanism in the Age of Henry VIII*, chs. 4–6.

21 Compare this to Richard Stanihurst's comments on Hiberno-English in his 'Description of Ireland', in R. Holinshed, ed., *Chronicles*, 6 vols. (1907–8), VI, p.4.

22 See also Annabel Patterson, 'Re-opening the Green Cabinet: Clement Marot and Edmund Spenser', *ELR* 16 (1986), 44–70; Harry Berger, Jr, 'Re-verting to the Green Cabinet: A Modernist Approach to the Aesthetics of Wailing', in *Revisionary Play: Studies in the Spenserian Dynamic* (Berkeley and Los Angeles: California University Press, 1988), pp.378–415, for other readings of the poem in relation to its sources.

23 See Helgerson, *Self-Crowned Laureates*, pp.62–3; O'Connell, *The Mirror and the Veil*, 'introduction'.

24 For a summary of sources and commentary see Paul G. Ruggiers, 'The Italian Influence on Chaucer', in Beryl Rowland, ed., *Companion to Chaucer Studies* (Oxford University Press, 1979), pp.160–84.

25 See 'Hugh Singleton' in *Spenser Encyclopedia*, p.659; Patterson, *Censorship and Interpretation*, pp.25–6, 45–6.

26 For details see *Variorum, The Minor Poems*, I, ed. Edwin Greenlaw *et al.* (Baltimore: Johns Hopkins University Press, 1943), p.252.

27 See Marotti, '"Love is Not Love"'; Waller, *English Poetry of the Sixteenth Century*, pp.79–80.

28 Julia Reinhard Lupton, 'Home-Making in Ireland: Virgil's Eclogue I and Book VI of the *Faerie Queene*', *Sp. St.* 8 (1990), 119–45.

29 See King, *Spenser's Poetry and the Reformation Tradition*, ch. 1. Paul E. McLane identifies Rosalinde as Elizabeth; *Spenser's Shepheardes Calender*, Ch. 3; 'Rosalind', *Spenser Encyclopedia*, p.622.

30 Sir Thomas Smith, *De Republica Anglorum*. For details of Smith's life, see Mary Dewar, *Sir Thomas Smith: a Tudor Intellectual in Office* (London: Athlone Press, 1964).

31 See Harry Berger, Jr, 'Introduction to *The Shepheardes Calender*', *Revisionary Play*, pp.277–89; John D. Bernard, *Ceremonies of*

Innocence: Pastoralism in the Poetry of Edmund Spenser (Cambridge University Press, 1989); Montrose, 'Of Gentlemen and Shepherds', for recent discussions.

32 For other discussions see Waldo F. McNeir, 'The Drama of Spenser's *The Shepheardes Calender*', *Anglia* 95 (1977), 34–59; David R. Shore, 'Colin and Rosalind: Love and Poetry in the *Shepheardes Calender*', *SP* 73 (1976), 176–88; Harry Berger, Jr, 'The Mirror Stage of Colin Clout', *Revisionary Play*, pp.325–46; John W. Moore, Jr, 'Colin Breaks his Pipe: A Reading of the January Eclogue', *ELR* 5 (1975), 3–24; Nancy Jo Hoffman, *Spenser's Pastorals: The Shepheardes Calender and 'Colin Clout'* (Baltimore: Johns Hopkins University Press, 1977), pp.43–53; A. C. Hamilton, 'The Argument of Spenser's *Shepheardes Calender*', *ELH* 23 (1956), 171–82, p.178.

33 Virgil, *The Pastoral Poems (The Eclogues)*, trans. E. V. Rieu (Harmondsworth: Penguin, 1949), pp.21–4. All subsequent references to this edition.

34 Michael Winterbottom, 'Virgil and the Confiscations', in Ian McAuslan and Peter Walcot, eds., *Virgil* (Oxford University Press, 1990), pp.65–8.

35 See, for example, McLane, *Spenser's Shepheardes Calender*; Louis Adrian Montrose, '"The Perfecte Paterne of a Poete": The Poetics of Courtship in *The Shepheardes Calender*', *TSLL* 21 (1979), 34–67; King, *Spenser's Poetry and the Reformation Tradition*, ch. 1; Harry Berger, Jr, 'The Moral Eclogues', *Revisionary Play*, pp.290–324; Hoffman, *Spenser's Pastorals*, ch. 4.

36 For speculations as to the identities of Hobbinoll and Thenot see McLane, *Spenser's Shepheardes Calender*, ch. 15 and 'Appendix'; William Nelson, *The Poetry of Edmund Spenser: A Study* (New York: Columbia University Press, 1963), p.22; 'Hobbinol', *Spenser Encyclopedia*, p.372.

37 On the May eclogue see King, *Spenser and the Reformation Tradition*, pp.35–41; Anthea Hume, *Edmund Spenser: Protestant Poet* (Cambridge University Press, 1984), pp.14–28; Hoffman, *Spenser's Pastorals*, pp.109–15; Robert Allen Durr, 'Spenser's Calendar of Christian Time', *ELH* 24 (1957), 269–95, pp.280–2.

38 See Norbrook, *Poetry and Politics*, pp.71–6; King, *Spenser and the Reformation Tradition*, pp.14–20; Hume, *Spenser: Protestant Poet*, pp.21–6, 36–8.

39 McLane, *Spenser's Shepheardes Calender*, ch. 4; 'Dido', *Spenser Encyclopedia*, pp.218–19.

40 See Miller, *The Poem's Two Bodies*, for an analogous reading of *The Faerie Queene*.

41 Berry, *Of Chastity and Power*, pp.78–81. See also Louis Adrian

Montrose, 'The Elizabethan Subject and the SpenserianText', in Parker and Quint, eds., *Literary Theory/ Renaissance Texts*, pp.303–40, for a related analysis of *The Faerie Queene*; Nairn, *Enchanted Glass*, ch. 1.

42 For alternative readings of the eclogue see Thomas H. Cain, 'The Strategy of Praise in Spenser's "April"', *SEL* 8 (1968), 45–58; Walter F. Staton, Jr, 'Spenser's "April" Lay as a Dramatic Chorus', *SP* 59 (1962), 111–18.

43 For details of the composition and publication of 'Colin Clout' see Sam Meyer, *An Interpretation of Edmund Spenser's Colin Clout* (Cork University Press, 1969), 'Introduction'; 'Colin Clout Comes Home Againe', *Spenser Encyclopedia*, pp.173–7.

44 See Hoffman, *Spenser's Pastorals*, ch. 4; King, *Spenser and the Reformation Tradition*, pp.31–46; Edwin A. Greenlaw, '*The Shepheardes Calender*', *PMLA* 26 (1911), 419–51.

45 The standard life of Spenser remains Alexander C. Judson, *The Life of Edmund Spenser* (Baltimore: Johns Hopkins University Press, 1945); see especially chs. 16–17.

46 On the identity of the 'New' English see Canny, 'Edmund Spenser and the Development of an Anglo-Irish Identity'; *The Formation of the Old English Elite in Ireland* (Dublin: O'Donnell Lecture, 1975); 'Identity Formation in Ireland: The Emergence of the Anglo-Irish', in N. P. Canny and A. Pagden, eds., *Colonial Identity in the Atlantic World, 1500–1800* (Princeton University Press, 1987), pp.157–212; T. W. Moody, 'Introduction: Early Modern Ireland', in T. W. Moody et al., eds., *A New History of Ireland*, III (Oxford University Press, 1976), pp.xxxix–lxiii; Ciaran Brady and Nicholas Canny, 'Debate: Spenser's Irish Crisis: Humanism and Experience in the 1590s', *P.&P.* 120 (1988), 201–15, pp.203, 212–13.

47 See Hamilton, ed., *The Faerie Queene*, p.22; Greenblatt, *Renaissance Self-Fashioning*, p.192.

48 See Andrew Hadfield and Willy Maley, 'Introduction: Irish Representatives and English Alternatives', in Bradshaw, Hadfield and Maley, eds., *Representing Ireland*, p.11.

49 For some comments on these lines in an Irish context see A. D. Hadfield, 'Spenser's *View of the Present State of Ireland*: Some Notes Towards a "Materialist" Analysis of Discourse', in Birgit Bramsback and Martin Crogan, eds., *Anglo-Irish Literature: Aspects of Language and Culture*, 2 vols. (Uppsala: Almquist and Wiksell, 1988), II, 265–72, pp.266–7.

50 See Hadfield and Maley, 'Introduction', in Bradshaw et al., eds., *Representing Ireland*, pp.7–11.

51 For some related comments on Spenser's Irish status see Ciaran

Brady, 'Spenser's Irish Crisis: Humanism and Experience in the 1590s', *P.&P.* 111 (1986), 17–49. A bibliographical guide to Spenser's relations with Ireland is provided by Willy Maley, 'Spenser and Ireland: A Select Bibliography', *Sp. St.* 9 (1991), 227–42.

52 On hybrid colonial identity see Albert Memmi, *The Colonizer and the Colonized*, trans. Howard Greenfield (New York: Orien Press, 1965); Homi Bhabha, 'Of Mimicry and Men: The Ambivalence of Colonial Discourse', *October* 28 (1984), 125–33. For other readings of the poem see Meyer, *Colin Clout*; Richard Mallette, 'Spenser's Portrait of the Artist in *The Shepherdes Calender* and *Colin Clouts Come Home Againe*', *SEL* 19 (1979), 19–41; Hoffman, *Spenser's Pastorals*, ch. 5.

53 For other analyses of this passage see Bernard, *Ceremonies of Innocence*, ch. 5; Humphrey Tonkin, *Spenser's Courteous Pastoral: Book VI of 'The Faerie Queene'* (Oxford: Clarendon Press, 1972), ch. 9; Isabel G. MacCaffrey, *Spenser's Allegory: The Anatomy of Imagination* (Princeton University Press, 1976), part 4 et passim; Edgar Wind, *Pagan Mysteries in the Renaissance* (New Haven: Yale University Press, 1958), pp.130–1; Berger, *Revisionary Play*, pp. 234–42.

54 See Hadfield, 'The English Conception of Ireland', pp.414–25.

55 See Montrose, 'The Elizabethan Subject', pp.322–3.

56 See Kathleen Williams, *Spenser's World of Glass: A Reading of 'The Faerie Queene'* (Berkeley and Los Angeles: California University Press, 1966), pp.119–20.

57 See Richard Neuse, 'Book VI as Conclusion to *The Faerie Queene*', *ELH* 35 (1968), 329–53.

58 For details of Florimell's role in the poem see Elizabeth Heale, *The Faerie Queene: A Reader's Guide* (Cambridge University Press, 1987), pp.81–4, 117–20; 'Florimell' and 'Marinell', *Spenser Encyclopedia*, pp.309–10, 453.

59 As it is, for example, by Alistair Fowler, *Spenser and the Numbers of Time* (London: RKP, 1964), pp.170–5; Nohrnberg, *The Analogy of The Faerie Queene*, pp.643–5.

60 See Cain, *Praise in The Faerie Queene*. See also J. W. Bennett, *The Evolution of The Faerie Queene* (Chicago University Press, 1942).

61 Harry Berger, Jr, *The Allegorical Temper* (New Haven: Yale University Press, 1957), pp.107–8.

62 See Carrie A. Harper, *The Sources of the British Chronicle History in Spenser's Faerie Queene* (Philadelphia University Press, 1910), pp.117–20.

63 Geoffrey, *History of the Kings of Britain*, pp.151–69, 186–94.

64 Wright, *Middle Class Culture*, ch. 9; Kendrick, *British Antiquity*, chs. 3, 6.

65 For analysis of this passage, see Hume, *Spenser: Protestant Poet*, ch. 7; Isabel E. Rathborne, *The Meaning of Spenser's Fairyland* (New York: Columbia University Press, 1937), chs. 2–3. See also Greenlaw, *Studies in Spenser's Historical Allegory*, ch. 1; Millican, *Spenser and the Table Round*.

66 Berry, *Of Chastity and Power*, pp.153–65. Berry is correcting Yates, *Astrea*; Roy Strong, *The Cult of Elizabeth: Elizabethan Portraiture and Pagentry* (London: Thames and Hudson, 1977).

67 *A View of the Present State of Ireland*, pp.106–9; Richard A. McCabe, 'The Fate of Irena: Spenser and Political Violence', in Patricia Coughlan, ed., *Spenser and Ireland: An Interdisciplinary Perspective* (Cork University Press, 1989), pp.109–25; H. S. V. Jones, 'Spenser's Defence of Lord Grey', *University of Illinois Studies in Language and Literature* 5 (1919), 151–219.

68 Dobin, *Merlin's Disciples*, pp.83–6, 139–54.

69 See Berger, *Revisionary Play*, pp.154–71; Paul J. Alpers, *The Poetry of 'The Faerie Queene'* (Princeton University Press, 1967), pp.215–28.

70 See MacCaffrey, *Spenser's Allegory*, part 3 ch. 4, for some relevant comments on Britomart's place in British history and prophecy.

71 Berry, *Of Chastity and Power*, pp.163–5. See also Marie Axton, *The Queen's Two Bodies*.

Select bibliography

Aers, David, 'Reflections on Current Histories of the Subject', *Literature and History*, second series, 2, ii (1991), 20–34.

Culture and History, 1350–1600: Essays on English Communities, Identities and Writing (Hemel Hempstead: Harvester, 1992).

Anderson, Benedict, *Imagined Communities: Reflections on the Origin and Spread of Nationalism* (London: Verso, 1990, rpt of 1983).

Attridge, Derek, *Well-Weighed Syllables: Elizabethan Verse in Classical Metres* (Cambridge University Press, 1974).

Peculiar Language: Literature as Difference from the Renaissance to James Joyce (Ithaca, New York: Cornell University Press, 1988).

Bakhtin, Mikhail, *The Dialogic Imagination: Four Essays*, trans. C. Emerson and M. Holquist (Austin: Texas University Press, 1981).

Bale, John, *The Actes of the English Votaries* (1546), STC 1270.

An Answere to a Papystycall Exhortacyon, Pretendynge to Avoyde False Doctrine (1548), STC 1274a.

The Epistel Exhortatatorye of an Inglyshe Chrystien (1544), STC 1291.

An Expostulation or Complaynte Agaynste the Blasphemyes of a Franticke Papist of Hampshire (1552), STC 1294.

The Pagent of Popes, trans. John Studeley (1574), STC 1304.

The Vocacyon of John Bale to the Bishoprick of Ossorie, STC 1307, reprinted in *Harlean Miscellany*, 10 vols. (1813), x, pp.437–64.

Select Works of John Bale, ed. H. Christmas (Cambridge: Parker Society, 1849).

Complete Plays of John Bale, 2 vols., ed. Peter Happé (Cambridge: Boydell and Brewer, 1985).

Barthes, Roland, *S/Z: An Essay*, trans. Richard Miller (New York: Hill and Wang, 1987, rpt of 1974).

Baukham, Richard, *Tudor Apocalypse, from John Bale to John Foxe and Thomas Brightman* (Oxford: Sutton Courtnay Press, 1978).

Berger, Harry, Jr, *Revisionary Play: Studies in the Spenserian Dynamic* (Berkeley and Los Angeles: California University Press, 1988).

Berry, Edward, 'The Poet as Warrior in Sidney's *Defence of Poetry*', *SEL* 29 (1989), 21–34.

'Sidney's "Poor Painter": Nationalism and Social Class', in Vincent Newey and Ann Thompson, eds., *Literature and Nationalism* (Liverpool University Press, 1991), pp.1–10.

Berry, Philippa, *Of Chastity and Power: Elizabethan Literature and the Unmarried Queen* (London: Routledge, 1989).

Bhabha, Homi, ed., *Nation and Narration* (London: RKP, 1990).

Blatt, Thora Balsler, *The Plays of John Bale: A Study of Ideas, Technique and Style* (Copenhagen: G. E. C. Gad, 1968).

Bradshaw, Brendan, Hadfield, Andrew, and Maley, Willy, eds., *Representing Ireland, 1534–1660: Literature and the Origins of Conflict* (Cambridge University Press, 1993).

Brady, Ciaran, 'Spenser's Irish Crisis: Humanism and Experience in the 1590s', *P. & P.* 111 (1986), 17–49.

Briggs, William Dinsmore, 'Political Ideas in Sidney's "Arcadia"', *SP* 28 (1931), 137–61.

Canny, Nicholas P., 'Edmund Spenser and the Development of an Anglo-Irish Identity', *YES* 13 (1983), 1–19.

Collinson, Patrick, *The Birthpangs of Protestant England: Religious and Cultural Change in the Sixteenth and Seventeenth Centuries* (London: Macmillan, 1988).

Crewe, Jonathan V., 'The Hegemonic Theatre of George Puttenham', *ELR* 16 (1986), 71–85.

Culler, Jonathan, *The Pursuit of Signs: Semiotics, Literature, Deconstruction* (London: RKP, 1981).

Davies, W. T., 'A Bibliography of John Bale', *Proceedings and Papers of the Oxford Bibliographical Society* 5 (1940), 201–79.

Dickens, A. G., *The English Reformation* (London: Fontana, rev. edn, 1986, rpt of 1967).

Dowling, Maria, *Humanism in the Age of Henry VIII* (London: Croom Helm, 1986).

Edwards, Philip, *Threshold of a Nation: A Study in English and Irish Drama* (Cambridge University Press, 1979).

Ellis, Stephen, 'John Bale, Bishop of Ossory, 1552–3', *Journal of the Butler Society* 3 (1984), 280–93.

'"Not Mere English": The British Perspective, 1400–1650', *History Today* 28 (1988), pp.41–8.

Fairfield, L. P., *John Bale: Mythmaker for the English Reformation* (Indiana: Purdue University Press, 1976).

Farnham, Willard, *The Medieval Heritage of Elizabethan Tragedy* (Oxford: Basil Blackwell, 1956, rpt of 1936).

Firth, Katherine R., *The Apocalyptic Tradition in Reformation Britain, 1530–1645* (Oxford University Press, 1979).

Fish, Stanley, *John Skelton's Poetry* (New Haven: Yale University Press, 1965).

Foucault, Michel, *The Order of Things: An Archaeology of the Human Sciences* (London: Tavistock, 1986, rpt of 1970).

Power/Knowledge: Selected Interviews and Other Writings, 1972–1977, ed. Colin Gordon (New York: Pantheon, 1980).

Fox, Alistair, *Politics and Literature in the Reigns of Henry VII and Henry VIII* (Oxford: Basil Blackwell, 1989).

Foxe, John, *The Acts and Monuments of the Christian Church*, ed. Josiah Pratt, 8 vols. (London: Religious Trust Society, 1853–70).

Garrett, Christina H., *The Marian Exiles: A Study in the Origins of Elizabethan Puritanism* (Cambridge University Press, 1966, rpt of 1938).

Giddens, Anthony, *The Nation State and Violence*, vol. II of *A Contemporary Critique of Historical Materialism* (Cambridge: Polity Press, 1985).

Goldberg, Jonathan, 'The Politics of Renaissance Literature: A Review Essay', *ELH* 15 (1982), 514–42.

Gosson, Stephen, *The Schoole of Abuse* (London, 1579), *STC* 12097.

Markets of Bawdrie: The Dramatic Criticism of Stephen Gosson, ed. Arthur Kinney (Universitat Salzburg, 1974).

Greenblatt, Stephen, *Renaissance Self-Fashioning: From More to Shakespeare* (Chicago University Press, 1980).

'Murdering Peasants: Status, Genre and the Representation of Rebellion', *Representations* 1 (1983), 1–29.

Greenlaw, Edwin A., *Studies in Spenser's Historical Allegory* (Baltimore: Johns Hopkins University Press, 1932).

Häbermas, Jürgen, 'The Public Sphere', trans. S. and F. Lennox, *New German Critique* 3 (1974), 45–55.

Haller, William, *Foxe's Book of Martyrs and the Elect Nation* (London: Cape, 1963).

Hamilton, A. C., ed., *The Spenser Encyclopedia* (London: Routledge, 1990).

Happe, Peter, 'Recent Studies in John Bale', *ELR* 17 (1987), 103–13.

Harper, Carrie A., *The Sources of the British Chronicle History in Spenser's Faerie Queene* (Philadelphia University Press, 1910).

Hechter, Michael, *Internal Colonialism: The Celtic Fringe in British National Development, 1536–1966* (Berkeley: California University Press, 1975).

Helgerson, Richard, *Self-Crowned Laureates: Spenser, Jonson, Milton and the Literary System* (Berkeley: California University Press, 1983).

Forms of Nationhood: The Elizabethan Writing of England (Chicago University Press, 1992).

'"Barbarous Tongues": The Ideology of Poetic Form in Renaissance England', in Heather Dubrow and Richard Strier, eds., *The Historical Renaissance: New Essays on Tudor and Stuart Literature and Culture* (Chicago University Press, 1988), pp.273–92.

Hill, Christopher, 'Censorship and English Literature' in *The Collected Essays of Christopher Hill*, vol. 1, *Writing and Revolution in Seventeenth-Century England* (Brighton: Harvester, 1985), pp.32–71.

Hoffman, Nancy Jo, *Spenser's Pastorals: The Shepheardes Calender and 'Colin Clout'* (Baltimore: Johns Hopkins University Press, 1977).

Hume, Anthea, *Edmund Spenser: Protestant Poet* (Cambridge University Press, 1984).

Jones, Ann Rosalind, and Stallybrass, Peter, 'The Politics of *Astrophil and Stella*', *SEL* 24 (1984).

Kantorowicz, Ernst, *The King's Two Bodies: A Study in Medieval Political Theology* (Princeton University Press, 1957).

Kendrick, T. D., *British Antiquity* (London: Methuen, 1950).

King, John N., *English Reformation Literature: The Tudor Origins of the Protestant Tradition* (Princeton University Press, 1982).

Spenser's Poetry and the Reformation Tradition (Princeton University Press, 1990).

Kinghorn, A. M., *The Chorus of History: Literary–Historical Relations in Renaissance Britain, 1485–1558* (London: Batsford, 1971).

Kipling, Gordon, 'John Skelton and Burgundian Letters', in Jan Van Dorsten, ed., *Ten Studies in Anglo-Dutch Relations* (Leiden: Sir Thomas Browne Institute, G. S. 5, 1974).

'Henry VII and the Origins of Tudor Patronage', in Guy Finch Lytle and Stephen Orgel, eds., *Patronage in the Renaissance* (Princeton University Press, 1981), pp.117–64.

Kohn, Hans, *The Idea of Nationalism: A Study in its Origins and Background* (Ithaca, New York: Cornell University Press, 1946).

Lawry, Jon S., *Sidney's Two Arcadias: Pattern and Proceeding* (Ithaca, New York: Cornell University Press, 1972).

Lentricchia, Frank, and McLaughlin, Thomas, eds., *Critical Terms for Literary Study* (Chicago University Press, 1990).

Levy, F. J., *Tudor Historical Thought* (San Marino: Huntington Library Publications, 1967).

Lewis, C. S., *English Literature in the Sixteenth Century, Excluding Drama* (Oxford University Press, 1954).

Loades, D. M., 'The Theory and Practice of Censorship in Sixteenth-Century England', *TRHS*, fifth series, 24 (1974), 141–57.

Love, Harold, 'Scribal Publication in Seventeenth-Century England', *TCBS* 9 (1987), 130–54.

McCanles, Michael, '*The Shepheardes Calender* as Document and Monument', *SEL* 22 (1982), 5–19.

McConica, J. K., *English Humanists and Reformation Politics* (Oxford University Press, 1965).

McCoy, Richard, *Sir Philip Sidney: Rebellion in Arcadia* (Brighton: Harvester, 1979).

McLane, Paul, *Spenser's Shepheardes Calender: A Study in Elizabethan Allegory* (Notre Dame University Press, 1961).

Maley, Willy, 'Spenser and Ireland: A Select Bibliography', *Sp. St.* 9 (1991), 227–42.

Marotti, Arthur F., '"Love is not Love": Elizabethan Sonnet Sequences and the Social Order', *ELH* 49 (1982), 396–428.

Memmi, Albert, *The Colonizer and the Colonized*, trans. Howard Greenfield (New York: Orien Press, 1965).

Millican, Charles B., *Spenser and the Table Round* (London: Frank Cass and Co., 1967, rpt of 1932).

Mills, Jerry Leath, 'Recent Studies in *A Mirror for Magistrates*', *ELR* 9 (1979), 343–54.

A Mirror for Magistrates, ed. Lily B. Campbell (Cambridge University Press, 1938).

    Parts Added to 'A Mirror for Magistrates', ed. Lily B. Campbell (Cambridge University Press, 1946).

Miskimin, Alice, *The Renaissance Chaucer* (New Haven: Yale University Press, 1975).

Montrose, Louis Adrian, 'Celebration and Insinuation: Sir Philip Sidney and the Motives of Elizabethan Courtship', *RD* 8 (1977), 3–35.

    '"The Perfecte Paterne of a Poete": The Poetics of Courtship in *The Shepheardes Calender*', *TSLL* 21 (1979), 34–67.

    'Of Gentlemen and Shepherds: The Politics of Elizabethan Pastoral Form', *ELH* 50 (1983), 415–59.

Mozeley, J. F., *John Foxe and his Book* (London: SPCK, 1940).

Myrick, Kenneth, *Sir Philip Sidney as a Literary Craftsman* (Lincoln: Nebraska University Press, rev. edn, 1965).

Nearing, Homer, *English Historical Poetry*, 1599–1641 (Philadelphia: University of Pennsylvania Press, 1945).

Nelson, William, *John Skelton, Laureate* (New York: Russell and Russell, 1964).

Neuse, Richard, 'Book VI as Conclusion to *The Faerie Queene*', *ELH* 35 (1968), 329–53.

Norbrook, David, *Poetry and Politics in the English Renaissance* (London: RKP, 1984).

O'Connell, Michael, *The Mirror and the Veil: The Historical Dimension of Spenser's 'Faerie Queene'* (North Carolina University Press, 1977).

Olsen, V. Norskov, *John Foxe and the Elizabethan Church* (Berkeley, California University Press, 1973).

Parker, Patricia, and Quint, David, eds., *Literary Theory/ Renaissance Texts* (Baltimore: Johns Hopkins University Press, 1986).

Patterson, Annabel, *Censorship and Interpretation: The Conditions of Writing and Reading in Early Modern England* (Wisconsin University Press, 1984).

Pitcher, John, 'Tudor Literature (1485–1603)', in Pat Rogers, ed., *The Oxford Illustrated History of English Literature* (Oxford University Press, 1987), 59–111.

Puttenham, George, *The Arte of English Poesie* (1589), ed. R. C. Alston (Menston: Scolar Press, 1968).

Raitiere, Martin N., *Faire Bitts: Sir Philip Sidney and Renaissance Political Theory* (Pittsburgh: Duquesne University Press, 1984).

Rathborne, Isabel E., *The Meaning of Spenser's Fairyland* (New York: Columbia University Press, 1937).

Ribner, Irving, 'Machiavelli and Sidney: The *Arcadia* of 1590', *SP* 47 (1950), 152–72.

'Sir Philip Sidney and Civil Insurrection', *JHI* 13 (1952), 257–65.

Ricoeur, Paul, *The Rule of Metaphor: Multi-Disciplinary Studies in the Creation of Meaning in Language*, trans. Robert Czerny *et al.* (Toronto University Press, 1984, rpt of 1977).

Scarisbrick, J. J., *Henry VIII* (London: Methuen, 1988, rpt of 1968).

Scattergood, V. J., *Politics and Poetry in the Fifteenth Century* (London: Blandford, 1971).

Sessions, William A., *Henry Howard, Earl of Surrey* (Boston: Twayne, 1986).

Sharratt, Bernard, 'John Skelton: finding a voice – notes after Bakhtin', in David Aers, ed., *Medieval Literature: Criticism, Ideology and History* (Brighton: Harvester, 1986).

Sidney, Sir Philip, *An Apologie for Poetry*, ed. Geoffrey Shepherd (Manchester University Press, 1973, rpt. of 1965).

The Poems of Sir Philip Sidney, ed. William A. Ringler, Jr, (Oxford: Clarendon Press, 1962)

The Old Arcadia, ed. Katherine Duncan-Jones (Oxford University Press, 1985).

The New Arcadia, ed. Victor Skretkowicz (Oxford: Clarendon Press, 1987).

Sinfield, Alan, *Literature in Protestant England* (London: Croom Helm, 1983).

'Power and Ideology: An Outline Theory and Sidney's *Arcadia*', *ELH* 52 (1985), 259–77.

Skelton, John, *The Complete English Poems*, ed. John Scattergood (Harmondsworth: Penguin, 1983).

Skinner, Quentin, *The Foundations of Modern Political Thought*, 2 Vols. (Cambridge University Press, 1978).

Smith, Anthony D., *National Identity* (Harmondsworth: Penguin, 1991).

Smith, George Gregory, ed., *Elizabethan Critical Essays*, 2 Vols. (Oxford: Clarendon Press, 1904).

Smith, Sir Thomas, *De Republica Anglorum, A Discourse on the Commonwealth of England*, ed., L. Alston (Shannon: Irish Universities Press, 1972, rpt. of 1906).

Sonnino, Lee A., *A Handbook to Sixteenth-Century Rhetoric* (London: RKP, 1968).

Spearing, A. C., *Medieval to Renaissance in English Poetry* (Cambridge University Press, 1985).

Spenser, Edmund, *The Poetical Works of Edmund Spenser*, ed. J. C. Smith and A. De Selincourt (Oxford University Press, 1965, rpt. of 1912).

The Works of Edmund Spenser: A Variorum Edition, ed. Edwin Greenlaw *et al.*, (Baltimore: Johns Hopkins University Press, 1932–49).

The Faerie Queene, ed. A. C. Hamilton (London: Longman, 1977).

A View of the Present State of Ireland, ed. W. L. Renwick (Oxford: Clarendon Press, 1970, rpt of 1934).

Stillman, Robert E., 'The Politics of Sidney's Pastoral: Mystification and Mythology in *The Old Arcadia*', *ELH* 52 (1985), 795–814.

Taylor, Barry, *Vagrant Writing: Social and Semiotic Disorders in the English Renaissance* (Hemel Hempstead: Harvester, 1991).

Veeser, H. Aram, ed., *The New Historicism* (London: Routledge, 1989).

Virgil, *The Pastoral Poems (The Eclogues)*, trans. E. V. Rieu (Harmondsworth: Penguin, 1949).

Walker, Greg, *John Skelton and the Politics of the 1520s* (Cambridge University Press, 1988).

Plays of Persuasion: Drama and Politics at the Court of Henry VIII (Cambridge University Press, 1991).

Waller, Gary, *English Poetry of the Sixteenth Century* (London: Longman, 1986).

Waller, Gary F., and Moore, Michael D., eds., *Sir Philip Sidney and the Interpretation of Renaissance Culture: The Poet in His Time and Ours* (London: Croom Helm, 1984).

White, P. L., *Theatre and Reformation: Protestantism, Patronage and Playing in Tudor England* (Cambridge University Press, 1993).

Wilson, Sir Thomas, *The Arte of Rhetorique*, ed. G. H. Mair (Oxford: Clarendon Press, 1909).

Yates, Frances A., *Astrea: The Imperial Theme in the Sixteenth Century* (London: RKP, 1985, rpt of 1975).

Young, Robert, *White Mythologies: Writing History and the West* (London: RKP, 1990).

Zeeveld, W. Gordon, 'The Uprising of the Commons in Sidney's *Arcadia*', *MLN* 48 (1933), 209–17.

Foundations of Tudor Polity (Cambridge, Mass.: Harvard University Press, 1948).

Index

Aers, David 13–15
Alcaeus 39
Alençon, Francis, Duke of 159, 177,
    186, 187
Anderson, Benedict 78
André, Bernard 41
Andronicus, Livius 135
Antin, David ix
Ariosto, Ludovico 123
Aristotle 40, 132, 134, 139, 143
Arnold, Thomas (Archbishop of
    Canterbury) 64
Aske, Robert 79
Askew, Anne 55, 70, 73, 144
Auden, W. H. 44
Augustine, Saint 58, 62
Augustus 178
Ayer, A. J. xiv
Aylmer, John 69

Bacon, Francis 12
Bakhtin, Mikhail 21, 89–91
Baldick, Chris 18
Baldwin, William 83, 91, 93–4, 98, 99,
    103–5
Bale, John 8, 19, 42, 51–80, 83, 92,
    103–4, 106, 126, 134, 139, 170
Barclay, Alexander 41, 70
Barker, Francis 14
Barthes, Roland 21, 68, 149
Beaufort, Edmund (Duke of Somerset)
    93–5
Beaufort, Henry (Cardinal) 95
Becket, Thomas 51–2, 77
Beckett, Samuel 138
Bede 70
Berry, Edward 141, 167

Bevington, David 77
Bhabha, Homi 21
Blenerhasset, Thomas 84, 101–2
Bloom, Harold 31
Blunden, Edward 44
Boccaccio, Giovanni 81, 84, 86, 87,
    135, 176
Bodin, Jean 51, 160
Boethius 139
Boniface (Pope) 63
Boudicca 119–20, 194
Brownlow, F. W. 26
Burckhardt, Jacob 15
Burdet, Sir Nicholas 101

Cade, Jack 96–7, 98, 101, 129
Caedmon 70
Calvin, Jean 98–9
Camden, William 12
Campbell, Lily B. 83, 86
Catesby, Sir William 104–5
Cato the elder 83
Catullus 35, 39
Caxton, William 47
Chaucer, Geoffrey 4, 9, 28–31, 34, 37,
    41, 47, 49, 84, 87, 88, 123, 135,
    142, 144, 145, 176
Cheke, John 165
Churchyard, Thomas 43, 48, 100,
    143
Cicero 28, 38, 110
Cobham, Eleanor 93–4
Collingbourne, William 102–7, 193
Collinson, Patrick 53, 57
Cotton, Sir Robert 12
Cox, Richard 53
Cranmer, Thomas 53, 54, 77

Cromwell, Thomas 7, 39, 54, 64, 76, 93
Culler, Jonathan 137–8

Daniel, Samuel 174
Dante, Alighieri 87, 88, 103, 123, 135, 176
Darwin, Charles 24
Davies, W. T. 52, 57,
Derrida, Jacques 21, 67
Devereux, Robert (Second Earl of Essex) 92, 143
Diodorus Sicilius 30, 40, 46, 47
Dollimore, Jonathan 19
Donne, John 154
Doyle, Brian 18
Drayton, Michael 9, 43, 174
Dryden, John 9
Du Bellay, Joachim 148, 175
Dudley, John (Duke of Northumberland) 60, 110
Dudley, Robert (Earl of Leicester) 174, 180
Duncan-Jones, Katherine 160–1
Dyce, Alexander 44

Eagleton, Terry 18
Edward III 122
Edward IV 60, 187
Edward VI 4, 5, 55, 59–60, 73–4, 83, 93, 110, 131
Edwards, Philip 17–18
Eliot, T. S. 13
Elizabeth I 55, 56, 76, 83, 103, 107, 112, 120, 126, 143, 151, 154, 157, 159, 161, 173, 177, 183–201
Elizabeth of York 187
Ennius 135
Erasmus, Desiderius 39, 41, 42
Evans, Maurice 149

Fabyan, Robert 82, 83
Farnham, Willard 86
Fawkes, Richard 26
Feasey, Eveline 93–5, 104
Ferrars, George 83, 93
Fillastre, Guillaume 40
Fiore, Joachim de 66
Firth, Katherine 58, 63
Fish, Stanley 39
Fisher, John 70

Foucault, Michel 13, 21, 68
Fowler, Alistair 70
Foxe, John 19, 55, 56, 57, 58, 59, 63, 66, 126

Gardiner, Stephen 95
Gascoigne, George 143
Geoffrey of Monmouth 62, 70, 83–4, 194–5
Gesner, Conrad 69
Gildas 62, 70
Glendower, Owen 96–8, 101
Goodman, Christopher 53, 64, 160
Googe, Barnaby 57, 143
Gosson, Stephen 8, 117–22, 123, 127, 131, 137, 177
Gould, Stephen Jay 23, 50
Gower, John 9, 28, 34, 37, 41, 84, 123, 135
Grafton, Richard 84
Graves, Robert 44
Green, Laurence 91, 100
Green, Peter 39
Gregory, Pope 62, 63
Greenblatt, Stephen 19, 21, 167
Greville, Fulke, Lord Brooke 141, 143, 168
Grey, Arthur, fourteenth Baron of Wilton 197
Gringore, Pierre 40
Gutierrez, Nancy 47

Häbermäs, Jurgen 5–6, 8, 14, 15, 21
Hakluyt, Richard 2, 59
Hall, Edward 2, 82, 83
Haller, William 57–8
Hardison, O. B., Jr 132–3, 141–2
Harington, John 143
Harvey, Gabriel 43, 174–5, 177, 180, 185
Hawes, Stephen 41
Helgerson, Richard 170–1
Hengist 195
Heliodorus 154
Henry II 77
Henry III 60
Henry IV 96
Henry VI 60, 88–9, 96
Henry VII 39–40, 45, 93, 187
Henry VIII 3, 7, 25, 39, 40, 60, 79, 123, 187

Herbert, George 9
Herodotus 81
Heywood, John 143
Higden, Ranulph 62
Higgens, John 83–4, 101–2
Hildebrand (Pope) 63
Hoccleve, Thomas 70
Holinshed, Raphael 2, 100
Holme, Wilfrid 7–8
Homer 35, 145
Horace 132
Horsa 195
Howard, Henry, Earl of Surrey 3, 4, 8, 49, 81, 123, 135, 142–8
Hooker, Richard 98
Huizinga, Johan 45
Humber (King of the Huns) 102
Humphrey, Duke of Gloucester 84, 88, 93–5

Illyricus, Marcus Flacius 56

James IV (King of Scotland) 101
Jeremiah 103
Jerome, Saint 39
John (King) 76–9
John II (King of France) 87, 89
John, Saint 66
Jones, Emrys 148
Jones, Roy Foster 47, 62, 114
Jonson, Ben 9, 174
Juvenal 27, 103

Kedourie, Elie ix, 2
Kett, Robert 129
King, John 4, 19, 20, 43–4, 49, 67, 144
Kipling, Gordon 39–41
Knox, John 53, 159

Langland, William 123
Langton, Stephen 77
Lawry, Jon 163
Leavis, F. R. and Q. D. 13–14
Leland, John 55, 70
Lewis, C. S. 44–5
Lily, William 41
Livy 28
Lodge, Thomas 143
Lovell, Viscount Francis 104
Lucian 28, 42
Lucius 62

Luther, Martin 52, 54, 98
Lyly, John 8
Lydgate, John 28–9, 30–1, 34, 37, 41, 83, 84–90, 93, 123

McCormack, William J. xiii
Machiavelli, Niccolo 160
Malory, Sir Thomas 9
Manley, Lawrence 126
Marlowe, Christopher 8, 174
Marot, Clement 43
Marotti, Arthur 150–1
Marsh, Thomas 26
Martial 104
Mary I 53, 55, 74, 83, 92, 95, 103, 107, 110, 159
Mills, Jerry Leath 81
Milton, John 9, 56
Minturno, A. S. 134
Montemayor, Jorge de 154
More, Sir Thomas 37, 42, 70, 83
Morison, Richard 54
Mortimer, John (pseudonym of Jack Cade) 96
Mortimer, Roger(s) 93

Nashe, Thomas 8
Nero 119
Noot, Jan Van Der 175
Norton, Thomas 98

Oldcastle, Sir John 52, 55, 63–5, 73
O'Leary, John 17
Ovid 27, 28, 144, 167, 177, 178, 181

Panofsky, Erwin 15
Parker, Matthew 56, 69, 70
Patterson, Annabel 166
Paul, Saint 73, 74
Peacham, Henry 44
Paul IV (Pope) 110
Pearsall, Derek 86
Peery, William 86
Petrarca, Francesco 3–4, 49, 87, 123, 135, 144, 145, 147–8, 175, 176
Philip II (King of Spain) 197
Philips, Edward 44
Pindar 39, 139, 150
Plato 117, 132, 134, 139, 143
Plutarch 134
Poggio Bracciolini 30
Ponet, John 53, 56

Pole, William de la (Duke of Suffolk) 94
Premierfait, Laurence de 84–5
Puttenham, Sir George 8, 25, 44, 49, 122–31, 144
Pynson, Richard 84

Quintilian 28

Raleigh, Sir Walter 173, 188, 191, 200
Ratcliffe, Sir John 104
Ribner, Irving 164
Rich, Barnaby 143
Rich, Sir Richard 7
Ricoeur, Paul 21, 153
Richard II 4, 63, 91–2, 94, 122
Richard III 103–5, 107
Robertson, D. W. 13

Sackville, Thomas 98, 99
Sampson, George 70
Sannazaro, Jacopo 154
Sappho 119
Scattergood, John 87
Schibanoff, Susan 35, 37
Seneca 28
Sessions, William 144–6
Seymour, Edward (Duke of Somerset) 93–5, 98
Shakespeare, William 14, 17, 31, 47, 81, 92, 177
Sharrat, Bernard 47
Shepherd, Luke 43
Sherry, Richard 117
Sidney, Sir Philip 4, 8, 10, 16, 49, 81–2, 84, 87, 98, 132–69, 170, 174, 176
Singleton, Hugh 177
Skelton, John 3, 8, 9, 23–50, 51, 52, 56–7, 65, 70–1, 76, 87, 101, 123, 124, 135, 144, 171, 172–3, 176
Smith, Anthony D. 2
Smith, Sir Thomas 3, 97, 98, 160, 179–80
Smith, Thomas of Lavenham 46
Spearing, A. C. 15
Spenser, Edmund 4, 8, 10–11, 16, 20, 43, 126, 170–201
Stafford, Henry (Duke of Buckingham) 103

Stanbridge, John 41
Starkey, Thomas 54
Statius 28, 177
Stow, John 26, 43, 84
Stubbs, John 177
Straw, Jack 129
Studeley, John 56
Surrey, Earl of (see Howard, Henry)
Syminides 39

Terence 28, 154
Tertullian 117
Theocritus 28
Thorpe, William 55
Tiptoft, John (Earl of Worcester) 95
Tottel, Richard 4, 144
Tillyard, E. W. M. 14
Tresilian, Robert 91–2, 94

Vergil, Polydore 12, 62, 63, 78
Virgil 36, 87, 144, 176, 177, 178, 181–2
Vortigern 195

Walker, Greg 25, 41, 45
Wayland, John 83
Webbe, William 44, 124–5
West, Rebecca ix
Whittingham, William 53
Widdowson, Peter 18
William of Orange 152
Wilson, Sir Thomas 8, 108–17, 120, 121, 126, 127, 128, 131
Wolsey, Thomas 24, 38, 44, 45, 46–7, 100–1, 172
Womack, Peter 78
Woodstock, Thomas of (Duke of Gloucester) 93
Wyatt, Sir Thomas 3, 4, 8, 49, 123, 135, 144
Wyatt, Sir Thomas the younger 53, 144

Xenophon 81

Yeats, W. B. 17
Young, Robert 49

Zuccaro, Federigo 134